# SITES OF PLURALISM

FIRAT ORUC
(*Editor*)

# Sites of Pluralism

## *Community Politics in the Middle East*

17 89
جامعة جورجتاون قطر
GEORGETOWN UNIVERSITY QATAR
Center *for* International *and* Regional Studies

HURST & COMPANY, LONDON

Published in collaboration with Center for International and Regional Studies, Georgetown University in Qatar.

First published in the United Kingdom in 2019 by
C. Hurst & Co. (Publishers) Ltd.,
41 Great Russell Street, London, WC1B 3PL

Printed in India



A Cataloguing-in-Publication data record for this book is available from the British Library.

This book is printed using paper from registered sustainable and managed sources.

ISBN: 9781787380226

www.hurstpublishers.com

# CONTENTS

# ACKNOWLEDGMENTS

This volume is the product of the "Pluralism and Community in the Middle East" research initiative convened by the Center for International and Regional Studies (CIRS) at Georgetown University-Qatar in 2016. I would like to thank Mehran Kamrava, the Director of the Center, and Zahra Babar, the Associate Director for Research, for launching and supporting this important and timely research initiative. The goal of the project was to examine the significance and dynamics of ethnic, linguistic, cultural, and religious communities in the Middle East through a variety of multidisciplinary perspectives that add original insight to the subject. I thank the authors of the individual chapters in this volume as well as other scholars who attended the working group meetings—Paolo D'Urbano, Amanda Garrett, and Shak Hanish—for generously bringing their expertise to the table to accomplish this goal.

I could not have survived without the wonderful staff members of CIRS. Suzi Mirgani, the Managing Editor of CIRS Publications, offered her incessant assistance in each and every step of the production of this book. I am indebted to Jackie Starbird, Elizabeth Wanucha, Misba Bhatti, and Umber Latafat for all the logistical support they provided from the inception of the project. I also benefited substantially from the constructive feedback of the anonymous reviewers and the editorial support of Michael Dwyer, Jon de Peyer, Daisy Leitch, and Kathleen May. I would like to acknowledge the Qatar Foundation for Education, Science and Community Development for its enduring commitment to support scholarly research on the pressing issues of our times in every field of inquiry.

Last, but not least, I am immensely grateful to my wife, Nurgül, and our children İkbal, Ebrar, and Tarık, for their plural ways of support while I was working on this book. I am blessed with their unfaltering love, care, and patience.

# ABOUT THE AUTHORS

**Ehsan Abdoh-Tabrizi** is an independent researcher. His research interests encompass state and society in Iran. He is the co-author, with Afshin Shahi, of the forthcoming book on *Iran, the Shia State and the Sunni Minority.*

**Taghreed Jamal Al-Deen** is an associate research fellow at the Alfred Deakin Institute for Citizenship and Globalization at Deakin University in Australia. Her disciplinary background is in the sociology of education, with research interests in migration, transnationalism, multiculturalism, ethnicity, class, and gender. Al-Deen is currently working on a research project assessing heritage destruction in Syria and Iraq. Her publications include: "'I Feel Sometimes I Am a Bad Mother': The Affective Dimension of Immigrant Mothers' Involvement in their Children's Schooling," *Journal of Sociology* 53, no. 1 (2016), and "The Involvement of Migrant Mothers in their Children's Education: Cultural Capital and Transnational Class Processes," *International Studies in Sociology of Education* 25, no. 4 (2015).

**Nezar AlSayyad** is an architect, planner, urban historian, and public intellectual. He is a Professor of Architecture and Planning at the University of California at Berkeley, where he was Faculty Director of the Center for Arab Societies and Environments Studies (CASES) and Center for Middle Eastern Studies (CMES) for two decades. AlSayyad holds a B.S. in Architectural Engineering and Diploma in Town Planning from Cairo University, an M.S. in Architecture from the Massachusetts Institute of Technology and a Ph.D. in Architectural History from UC Berkeley. He serves as editor of *Traditional Dwellings and Settlements Review*, and is the author, co-author, editor, or co-editor of many books, including: *Making Cairo Medieval* (2005); *Cinematic Urbanism* (2006); *The Fundamentalist City* (2010); *Cairo: Histories of a City*

(2011); and *Traditions: The Real, the Hyper and the Virtual* (2014). AlSayyad has written, co-produced and co-directed two NEA-funded public television programs, and in 2008, the University of California at Berkeley awarded him the Distinguished Teaching Award. In 2014–15, he was awarded a Distinguished Guggenheim Fellowship.

**James Barry** is a research fellow at the Alfred Deakin Institute at Deakin University, Melbourne, Australia. Barry was awarded a PhD in anthropology from Monash University in 2013, and is currently working with the Chair of Islamic Studies at Deakin University. His book, *Armenian Christians in Iran: Ethnicity, Religion, and Identity in an Islamic Republic*, is published with Cambridge University Press (2019). In addition, James has published widely on Iranian ethnic and religious identities and the role of Iranian identity in foreign policy. James speaks Armenian and Persian and has recently expanded his research to analyze contested notions of ethnicity and diaspora in the case of Iran.

**Kathleen A. Cavanaugh** is socio-legal scholar and currently a Lecturer in the Faculty of Law, Irish Centre for Human Rights (ICHR), National University of Ireland, Galway. Her areas of expertise include: nationalism, ethnic conflict, political violence, states of emergency, narratives on Islamic law and rights, freedom of religion, and militant democracy. Selected recent publications include: "Turkey's Hidden Wars," *Harvard Human Rights Journal* (Winter 2018); "Rethinking What is Necessary in a Democratic Society: Militant Democracy and the Turkish State," *Human Rights Quarterly* (August 2016); *Unspoken Truths: Accessing Rights for Victims of Extraordinary Rendition, Columbia Human Rights Law Review* (Winter 2015); and *Minority Rights in the Middle East* (Oxford University Press, 2013) with Joshua Castellino. Recent grant awards include a two-year Leverhulme/British Academy of Sciences project grant on Militant Democracy in Turkey.

**Islam Hassan** is Research Analyst at the Center for International and Regional Studies, Georgetown University in Qatar. His current research interests include state-building in the Gulf states, and comparative politics and international relations of West Asia and North Africa. He coedited a special issue of *The Muslim World* (2017) on "The State of Middle Eastern Youth," and authored "Social Stratification in Qatari Society: Family, Marriage, and Khaleeji Culture," *Hawwa* (2018); "GCC's 2014 Crisis: Causes, Issues and Solutions" (in Arabic and English, with Al Jazeera Research Center 2015); and "Jordan on the Brink," *International Journal of Culture and History* (2016).

**Benjamin Isakhan** is associate professor of politics and policy studies and founding director of POLIS, a research network for politics and international relations in the Alfred Deakin Institute for Citizenship and Globalization at Deakin University, Australia. He is also adjunct senior research associate, Department of Politics and International Relations at the University of Johannesburg, South Africa. Isakhan is the author of *Democracy in Iraq: History, Politics, Discourse* (London: Routledge, 2016), and the editor of six books including, most recently, *State and Society in Iraq: Citizenship under Occupation, Dictatorship and Democratization* (London: I. B. Tauris, 2017).

**Firoozeh Kashani-Sabet** is Walter H. Annenberg Professor of History at the University of Pennsylvania. She is the author of *Frontier Fictions: Shaping the Iranian Nation* (Princeton University Press, 1999), and *Conceiving Citizens: Women and the Politics of Motherhood in Iran* (Oxford University Press, 2011). She is completing two book manuscripts titled, *Between Heroes and Hostages: Reflections on US–Iranian Relations*, and *Tales of Trespassing: Borderland Histories of Iran, Iraq, and the Persian Gulf.*

**Firat Oruc** is Assistant Professor of World Literature at Georgetown University School of Foreign Service in Qatar. His research center on cultures and literatures of the Middle East through two ongoing book projects: one on translation and national humanism in Turkey, and the other on the history of cinema in the Arabian Peninsula. His scholarship has appeared in peer-reviewed journals *English Language Notes*, *Criticism*, *Postcolonial Text*, *Journal of World Literature*, *HAWWA: Journal of Women of the Middle East and the Islamic World*, and *Comparative Literature Studies*. He is also the author of two widely used reference articles on "Cultural History of Reading in the Modern Middle East," in *The Cultural History of Reading* (2008), and "Middle East Literature and Theory," in *The Blackwell Encyclopedia of Postcolonial Studies* (2016). Oruc holds degrees from Boğaziçi (Bosphorus) University (B.A.), State University of New York (M.A.), and Duke University (Ph.D.). Before joining Georgetown-Qatar, he taught in the Comparative Literary Studies program at Northwestern University (2011–2013) and the departments of English and Comparative Literature at University of California, Los Angeles (2010–2011).

**Annika Rabo** is professor in the Department of Social Anthropology at Stockholm University since 2007. She received a Ph.D. in Social Anthropology in 1986 after completing a thesis on the political and social effects of a gigantic irrigation scheme along the Euphrates in northeast Syria. Rabo has worked on numerous projects in the Middle East, mainly in Syria, since the late 1970s, as well as in Sweden, focusing on a variety of topics such as, gender, kinship, family law, and education as well as urban and rural development and transnational migration. Her recent publications include: "Anthropological Methods and an Analysis of Memory: Migration, Past and Present in Raqqa Province," *Middle East Journal of Refugee Studies* (2017); "Conflicts and Identities among Assyrians/Syriacs in Sweden," in *Identity and Conflict in the Middle East and its Diasporic Cultures* (2016); and "'It has all been Planned:' Talking about us and Powerful Others in Contemporary Syria," in *Conspiracy Theories in the United States and the Middle East: A Comparative Perspective* (2014).

**Afshin Shahi** is a senior lecturer in Middle East Politics at Bradford University. His research interests include Middle East politics and security, political Islam, and religious sectarianism. Shahi's publications include *The Politics of Truth Management in Saudi Arabia* (Routledge, 2013), and he is also working on a forthcoming book, co-authored with Ehsan Abdoh-Tabrizi, titled *Iran, the Shia State and the Sunni Minority*. His articles include "Andalusiasation: Is Iran on the Trajectory of De-Islamisation?," *British Journal of Middle East Studies* 42, no. 4 (2015), and "The Paradoxes of Iranian Messianic Politics," *Digest of Middle East Studies* 22 (2012). He received his PhD in Politics from Durham University.

**José Antonio González Zarandona** is an associate research fellow at the Alfred Deakin Institute for Citizenship and Globalization at Deakin University in Australia. He is also an associate researcher in the History Department at the Center for Research and Teaching of Economics, Mexico. His research interests include iconoclasm, the destruction of art, and heritage destruction. He recently completed a Visiting Fellowship (funded by the British Academy) at Forensic Architecture (Goldsmiths, University of London) where he collaborated with the Victoria & Albert museum to produce Maps of Defiance, an exhibition for the London Design Biennale on the destruction of Yezidi mausoleums in Sinjar.

# INTRODUCTION

## COMMUNITIES IN THE PLAYING FIELD OF PLURALISM

*Firat Oruc*

> The very strength of the cultural disposition to pluralism in numerous zones of life today mobilizes a series of movements against it.[1]

How can we approach the concepts of pluralism and community in the Middle East without treating them as either self-evident facts or normative values that each society must reflect? The Middle East is viewed either as a region that is entrapped in the abyss of fundamentalism and authoritarianism and dreadfully lacking in the recognition of pluralism in religion, culture, law, and politics, or as a bygone mosaic of communities that co-existed peacefully for centuries. How, many analysts wonder, has "a region that for half a millennium was a global exemplar of pluralism and religious harmony ... become the least tolerant and stable place on the planet?"[2] The same pundits advocate for a revival of pluralism as a sure recipe to fix the so-called democracy deficit of the Middle East.[3]

But the policy circles have failed to appreciate that rather than a mere pragmatic approach to accommodate difference among and across different groups, pluralism is a multidimensional site of negotiation and contestation. To use Middle East historian Orit Bashkin's helpful definition, pluralism involves "the rejection of a singular concept of the philosophical or political domain, the acceptance of the diversity of the social realm, and the view of the social subject as a site of multiple group memberships."[4] While overlapping with related notions of identity politics, multiculturalism, diversity, and minority rights, the concept of pluralism refers specifically to the inherent co-existence of multiple community formations (religious, ethnic, legal, civic, and so on) in a given social site. A site is a location of construction, occurrence, activity, and interaction. As the binding metaphor of this volume, "sites" designate a range of heterogeneous domains and platforms of collective action and engagement. Sites of pluralism, therefore, encompass all the material areas where individuals and groups perform, claim, regulate, and contest power relations within polities and communities. Equally important, rather than assuming diversity, tolerance, and dialogue as a mere given, pluralism calls for an engaged commitment to recognize and understand others across perceived or claimed lines of difference.[5]

While it is common to understand pluralism as a form of regulating state–civil society relations through different forms of accommodations in the public sphere, "different constellations of institutions and actors shape the conditions of interaction."[6] As political theorists Maria Baghramian and Attracta Ingram aptly point out, "strategies of assimilation, integration, and politicization of cultural difference all have adherents and opponents in the practical arenas where disputes over the treatment of minorities, claims to self-determination, or identity rights, are fought out. And these practical disputes often feed on assumptions that are matters of vigorous theoretical dispute."[7] There are typically two major models through which social scientists have studied pluralism: the equilibrium model and the conflict model.[8] While the first model defines pluralism as the co-existence of multiple loyal groups in a consensual balance of power, the second looks at plural societies in which one community dominates the others. Based on the historical experience of the colonial governance of different native and indentured immigrant groups, the conflict model highlights the fact that a pluralistic society may not be exempt from dominance. In order for pluralism to take over some divisions in a truly democratic manner, it is imperative that the distribution of social, political, economic, and cultural resources does not lead to the monopolistic dominance of one group over others.[9]

Whether one adheres to the equilibrium or the conflict model, pluralism manifests itself in processes of inclusion and exclusion that are performed in specific political and historical contexts. It is therefore a mode of "historical reckoning" that would inevitably be "both contentious as a political project and unsettling in its effects."[10] Thus, any attempt to produce a prescriptive framework of pluralism would be fallacious precisely because this would only "lead us to mark the deficiencies of its actual use, rather than to an understanding of what its invocation contextually signifies."[11] In a similar manner, rather than a natural, non-voluntary collective with a set of shared features, a community is always relational and is formed by certain differences from, as well as affiliations with, other entities.[12] As sociologist Gerard Delanty aptly points out, "lying at the heart of the idea of community is an ambivalence. On the one side, it expresses locality and particularness—the domain of immediate social relations, the familiar, proximity—and, on the other, it refers to the universal community, in which all human beings participate."[13] Somewhere between kinship and society, community is a realm in which individuals experience physical as well as symbolic boundaries that regulate their interactions with others. The dynamics of inter-community relations, moreover, frequently shuttle between what political scientist James Scott calls "public" and "hidden" transcripts.[14] In other words, marginalized or subordinate communities often find themselves in a position of employing a dual discourse of conformity (public) and defiance (hidden) in their relations with their dominant counterparts.[15]

Pluralism is commonly regarded as the hallmark of liberalism.[16] As the embodiment of the political modernity of post-theological societies, the liberal nation-state is taken for granted as the ideal form of granting legitimacy to multiple groups with different normative values, dispositions toward self-realization, and conceptions of public existence. Yet, in a somewhat paradoxical way, nation-state formation in the Middle East has posed significant challenges to pluralism. Efforts to standardize and create a particular national identity have led to the suppression of differences for the sake of "the ideal citizen." National belonging has imposed internal homogeneity as a non-negotiable imperative at the expense of difference. If few attempts have been made to reconcile seemingly primordial divides that have defined relations between communities, this is in large part a product of political rhetoric that seeks to promote a narrative of a homogenous Middle East at the expense of the erasure of the rich fabric of communities in each country.

With the demise of the legal pluralism of traditional empires—which recognized the legitimate availability of different bodies of law for different groups, usually due to the pragmatic necessity of the territorial and economic expansion—religious and political communities can no longer design an autonomous jurisprudence of their own.[17] Cultural anthropologist Kabir

Tambar raises a significant question for this study: "What, then, are the limits of pluralism when it is organized within the institutional and ideological frameworks of the nation-state?"[18] The rhetoric of inclusion that is employed by the ruling powers does not automatically guarantee an expanded space for heterogeneous populations in the public life of the nation. Even under the regime of inclusivism, social groups can experience political vulnerability. "Increasingly and in many locales, the discourse of inclusion represents a modality of governance that disciplines the boundaries within which social difference is permitted to authenticate itself."[19] The state apparatuses (education, law, and so on) regulate the plural field of social, religious, economic, and ethnic differences among the existing communities of the nation. Examining the complex relationship of the Alevi community to the modern Turkish Republic, Tambar explains the double bind of pluralism to the nation-state as follows:

> To conceptualize pluralism as a tactic of inclusion within a regime of governance requires attention to the regulated forms of social difference—its key terms, its discursive and affective modalities, and its sites of institutional modalities, and its sites of institutional manifestation and mooring. For many Alevis today, this assemblage at once binds and empowers them. It created tools of political maneuver and possibilities of political engagement for a community that has long been excluded from participation in state planning and policy formulation. Yet these empowering forces also set the terms of reference necessary for Alevi discourse to be validated as legitimate. They incite but also monitor and regulate displays of collective difference.[20]

The crucial question at stake, therefore, is how communities can participate in shaping the public and political culture of the nation to which they belong, without just being fixated in the social hierarchy through some granted rights and space. While liberal norms will certainly continue to inspire how contemporary societies can achieve ethnic, linguistic, and religious diversity, the mere macro-level democracy afforded by liberalism on the basis of citizenship equality cannot in itself secure pluralism. In Monique Deveaux's words, "unlike *cultural diversity*—a merely descriptive term denoting the presence of different cultures—a commitment to *cultural pluralism* ... describes a normative position that accords basic respect and recognition to culturally diverse groups."[21]

The era of globalization has led to fundamental changes in the nation-state-based conceptions of pluralism and community. Transnational spatial formations have given rise to new forms of hybridization as well as marginalization of communities.[22] The Muslim communities in the West are an emblematic example of this double bind. Arguably, one of the most significant semantic shifts occurred in the emergence of "identity politics" and "multiculturalism."[23] While globalization has promised to produce a "world culture" that seeks to encourage diversity, the result has been less inclusive. As cultures have become increasingly deterritorialized, culture has come to be reproduced through the flow of information rather than through physical experiences in place and space. Thus, different outlets for the construction and articulation of complex identities will have to emerge. The coalescing of all these factors affirms that the Middle East will continue to be a critical region in terms of tracking how local cultures mediate global transformations.

At the current post-Arab Spring juncture, much of the study of pluralism and community in the Middle East revolves around examining identity as a source rather than a consequence of failing national projects. Numerous countries in the Middle East are currently in the grip of intense civil conflict that is tearing apart the social and cultural fabric that has held these societies together. With increasing sectarianism spreading across much of the region, the collapsing of state structures and evaporation of national borders, and open conflict and warfare engulfing whole swathes of the region's geography, questions of the resilience of ethnicity and religious identity are becoming increasingly relevant. Within some policy circles, the argument holds that it is the fundamental incompatibility between different ethnolinguistic and religious communities that is at the heart of the issue, and that these atavistic cleavages are impeding any form of political resolution and social cohesion. But one can also argue that the Arab Spring has made communities ever more visible and has shown the inescapable necessity for new modes of framing difference both practically and theoretically.[24] Since then, state–community relations in many Middle Eastern countries have changed dramatically. More importantly, the political turbulence in the region has led to seismic demographic changes, which forced many local communities to migrate elsewhere. The ongoing crisis of displaced communities of refugees, asylum seekers, migrant workers, and trafficked persons both within and beyond the region will sit at the heart of the issue of pluralism and community in the Middle East. Who would have thought until a few years ago that virtually each Turkish city would have its own Syrian community?[25]

The question of migration and forced displacement is not only bound to transform all social, economic, and political life in the region but will also pose new challenges to the politics of accommodation, especially to the extent that it challenges the presumed linkage between citizenship and pluralism.[26] Despite all the suffering and uncertainty of being uprooted, displaced communities are actively seeking and creating new forms of "survival units" in new "impermanent landscapes" in the aftermath of their deprival of the safety and welfare net afforded by the state and kinship ties.[27] Ultimately, it remains to be seen whether a pluralist sociopolitical paradigm based on increased empowerment of communities through new forms of mobility, agency, and cohesion can play a role in peace-building and state-reconstruction in the so-called new Middle East. In any case, this would require a different understanding than what Imad Salamey calls "state communitocracy," a framework for post-conflict resolution through the power-sharing distribution of different communitarian groups within a state.[28] Communities are not merely territorially marked entities that are in need of accommodation by the state and "mainstream" society. As opposed to the idea of state-sanctioned communitarianism that places communities under fixed historic narratives, symbolism, values, traditions, and practices, the new pluralist paradigm would have to account for the variable, flexible, adaptable, and malleable texture of the region's communities. Otherwise, we are always at the risk of producing "*an ideology of pluralism* that articulates and naturalizes the very boundaries of difference that seeks to diminish, overcome, or mediate."[29]

## *This volume*

One of the distinguishing features of this collection is that each chapter looks beyond the present and provides a historically grounded explanation for the topic it addresses. The chapters share a consensus that the Middle East has historically been a vastly diverse region that witnessed peaceful co-existence among different communities. Yet a glaring gap in research about the concrete sites of pluralism seems to be pervasive, too. The chapters address the impact of state policies on the diversity and heterogeneity of national identities as manifested at multiple levels, including education, law, cultural heritage, architecture, economic activities, citizenship, and identity formation. Thus, this volume does not limit its focus to religious and ethnic minorities in the region.[30] Nor does it repeat the case for the diversity of Muslim societies and epistemological plurality of Islam.[31] Rather, the contributors approach the question of pluralism and community in the Middle East as the lived experience of populations constantly navigating the boundaries of inclusion and exclusion mechanisms.

Part 1 of the volume focuses on "State–Community Relations" to analyze the role of governance apparatuses and institutions in the configuration of pluralism in civil society. In the first chapter of this section, Kathleen Cavanaugh highlights governance and law as two fundamental areas in which policies of inclusion are designed and implemented. Writing with a strong command of the political and theoretical dimensions of law, Cavanaugh attempts to open up a space for faith in the contemporary human rights project. Is it possible to think of religious community beyond its current problematic association with violence and extremism? What place is "religion" offered in the framework of law and rights? The secularist mandates of contemporary liberal democracy, observes Cavanaugh, have excluded faith and faith-based communities from the human rights project.[32] The idea, in particular, that Islam could provide certain organizing and socializing guidelines to a community has been received with great suspicion by both regional and international political actors. Especially in the aftermath of the 9/11 attacks, Muslim communities in Europe and the United States have been subjected to policing and surveillance in the public as well as legal spheres. Cavanaugh refers to several court cases, claiming that the lawmakers actively partake in limiting the public presence of Islam on the grounds that Islamic expressions, such as the veil, may violate citizenship equality. In the case of Fereshta Ludin, an Afghan-born naturalized German Muslim schoolteacher, the court decided that she could not enter the classroom with her headscarf, claiming that the hijab conveyed a "signaling effect" that could not be accommodated within the framework of state neutrality. Rather than a sartorial choice, the veil was treated as a divisive marker in the public sphere.

As a way of overcoming the faith-versus-reason binary, Cavanaugh puts together the two readings of human rights discourse: the first as a universalizing discourse that erases differences under the weight of equality, and the second as one that requires culture and norms to inform and help understand international norms and principles. From these readings, it follows that differences must either be promoted within the project or exist parallel to it. Cavanaugh's main contention is that the law is neither fixed nor stable and that Islam's presence in the public sphere remains a test case for rethinking the exclusionary zones that are embedded in the human rights project. The abstract categories of the hegemonic paradigm of secularism have mostly served to institute a monist perspective that aims to relegate religion to the private sphere. As an alternative to the regime of secularism, Cavanaugh proposes secularity as a pluralistic framework that would facilitate the co-existence of different belief and legal systems. Exposing the dichotomous positioning of faith and reason as a tension between cultural pluralism and

Eurocentric monism, Cavanaugh argues that contemporary international law carries on the negative legacy of the colonial project. Instead of ensuring non-violative relations, the law itself acts as a form of imposing what one community believes is good for all. This colonial logic reaches a climactic point especially in the legal policing of Muslim communities in the West and the sovereign states in the Middle East.

In tandem with the marginalization of Islam and Muslim communities in the Western legal framework, states in the Middle East have engaged with the international legal machinery on issues related to their minority groups and religious communities, while also drawing on Islamic legal practices to either propel or discard the rights paradigm. There is an enormously wide spectrum of voices and interpretations that inform these practices both by state legislators and religious jurists. According to Cavanaugh, this plurality has to do with the historical formation of the shari'a. Since the sources of Islamic law-making (the Qur'an and the sunna) did not provide complete legal content, hermeneutic endeavor became inevitable. More importantly, this led Islamic law to maintain strong interaction with the Muslim community and allowed a great margin for adaptation to different social and cultural contexts. In making a case for Islamic legal pluralism, however, Cavanaugh cautions against romanticizing the concept. States and individual actors draw on Islamic law for both rights-based good governance and legitimizing restrictions on women, ethnic minorities, and other religious communities. At any rate, it is important to note that Islamic legal hermeneutics will continue to evolve. The issue once again is the problematic reluctance of the international human rights regime to acknowledge them. As Cavanaugh reminds us, in the post-Arab Spring conjuncture, an important opportunity of fostering dialogue between Islamic law and the human rights project was wasted.[33] Instead of engaging with the political communities that emerged from the fraught political terrain of the Arab Spring, the power elite fell back on the good old argument that religion was an obstacle to the democratization of Middle Eastern societies.

Another significant yet overlooked site where the state regulates the plural structure of communities under its territorial sovereignty is national education. Education has been an instrument of power by which states shape and direct narratives of inclusion and exclusion, on the one hand, and an essential means for numerous communities to teach their traditions and culture to their youth, on the other. The promotion of public education in the region, as in most of the world, has been seen as part of the state- and nation-building project. Yet, even with most Arab countries investing heavily in education in the twentieth century, the 2002 Arab Human Development Report brought attention to the region's inadequate educational policy, which is seen as being incapable of supporting the individual communities and national development. The report notes that education in the region has defined "the new citizen" in rather narrow terms, with education being primarily Arab-centered in nature to the exclusion of linguistic, ethnic, and religious pluralism. Diversity, in these case-study countries, has not been seen as an asset in the classroom.

Through the case studies of Lebanon and Syria, Annika Rabo argues that the school curricula exclude certain perspectives, subjects, and histories that are either contradictory or contentious. While both countries are linguistically, religiously, and ethnically heterogeneous, they have completely different methods of managing pluralism. Syria, until the Civil War, had an extremely centralized education system that was similar in form and content across the country. Meanwhile, in Lebanon, the case is almost the opposite, with differentiated private schools assuming dominance. Lebanon's heterogeneous education system is in large part the product of national educational policies that have been either weak or non-enforceable. Foreign schools and institutions of higher learning, moreover, have been a consistent feature in the country since the mid-nineteenth century. In addition, by the end of the Ottoman period, all religious groups had their own educational institutions. Consequently, public spending in education in Lebanon has been low and the private sector has been much larger than that of the public one. French-language schools still tend to dominate, although English-language schools are becoming more popular as English is increasingly seen as a language of global use. Yet, despite being enrolled in these foreign language schools, Lebanese students still have to pass the ninth-grade brevet and the twelfth-grade baccalaureate to qualify for local universities or to join a professional association. By comparison, formal education in Syria during the late Ottoman period developed much slower. The French mandate made small investments in education that was primarily conducted in French and focused on knowledge of France. It was not until the first few years after independence that foreign and private schools became much more controlled and efforts began to make Arabic the primary language of instruction. These educational policies were strengthened after the Ba'th Party coup in 1963, when education became state controlled, mandatory for six years, free of charge, and an important instrument through which to produce modern and Arab nationalist citizens.

Because most of the education in Lebanon is non-standardized and schools often use foreign textbooks, many students are not familiar with the history and geography of their own country. However, following the end of the civil war in 1990, the decision was made to standardize history textbooks to reflect a history that was simultaneously precise and vague—a product of the many conflicting versions of history that the different groups who participated in the civil war have. Nevertheless, even two decades after the civil war, there is no agreement on how to present Lebanese history. Alternatively, civics, which is intended to promote a unified Lebanese identity and sense of the role of the Lebanese citizen, has had greater success. In comparison, in Syria, up until the 2011 civil war, debates over citizenship and history were much more muted because of the prevailing ideological dominance of the Ba'th Party. The curricula in geography, history, and religious education were carefully honed to promote the party message. History and geography lessons focused on national and regional history and always emphasized a pan-Arab outlook. Ideologically, the most important school subject was "national upbringing," in which the Ba'th ideology was taught by teachers who were experts on the subject. To fail the subject was to declare oneself as a potentially dangerous opponent to the political system. More importantly, one could not pass the ninth- or twelfth-grade exams without passing the subject.

Through this case study, Rabo contends that difference is managed through silence about contentious issues and the diversity of the country. Unity is promoted through civic or "national upbringing" lessons. There is a glaring level of exclusion in both contexts of migration and mobility, even though both countries had to cope with these issues as a result of civil war. Education is very much regarded as bounded within national borders and only a concern of the citizens who live there. In the case of Syria, we must note, the educational system has rapidly deteriorated since the civil war as students do not have access to stable education and many continue to be underserved in Lebanon and Jordan, as schools are unable to accommodate the growing number of Syrian refugees.[34]

In the third chapter, Islam Hassan offers us another case study on the role of the state in the reproduction of marginalization against certain communities in national identity construction. He argues that the Qatari ruling elite has been able to maintain continued hegemony within Qatari society through a socially conservative approach that privileges Arab tribal social values, culture, traditions, and customs, and that promotes a scheme of exclusion and inclusion on the basis of proximity to these traits. Moreover, through a narrow definition of what constitutes "Qatari," insofar as national identity is concerned, a distinction between citizens and "Qataris" is made. Individuals who are descendants of Abid (slaves), Huwalah (Sunnis of Iranian origin), and Persians may enjoy the rights of citizenship but do not figure highly on the social hierarchy, nor are they regarded as legitimate representatives and ambassadors of Qatari culture. Marriage between "nationals" and foreigners—although not illegal—is socially regulated and often seen as disadvantageous for Qatari women, who experience downward social and political mobility as a result of such marriages. On a national level, the Qatari state directly influences the marriage choices of women by making it legally difficult for them to confer Qatari citizenship onto their children if they marry foreigners.

Maintaining the political and social dominance of the Al Thani tribe and other Arab tribes, by way of what Hassan describes as "Gramscian hegemony," has meant that the Qatari state has constructed an exclusionary historical narrative that highlights the contributions of the Arab tribes to state-building while disregarding contributions made by the Abid, Huwalah, and Persians. Arab tribes have a vested interest in maintaining this structure because it is set up to confer material wealth to them. The ruling family is able to depend on their support by prioritizing Arab tribes when it comes to governmental and military positions. Therefore, according to Hassan, the Qatari society described and promoted by official narratives is "imaginary" and in considerable conflict with people's memories and lived realities. The portrayal of Qatar as a historically homogenous society overlooks the fact that it has been a mélange of Arab, Persian, Abid, and Huwalah for centuries.

In the last chapter of Part 1, Afshin Shahi and Ehsan Abdoh-Tabrizi shift the frame of analysis to the socioeconomic aspects of state–community relations. Through a detailed study of the Sunni populations such as the Turkmen, Kurds, and Baluch, they examine the influence of sectarian state policies on the development of communities in Iran. While their study refers to earlier historical periods, their main focus is the impact of the 1979 Iranian Revolution on Sunni populations, particularly in Sistan-Baluchistan, most of which became economically disadvantaged and remained developmentally underserved by the new government.

The centralization of government during the Pahlavi reign in the early twentieth century meant that the state's power to demand revenues through taxation and custom increased and were felt by all levels of Iranian society, but particularly the Sunni tribal populations. Moreover, these populations played no more than a manual role in the developmental projects that were introduced to connect Sistan-Baluchistan to the rest of the country. Forced land grabs and tribal resettlement by the government weakened tribal organizations and had a detrimental economic and social impact. The Baluch tribal elders, known as *sardārs*, were, to a certain extent, spared the worst effects of these measures as they formed a patron–client relationship with the modern state. This relationship was formed as a consequence of the priorities and the inability of the central government to afford a ward with the Baluch tribes. For the most part, the modern nation-state's seizure of control in these regions involved arbitrary violence, brutal resettlement with little economic relief, and the destruction of an entire way of life for the majority of Sunni Iranians.

With the ascension of Reza Shah to the throne, the state's heavy-handed policies were somewhat diminished but, for the most part, forced resettlements continued. Reza Shah used different policies from his predecessor to form an ideal nation. Rather than simply using arbitrary force against these groups, he attempted to assimilate them into the new Persianized Iranian state by moving more "reliable" ethnicities to those regions. However, like his predecessors, he did not extend developmental schemes or distribute any of the economic wealth gained through the oil boom to these regions. Instead, he preferred to concentrate wealth and development in urban and industrialized areas, thereby exacerbating the uneven development between Shi'i urban centers and Sunni rural areas.

The Iranian Revolution of 1979 would once again lead to a change in state policy toward Sunni minorities in the country. The Islamic Republic's commitment to social justice and economic equality did indirectly improve the lives of Sunnis as the regime embarked on an ambitious program to provide electricity and piped water to rural and provisional households. Yet revolutionary policies of nationalization and redistribution did not extend to include Sunni regions of the country, which largely remained economically marginalized and underdeveloped. Thus, despite its rhetoric, the revolutionary government has failed to overturn the continuing economic marginalization of ethnic Sunni Iranians that has existed since the Pahlavi period. Instead, it has compounded the problem of ethnic discrimination by introducing discrimination on religious grounds. The religious bias of the regime quickly became obvious when the revolutionary government officially forbade nominations of non-Shi'a for presidential elections. Moreover, the Shi'i bias in the public sector has meant that many Sunnis who were able to ascend to the middle class during the Pahlavi period have had those opportunities stripped away from them. The Shi'i discourse that emerged and defined the nation in the aftermath of the revolution has exacerbated the rate of underdevelopment in ethnic Sunni regions in Iran. As a consequence of systematic alienation and economic exclusion, the informal economy in these regions has taken hold.

Part 2 of the volume, "Frontiers of Identity," brings forth four distinct cases of community identity in the Middle East. A theme that spans across the chapters in this section is the role of human geography—urban spaces, heritage sites, ancestral lands, and frontiers—for communal and individual affirmation. Identities are constructed or suppressed through spatial processes of inclusion and exclusion. What is the place of the Jews or the Copts in the Arab city; the Islamized Armenians of Hopa Hemshin in the Turkish and Armenian official narratives; the racialized ethnic frontier communities of southern Iran in the Persian national imagination; and the Yezidis and Assyrians in the future of Iraq and Syria after the destruction of their heritage sites by the Islamic State (IS)? These cases direct our attention to areas that have been missing in the reckonings of pluralism in the Middle East.

The manner in which cities are built and communities integrated often speaks to how different communities interact. It may be the case that certain quarters within the city become exclusively associated with particular ethnoreligious identities, whether they be ghettos or spaces within the city where minorities feel like they have some control over place and communal traditions. In his contribution to the volume, Nezar AlSayyad attempts to map out urban transformations of the Middle East over the course of the twentieth and twenty-first centuries. He contends that the social and architectural evolutions of the Arab city have taken place during three distinct time periods—the colonial, the era of independence and nation-state building, and globalization—each of which corresponded to a particular urban design: respectively, the hybrid, the modern or pseudo-modern, and the postmodern. In conceptualizing this particular framework to analyze and understand urbanism in the Middle East, AlSayyad argues that while the fluidity of identities in the region becomes evident, the reasons for ethnic and religious conflict and the manner in which these conflicts translate into particular forms of social inclusion and exclusion become much more discernible.

The Western influence on Middle Eastern urbanism has historically produced contentious social and aesthetic categories and cities that proved to be ill-suited for the traditional sociocultural needs of the inhabitants. AlSayyad notes that even though these societies have had Western notions of modernity imposed on them, and at other times have, of their own volition, appropriated and adapted particular architectural and design trends, the tension between the traditional and the modern continues to exist. The critical question that AlSayyad's chapter invokes is a pertinent one: can alternative modernities emerge out of these contradictions?

Central to the question of Middle Eastern modernity and social transformation in the Middle Eastern city is the issue of social inclusion and exclusion. Examining the cases of Jews in Morocco and Coptic Christians in Egypt, AlSayyad attempts to capture how these minorities navigate and perform their identities in the Middle Eastern city. He notes that many Coptic women have started to veil in the streets of Cairo as a way to avoid attracting attention to themselves. This exemplifies what AlSayyad has termed "a survival tactic within a hegemony of sameness." Alternatively, in Morocco, the in/exclusion of minorities, namely Jews, takes place not through assimilation but through self-imposed segregation. Drawing on the history and conception of the traditional Islamic city, AlSayyad argues that segregation was historically a way for minorities to carve out a place of their own without giving up the right to the rest of the city. The *mellah*, Jewish quarter, in Middle Eastern countries such as Morocco, stands in stark opposition to the ghettos of Western Europe, which seemed more like punitive spaces than ones for positive communal affirmation. The *mellahs*, unlike ghettos, were locked from within, and the community exercised control over which days and times non-Jews could enter, often closing the gates to their quarter during the Sabbath and other religious holidays. Moreover, because their presence was believed to bring financial and commercial prosperity to the city, Jews were often protected from harassment, and their presence was valued. Consequently, AlSayyad argues that the Jewish example in Morocco refutes normative perceptions of exclusion always being a negative and that in this particular case it served to empower and carve out a space for a minority community.

In the following chapter, James Barry studies another minority group—Muslims of Armenian descent—in relation to modern interpretations of the Ottoman millet system (which categorized the subjects of the empire according to their religious affiliations) and its continued influence on the construction of Turkish Muslim and Armenian Christian identities and the perception of Islamized Armenians. Throughout his analysis, Barry emphasizes how Christianity has historically been regarded as essential to being Armenian and making claims to Armenian-ness, and how Islam was often perceived as the religion of the oppressor, and conversion to it as a forfeiture of one's Armenian identity.

Barry argues that the Ottoman millet structure was kept in place when the republic took over, with the Muslim millet becoming the Turkish nation and the non-Muslim millets, which comprised Jews, Greek Orthodox, and followers of the Armenian Gregorian church, being maintained as they were. But in this transition from empire to nation-state, the millet system became ethnicized. According to Barry, the continuation of the system in strict ethnoreligious categories is the primary reason for the Hopa Hemshin—a sub-ethnic group that resides in northeastern Anatolia—to identify as Turks and deny their Armenian origins. Most of the studies published about the Hopa Hemshin make no reference to their Armenian heritage and instead refer to them as a "Turkish tribe." Barry makes the argument that this is a demonstration of the ethnicizing effect of the modern millet system, whereby the Hopa Hemshin, because of their Muslim identity, do not have their Armenian origins acknowledged. Their relationship to Islam is very different from Islamized Armenians who did not willingly convert. For Islamized Armenians, conversion was a means through which to escape violence during times of persecution.

Barry also traces the salience of the synonymy between Christianity and Armenian identity to the founding myth of the Armenian national church and the millet system. Armenians claim to be the oldest Christian nation, and the church was able to maintain its exclusivity and hierarchy due to its adherence to non-Chalcedonic doctrine and liturgy written in classical Armenian. Unlike other churches and orders, the Armenian Church defines itself as the national church, solely serving the needs of the Armenian nation, which is defined by territorial dispersion as well as a lack of sovereignty over a homeland. As a consequence, the Armenian identity and nation have come to be defined in terms of a shared language, ancestry, symbolic link to a homeland, and a sense of solidarity. In the absence of an actual kingdom, the church has taken over the role of national government. Thus, the church has become the foremost authority in defining and maintaining the Armenian identity, and exploits and solidifies the connection between Christianity and the Armenian identity.

Despite their continued existence throughout the Middle East, their histories are largely absent from national historical narratives. Meanwhile, Muslims tend to feature as peripheral elements in Armenian history, and the contributions of Armenian converts to Islam are largely overlooked. Interactions between Muslims and Armenians were primarily within the academic sphere up until the fourteenth century, with Armenian intellectuals showing limited interest in dealing with questions of Muslim–Christian relations. By the fourteenth century, polemic writings that touted Armenian superiority began to circulate. "Imaginary arguments" with an Islam or Judaism of their own invention were used to define Armenian identity in terms of that which it was not—Islamic or Jewish. While Armenians may have adopted Arabic, Turkish, or Persian names that made them indistinguishable from the people among whom they lived, religion would continue to be a gulf between them and their neighbors. In large part, the gulf has persisted until today because of the continued oppression and persecution of Armenian communities. It is with this history in mind that Barry utilizes the case study of Armenian Muslims to understand the changes around identities and perceptions of self that have taken place within the Armenian community in the Middle East.

Contrary to religion, sect, ethnicity, and language, the concept of race has not typically been at the center of studying Middle Eastern societies. There is limited discussion of how narratives of race and color translated into political, social, and cultural realms. The role of racial discourses in national myth-making has not received the same scholarly attention that it has in the United States, France, South Africa, and Britain. Our volume addresses this significantly understudied question through Firoozeh Kashani-Sabet's chapter on the employment of racial discourses in the formation of modern Iran by a vast range of actors, including nineteenth-century European Orientalists, nation-state builders, anti-colonial intellectuals of the 1960s, and the post-1979 Islamic government. Kashani-Sabet argues that discrimination in differences of skin color, culture, or ethnicity remains common in certain Iranian regional communities. In fact, in the popular imaginary, as exemplified by the film *Bashu*, blackness continues to be equated with deviousness. Iran's case has its particularities, but the continued incorporation of racial discourse is not something that makes it distinct from other Middle Eastern countries, which drew heavily from Western concepts of nationhood that emphasized the racial superiority of one group over another.[35] In addition, like other Middle Eastern countries, the use of racist discourse was "often defensive in nature as states attempted to cohere the ethnically diverse territories they had acquired." Invariably, this led to the imposition of "cultures of ethnolinguistic homogeneity that led to the expurgation of minority cultures and languages."

Kashani-Sabet notes that while this occurred in almost all post-First World War Middle Eastern countries, the promotion of a racial discourse was particularly emphasized and had incredibly detrimental results in the Persian Gulf, where British officials and anthropologists often erroneously affixed racial designations such as "Arab," "Turk," and "Persian" with limited understandings of local cultures and languages. Moreover, they tended to overstate the ethnolinguistic differences among the Kurds, Baluchs, Lurs, and other communities in Iran from the Persians, despite the difficulty of identifying or tracking anyone of Persian origin that had not intermixed with these groups. These ethnolinguistic divisions became pervasive, and, in the nineteenth century, at the height of the Persian nationalist movement and the debate over Aryanism, were often exploited to promote agendas of racial superiority. Kashani-Sabet's chapter traces how the production of knowledge about race and identity produced by colonial actors and institutions was appropriated by the Iranian state and developed to include an Aryanist discourse that sought to maintain social hierarchies and divisions.

One of the main ethnolinguistic dividing lines, which dates back to the medieval period, has been between Persians and Arabs. The Arab was often constructed and conceived as the morally bankrupt alterity to the Persian, even though, based on physical features, it is often difficult to distinguish between an Arab and a Lur or those who inhabit the southern regions of modern-day Iran. The subject of ethnicity became a particularly contentious issue between Iraq and Iran in the early twentieth century as both countries began to assert their sovereign rights. The unease about these ambiguities and the unresolved disputes over ethnicity and sovereignty increased the fervor around Aryanism and Persian exceptionalism during the interwar period. In the 1960s, as Iranians began to engage with global discourses on decolonization, Third Worldism, Islamism, and socialism, conversations surrounding race, culture, and identity began to differ in content and tone. Ironically, as intellectuals like Jalal al-Ahmad, Ali Shariati, and Manuchehr Hezarkhani began to contribute to these global discussions, the Iranian state consumed itself with an ostentatious embrace of Aryanism, most flagrantly demonstrated in the coronation of Muhammad Reza Shah Pahlavi and his adoption of "Aryamehr" as a royal epithet. It was not until the 1960s that key Iranian intellectuals began to move away from the Persian superiority-oriented discourse of the state and to concern themselves with the struggles of peoples and nations that had endured colonialism and racial discrimination.

The emergence of IS has shaken the pluralistic fabric of the Middle East in recent times. Thus, the volume concludes with Benjamin Isakhan, Antonio González Zarandona, and Taghreed Jamal Al-Deen's chapter on the interplay between human suffering and heritage destruction unleashed on religious minorities by IS. The authors document and explore the "cultural cleansing" undertaken against the Yezidi and Christian populations in northern Iraq and Syria. Their discussion of the topic is situated within the conceptual framework of heritage, community, and violence, and considers the impact of such destruction on the cultural mosaic of the Middle East. The destruction of heritage sites in conjunction with genocidal pogroms, the authors argue, is central to ethnoreligious conflict because heritage plays a crucial and tangible role in the manifestation of community. Therefore, destruction of heritage monuments necessarily functions as a form of actual and symbolic violence that destroys identities and tears apart the social composition.

Yezidis have been subjected to a long history of persecution and genocide with the last campaign against them, before the IS onslaught, being initiated by Saddam Hussein who destroyed their villages during his brutal campaign against the Kurds in 1988. The attack also led to the displacement of many Yezidis. As a result of forced migration to urban centers in Iraq and abroad, their religious sites have become even more critical locations for rituals and public gatherings. Similar to the Yezidis, Christians have endured religious persecution and oppression even in the aftermath of secular nation-states in the Middle East. As a result, Christian populations in the region have fallen dramatically over the last century.[36] IS's renewed assault on Christians has seen their monuments, statues, murals, cemeteries, and churches destroyed, desecrated, and defaced. Again, the assault on these groups seeks both to erase their history and collective identity.

These new waves of violence bring forth painful memories of persecutions and genocides, invoking traumas of the past. They also erase, and make increasingly unlikely, the possibility of diversity in the Middle East. IS becomes the culmination of a program and ideology that promotes the suppression and rejection of difference. Given how explosive conflicts have become in the region, and how sectarian, religious, and ethnic divides are often at the heart of these conflicts, the authors rightfully caution that:

> What the Middle East (and Iraq and Syria more specifically) needs is a robust and sensitive process in which the traumas of the past are openly and honestly engaged with. This would serve as but one antidote to the ongoing chaos and as a critical first step towards mending inter-ethnic and religious relations, creating a cohesive region and a modern, peaceful, and multicultural Middle East where all citizens are free to live in peace regardless of their ethnicity, religion, or political leanings.[37]

Thus, while a heterogeneous Middle East may have been preserved despite efforts to mute and erase difference, what the ongoing conflicts and those of the twentieth century demonstrate is that without clear policies to promote difference in a more inclusive and conciliatory way within different spheres of the civil society, conflicts will continue to erupt. The historical genealogies and sites that are highlighted in this volume demonstrate that the work of pluralism itself requires multi-vectoral participation by communities on the ground. The notions of pluralism and community are of course in a state of transition both in the Middle East and other parts of world. But far from disappearing, community spheres still continue to define our sense of belonging and guide us in an increasingly insecure and uncertain world.

# PART 1

# STATE–COMMUNITY RELATIONS

1

# BETWEEN FAITH AND STATE*

## CONTEMPORARY CONFLICTS OVER DIVERSITY

*Kathleen A. Cavanaugh*

Essentialist thinking about religious tensions and inequalities in the Middle East often attributes divisions to culture and atavisms within Arab societies that, in turn, are inextricably linked to the nature of Islam. Placing religion at the heart of extremism and violence in the region has generated ever more pressure to develop secular political practices. Although the merits of the secular project as a remedy to conflict in the Middle East have been challenged,[1] the idea that religion sits uneasily with the requirements of good governance—with secularism and democracy as the defining features of modern statehood and modern politics—remains.

* The author would like to thank members of the Pluralism and Community in the Middle East working group, convened by Georgetown University in Qatar, for their comments on early versions of this chapter; and special thanks to Matthew McManus and Julia Hall who kindly read subsequent drafts.

To the extent that the policing of religion in the public square is particularly acute in the human rights project, it conforms to the state-oriented approach of public international law where law achieves legitimacy, in part, through the exclusion of other forms of social regulation (for example, customs, mores, morality, and religion). Within the human rights discourse, the pull of secularism "encourages people to seek emancipation in the vocabularies of reason rather than faith,"[2] and has been used to promote equality (political and civil), minority rights, religious freedom in the private sphere, and the legal separation of the private and public domains. This secularization of human rights, where faith is read out of the rights-oriented discourse, has led some to suggest that the human rights discourse itself has become a new religion, reflecting a particularly Western liberal reading of rights.

There is a significant body of work that provides details of "the assertions, worries, [and] polemical charges" of the human rights project,[3] but it is when we turn to the interplay between politics and religion, and religion and rights, that we enter some of the most contested terrain. Of course, while the debate around faith and/in reason—religion and/in human rights—is not unique to the Middle East and North Africa (MENA) or Islam, the contestation between the so-called "East" and "West" is often understood as a struggle between "Islam" and "modernity." In piercing the public sphere, Islam has pressed against the liberal secular norm that divides faith and democracy and is read as a belief system that is intolerant, premodern, and rigid. That Islam is irreconcilable with "the fundamental principles of democracy" was mapped out in the seminal case of *Refah v. Turkey* at the European Court of Human Rights (ECHR).[4] In this case, the court opined:

> that sharia, which faithfully reflects the dogmas and divine rules laid down by religion, is stable and invariable. Principles such as pluralism in the political sphere or the constant evolution of public freedoms have no place in it ... It is difficult to declare one's respect for democracy and human rights while at the same time supporting a regime based on sharia, which clearly diverges from Convention values, particularly with regard to its criminal law and criminal procedure, its rules on the legal status of women and the way it intervenes in all spheres of private and public life in accordance with religious precepts.[5]

This understanding of Islam (and its othering in human rights law) has reinforced notions that the human rights project has a deeply embedded secular Western liberal agenda.[6]

Against this backdrop, this chapter will endeavor to examine the politics of law that are mapped out within the various trends of analysis within both

Islamic and international law. Disrupting the notion of a "fixedness" in these legal discourses and reimagining each in their political self is, I argue, a critical first step in addressing the challenge—one that preoccupies much of the literature that looks at Islam and rights—of opening a space in the human rights project where faith and reason can be accommodated. The chapter's first section will broadly examine how the human rights project engages with religion in the public sphere. It will define the concepts of secularism and secularity and examine the nature of faith–state relations. It will turn to how these concepts have been engaged where Islam and human rights intersect generally, and then specifically when applied to states in the Middle East. Depending on the point of departure of the narrator, human rights are read in one of two ways: in the first reading, human rights are posited as a universalizing good that requires the public space be policed, with differences extinguished under the weight of notions of equality. In contrast, the second reading requires culture and context to be considered in order to understand, as well as apply, international legal norms and principles. It follows, then, that difference must be protected (indeed promoted) within the project or exist in parallel to it.

Section two focuses on the plural readings of Islamic formulations of law. Differentiated readings of Islamic law, something I argue is shared with international law, yield differentiated approaches to the interpretation and applicability of the norms and principles of Islamic international law. Approaching law in this way—where law is neither fixed nor stable—recalibrates how we understand Islam in the public square and, additionally, pushes us to rethink some of the exclusionary zones that have traditionally been read into the human rights project. The third section of the chapter will focus on the trends of analysis within Islamic criminal law and procedure. As there are authoritative texts that undertake this task, this section will not replicate these endeavors but will provide an overview of the public law injunctions of (ostensibly) Islamic legal principles and examine just where (and how) these readings have led to "Islamic" restrictions with regard to human rights. The chapter will then look at how the tensions between religion and what is understood as "necessary in a democratic state" have mapped out in the political transformations that have unfolded, and continue to unfold, across the MENA region in the wake of the so-called Arab Spring. As the hegemonic contestation of these legal and political narratives plays out, the conclusion will revisit the question of faith in reason.

*Decaffeinating the public square*[7]

Whatever the understanding of the origins of human rights,[8] in its contemporary clothing, its vocabulary is secular. As a secular project, human rights divide faith and rights-based discourses, protecting the private while policing the public space. Part of the universalizing process of the human rights project has embedded a "hegemonic knowledge regime of secularism,"[9] where expressed will is read as derivative of the "coercive" influences of powerful religious expressions. And as David Kennedy notes,

> If you thought secularism was part of what is bad about the modern West, you might assert that human rights shares the secular spirit, that as a sentimental vocabulary of devotion it actively displaces religion, offering itself as a poor substitute. You might claim that the enforcement of human rights, including religious rights, downgrades religion to a matter of private and individual commitment, or otherwise advances the secular project.[10]

The debate over the extent to which religion and law interface is hardly new. Henry Maine's classic late nineteenth-century work posited that religion and law are wedded: "there is no system of recorded law, literally from China to Peru, which, when it first emerges into notice, is not seen to be entangled with religious ritual and observance."[11] Secularization, then, was necessary to divest law from religion's grasp. For Maine, progress was to be measured when the blurring of law and religion moved toward a demarcation between the realms of law and religion. Such a view of religion's relationship with law in early cultures was quite aggressively challenged by A. S. Diamond, who contended that law was secular *ab initio*. While Diamond acknowledged that the influence of religion was to be found in two specific areas—sacral crimes and oaths or ordeals in litigation—he argued that these were the exceptions to what otherwise were secular laws.[12] In revisiting these works, Javier Martínez Torrón and W. C. Durham Jr. note that the divide between Maine and Diamond obscures "a deeper methodological point."[13] They argue that the assumption of Maine and Diamond's theses—that law is either secular, or it is underpinned by religion or moving in between—fails to take account of the individual's relationship with "the" law, which may have a secular meaning for some and a religious meaning for others, and this relationship may shift and change over time.[14] Applying this reasoning to the current debate on the private/public divide, Torrón and Durham suggest that, similarly, the relationship between religion and the secular state must account for individual differences across plural societies, as well as "the rich variation over time and space within individual lives and communities."[15]

This rich variation is, in fact, what emerges when examining the relationship between faith and state, as all states adopt a particular discourse with regard to church–state relations, usually articulated at the level of constitutional and statutory law, together with judicial and administrative decisions. Although these positions are never fixed or immutable and often exist in a contested space, it is often possible to position them along a continuum. At one end, there are states that are strongly secular, exhibiting what José Casanova refers to as an illiberal secularism.[16] At the other end are those regimes that are secular and have a particular neutral position (both in rhetoric and law) but exhibit rather high levels of cooperation with religious groupings, and finally, those states that have a non-secular (for example, religious) orientation. Where states lie along this continuum affects how questions related to freedom of religion—especially the manifestation of religion—are engaged and, relatedly, how religious communities are accommodated in that state.

Research that has endeavored to provide an audit on the relationship between religion and state within liberal democratic states has revealed two broad patterns or models—defined as "secularism" (or secularization) and "secularity." While these patterns can shift and change over time, and some states may not affix to either side of the spectrum—that is, they may display tendencies toward each—these points of inquiry are useful in providing some method of categorizing current trends within individual states and indeed regions. The first category, secularity, applies to systems of governance in states that "favour substantive over formal conceptions of equality and neutrality, taking claims of conscience seriously as grounds for accommodating religiously-motivated difference."[17] This model provides a pluralist framework within which the state endeavors to accommodate different belief systems, which may take the form of legal pluralism.

The second trend is that of secularism. Historically, this concept of a secular society meant the absence of religious involvement in government affairs as well as the absence of government involvement in religious affairs. However, more contemporaneously, and this is especially true in so much of the language embedded in the human rights discourse, secularism is read as ideology or belief, that is, as an end in itself. In such a system, it is this belief that has supplanted religion as in need of protection and indeed enforcement. This form of illiberal secularism, as Casanova quite rightly termed it, polices religion, confining it to the realm of the private and communal sphere, keeping the public square free from religious manifestations.

This is particularly evident in Europe, which, on the one hand, has promoted a pluralist model at the EU level, while on the other, national jurisdictions have responded to the challenges posed in the wake of the events in the United States and Europe after 9/11 by attempting to more rigorously police the public sphere of religion. While these arguments within a wider EU context are not new—and have been raised before in Turkey, France, and Spain—the current geopolitical terrain is fertile for giving increased succor to this argument.

Although European states have, in general, protected the freedom to hold one's beliefs, when the expression of those beliefs enters in the public sphere or "public square," the freedom to manifest religion has been subject to limitations. Limitations on religious expression are often justified by states as necessary to ensure equality (for example, prevent discrimination) or to preserve the stability of a state (Turkey springs to mind here). At its core, the debate around religion in the public sphere centers on the extent to which the particular manifestation of religious belief is an individual's freely chosen act warranting protection or one that represents the religious coercion of individuals. This question has been captured at the national level in two seminal court cases (in Germany and Turkey) that involved a state restriction on the wearing of the hijab (headscarf).

In the first case, Fereshta Ludin, a twenty-six-year-old German schoolteacher of Muslim faith, was turned down for a teaching position in the Baden-Württemberg school system because she wore the hijab while teaching, and this, in the board's view, was incompatible with the principle of separating church and state in the German Basic Law (*Grundgesetz*). The board argued that the hijab had a "signaling effect" (*Signalwirkung*), which it considered incompatible with the principle of state neutrality (*staatlichen Neutralitatsgebot*).[18] It further argued that the headscarf was an expression of cultural demarcation and therefore a political, as well as a religious, symbol.[19] Ludin appealed this ruling through three avenues of the German administrative courts. The first two levels—the administrative court (Verwaltungsgericht) of Stuttgart, in a 24 March 2000 decision and the administrative court (Verwaltungsgerichtshof) of Baden-Württemberg, in a 26 June 2001 decision—upheld the board's ruling. In her final appeal to the highest court of appeal in Germany, the Federal Administrative Court (Bundesverwaltungsgericht) on 4 July 2002 the decision was finally overturned, but, crucially, the ruling itself left open the distinct possibility—indeed, the wording suggests inevitability—that given the increased diversity within Germany and the possible conflicts that might result from it, there may be conditions that arise in the future that will make it necessary to govern the "outward appearance" (*auberes Auftreten*) of instructors.[20]

A similar approach was adopted within the Turkish Constitutional Court in the case of Leyla Şahin, a twenty-four-year-old woman then in her fifth year of studies in the Cerrahpaşa Faculty of Medicine at the University of Istanbul.[21] In March 1998, Şahin was denied access to one of her written exams because she was wearing a hijab, which was in contravention of a 1997 decision by the vice chancellor of the University of Istanbul that stated:

> By virtue of the Constitution, the law and regulations, and in accordance with the case-law of the Supreme Administrative Court and the European Commission of Human Rights and the resolutions adopted by the university administrative boards, students whose "heads are covered" (wearing the Islamic headscarf) and students (including overseas students) with beards must not be admitted to lectures, courses or tutorials.[22]

Şahin was subsequently denied entry to the university on several occasions for defying the ban on wearing the hijab. The Turkish Constitutional Court ruled that the ban was necessary to protect the individual from external pressure on matters of religion by upholding the principles of freedom of religion and equality before the law.[23]

Such policing of the public square by states is also undertaken at the regional level, where a margin of appreciation on interferences in religious manifestation is often given to the state. At the ECHR, the definition of the requirements of secularism, mapped out by the Turkish Constitutional Court in the Sahin case, was adopted by the ECHR.[24] Having exhausted domestic remedies, Sahin subsequently lodged a complaint to the ECHR, and, in 2004, a seven-judge chamber rejected Sahin's arguments that the ban on the Islamic headscarf in higher education institutions violated her rights and freedoms under several ECHR provisions, including Article 9. In its ruling, the court argued that "the University of Istanbul's regulations imposing restrictions on the wearing of Islamic headscarves and the measures taken to implement them were justified in principle and proportionate to the aims pursued and, therefore, could be regarded as necessary in a democratic society." The case was later referred to the Grand Chamber where the decision was upheld.[25] Importantly, in arriving at its decision, the court drew on a number of other European states' court decisions and legal debates concerning the Islamic headscarf and state education in Belgium, France,[26] Germany, the Netherlands, Switzerland, and the United Kingdom. A closer look at the reasoning of the court in the *Sahin* case suggests that the court attributed "a perceived *political*, and potentially negative, meaning of the Islamic headscarf in a democratic society."[27] "Taken together," as one commentator has noted,

> these cases raise critical questions about the possibility, and limits, of religious freedom in increasingly diverse polities, within the European Union and beyond. On the one hand, they signify a growing tension between a "coming world order" that aims at the "cultural extension and legal enforcement of human rights," including freedom of religion and belief. On the other hand, the cases reflect both an increased vigilance of religious practices that are considered indicative of a "clash of civilizations," and the resulting restrictions on religious freedom in the name of public order. The cases also demonstrate the growth of a pan-European legal discourse of religious symbols not only as text, but as a mechanism, however broad and ambiguous, of social control.[28]

Since this ruling, the political landscape in Turkey has significantly transitioned as the election of the Adalet ve Kalkınma Partisi (hereafter the AK Party) in 2002 has brought religion in from the political cold.[29] This shift, however, has not been reflected in other parts of Europe where states continue to try to fit immigrant communities, which are predominately Muslim, into a secular normative model that increasingly favors privatizing religion. The legal narratives that have accompanied this privatization intertwine a secular hegemonic regime with what is necessary in a democratic society. What is interesting to note, however, is that the within this secular "democratic" pull lies "an implicit, diffused and submerged Christian cultural identity. In this respect, 'secular' and 'Christian' cultural identities are intertwined in complex and rarely verbalized modes among most Europeans."[30]

### *Between faith and state*

Although international law's secular policing of states in the Middle East is often framed in a rights-oriented discourse that proffers notions of equality, gender parity, and the necessary boundaries in a democratic regime that divides religion and politics, its attendant policies (and policing) historically have been extensions of colonial interests. Situating the application of law in the "colonial present" suggests a narration of modern international law that cannot be separated from the historical, cultural, economic, and political backdrop of the European colonial project. Although the "repertory companies" may differ, the conquest and domination between the "Occident and the Orient" can be found, contemporaneously, within public international law—from international economic and trade law and human rights to the laws governing the use of force (*jus ad bellum*) and international humanitarian law (*jus in bello*) in the context of the state of exception established during the "global war on terror;" and, of relevance here, to the struggle over the secular soul of the rights-orientated discourse.

Secularism, read within a colonial present, is no longer an idea or value that promotes tolerance, broadmindedness, and pluralism—qualities the ECHR has stated are necessary in a democratic society.[31] Rather it is a concept that is "closely connected with the rise of a system of capitalist nation-states—mutually suspicious and grossly unequal in power and prosperity, each possessing a collective personality that is differently mediated and therefore differently guaranteed and threatened."[32] As Talal Asad rightly observes, "a secular state does not guarantee toleration; it puts into play different structures of ambition and fear."[33] Moreover, these projects are built on the flawed assumption that states can be ascribed a morality: that there are "genuinely 'non-violative' relations between the Self (the 'West') and its Other."[34] The reality, as John Esposito and Azzam Tamimi argue, is that,

> Today throughout the Muslim world we are witnessing a domestic war over national/cultural identity. It is a battle to define the very identity and soul of nation states, which pits entrenched regimes and elites against new social forces, an alternative sector of society wishing to see its societies modern but Islamic rather than secular in orientation. Increasingly the struggle incorporates calls for greater political participation and democratisation. Ironically the forces of secularism often opt for great authoritarianism rather than democratization in order to retain their power and privilege. Western governments more content with short term gains than facing long term realties and strategies quietly acquiesce.[35]

While other regions of the postcolonial world have faced periods of colonial domination that have shaped the contemporary contours of their identity, the MENA region has been characterized by waves of different kinds of domination and a sustained external influence within the modern states. Situating international law within, rather than apart from, these political realities necessitates that before we begin to explain "universal" international law, we must first clarify "what or whose view of international law is meant."[36] While rights have "long existed," as Samuel Moyn argues, "they were from the beginning a part of the authority of the state, not invoked to transcend it."[37] Challenging the assumption of international law and related doctrines as "a stable set of normative demands opposed to international politics" reveals a "process of articulating political preferences into legal claims" that "cannot be detached from the conditions of political contestation in which they are made."[38] States often articulate political claims in the form of rights, endeavoring to marginalize the political cost for either adopting or discarding rights. Yet even where states choose to discard international law, its residue remains.

The deeply performative nature of how legal rules operate in international law reveals a constructive ambiguity that opens a space where the contestation over the "what" and the "whose" reading of the law plays out. Although the primary sources of international law identified under the Statute of the International Court of Justice (ICJ), Article 38 (treaty, custom, general principles, and judicial decisions), are not contested, much like Islamic law, its norms and principles are subject to interpretation and different trends of analysis. The differentiated approaches to interpreting international law are captured in three ways. The first is a textualist approach, in which a restrictive interpretation based on an "ordinary meaning" of the text is applied. Similar to a textualist reading of Islamic law, this approach places a great deal of weight on the literal meanings of the texts. The second, "subjective" approach factors the underpinning of a treaty, the intent of its drafters, and reads a treaty "in its context" when interpreting respective principles. A third approach is interpretative—sometimes called effective interpretation. Here, a text is read "in the light of its object and purpose," similar to what I have described as a contextualist approach within Islam. As detailed in the next section, the different trends of analysis that are evident in public international law are also present in Islamic legal discourse and also give rise to competing narrations whenever Islam enters the public square.

*Islam in the public square*

Even a cursory review of literature that endeavors to either unpack or marry Islamic law with various international legal norms and prescriptives will unveil contradistinctions, overlaps, and, at times, the "ambient noise" so wonderfully described by Ann Mayer. As Islam is not an actor, the various readings of Islam both depart and arrive at different interpretations of prophetic revelations. The struggle between "textualist" readings and those of "contextualists" moves between a reading of Islam that is fixed and immutable,[39] to one that endeavors to read the text within a specific historical context. Although "there is one Islam, and the fundamental principles that define it are those to which all Muslims adhere,"[40] there is an "important margin allowed for evolution, transformation, and adaptation to various social and cultural environments."[41] This margin gives rise to these plural readings and respective (and often distinct) "doctrinal and social attitudes." While the various tendencies within Islam spring from the same normative criteria, these differentiated readings yield differentiated approaches to the interpretation and applicability of the norms and principles of Islamic international law.[42]

This approach to understanding Islamic law suggests that the question posed earlier as to the "what" or "whose" version of law is adopted can also be applied to how we engage with the various readings and interpretations drawn from Islamic law. As Anver Emon, Mark Ellis, and Benjamin Glahn rightly argue, to negate the "effect of the state on the content, scope and application of Islamic law today,"[43] is to "address abstract ideas in a vacuum and to turn the risk of pursuing 'red herrings.'"[44] Disrupting the idea that these legal regimes are fixed, stable, and pre-political moves us beyond the reproduction of rather worn arguments on Islam and human rights and requires that we emancipate some of the concepts seen as inextricably linked to each.

Distilling the "ideals" expressed within the different readings of Islam from "the actual laws, legal institutions and policies in Muslim countries" reveals that the legal practices specific to an individual country—including the rhetorical use of human rights as well as the adoption of formal rights-based language in constitutions, etc.—draw on a variety of sources that can shift over time in ways that are not identical to Western experiences and may not be consistent across Muslim cases.[45] And, as studies have shown, there is a multiplicity of views on human rights among Muslims living in the Middle East, suggesting, as Mayer has argued, that we should not "speak of 'Islam' and human rights as if Islam were a monolith or as if there existed one established Islamic human rights philosophy that caused all Muslims to look at rights in a particular way."[46] Although purportedly drawing from the same sources, these shifting constructions and "plural readings" of Islam are critical to understanding why Muslim voices are complex and varied when engaging with questions of human rights. It also explains why Muslim state practice with regard to public law implementation and interpretation also varies. This is, in fact, the contradiction inherent in this debate—a plurality of readings of Islam with each argued to be fixed and stable. This may well also explain why some scholars assert that "the sources and methods of Islamic law contain common principles of good government and human welfare that validate modern international human rights ideals,"[47] while public law injunctions of, ostensibly, Islamic legal principles are used to restrict or define women's legal status, criminal procedure, select penal laws and procedures, and legal rules related to freedom of religion and religious minorities.

While it is not possible or necessary to discuss the doctrines (or minor techniques) in any detail, as there are other authoritative texts that undertake this task, it is important to understand the nature of Islamic law in order to understand "Islamic" restrictions with regard to human rights. Against this, there are a few points related to the development of shari'a and its intervention in the public space that merit some review. Shari'a draws on two formal sources—the Qur'an and the sunna of the Prophet.[48] There are, additionally, tools or methods that were developed (referred to as *fiqh*) that have been used to provide an evolutive form to the formal sources. The process of *ijtihad* (or legal reasoning) gave rise to two legal methods of *ijma* and *qiyas*,[49] and additional doctrines such as *istihsan* (juristic preference), *istislah* or *maslaha* (welfare), *istishab* (presumption of continuity), *darura* (necessity), and *urf* (custom).[50] What is important to note is that the Qur'an has a small number of verses that deal directly with legal subject matters, and only in a few specified cases (*hudud* and *qisas*) does it set out the legal consequences of a particular action.[51] This has led one scholar to note that "the primary purpose of the Qur'an is to regulate not the relationship of the man with his fellows but his relationship with his Creator."[52] What legal content the Qur'an has provided has been drawn to exact the most from the rather limited measures but, even in these instances, and "with very rare exceptions, [Islamic principles are] general, and give guidance in a certain direction, rather than fixing a restricting framework."[53] Some non-legal verses have also been constructed to provide legal guidance.

The contributions to shari'a by the sunna open up greater avenues of contention. Putting aside the legal implications for the moment, the authenticity of the sunna has led to questions of possible fabrication. The questions have been raised to suggest possible mediation by those who may have believed to have known the Prophet's thinking on certain matters and from this belief have recorded their beliefs as opposed to the sayings or actions of the Prophet himself. This human construct leaves open the possibility of fabrication and questions as to the genuineness of a particular report. Since most of the authentication of the sunna was undertaken during the second century, returning to this task today would prove impossible. Nonetheless, some scholars query the authentication process even when referencing the compilations by the six scholars accepted by sunni Muslims.

The two final parts for review are the legal methods of *ijma* and *qiyas*. Unlike the primary sources of the Qur'an and sunna, these are considered secondary sources of Islamic law as they are the "products of human reasoning" rather than (solely) divine revelation,[54] but are limited to specific situations. *Ijma* is best understood as "consensus" and "constitutes a strong 'source' of law in the absence of a direct text of the Qur'an or the sunna on any issue."[55] That said, it is the source of this consensus that has raised additional questions: for example, is it the consensus of *mujtahidun* (Islamic legists),[56] the companions and their community in Medina, or is it the consensus of the community of Muslims?[57] Mashood Baderin suggests that *ijma* may, contemporaneously, source its consensus from the practice of Muslim states (much like customary law).[58] The second subsidiary source is *qiyas* or analogy. As this process is based on human reason (and as noted, *ijtihad* was to have closed at the end of the ninth century AD), there is some controversy when using *qiyas* as a source for shari'a. However, the process of *qiyas* is confined to those cases where "none of the other sources is applicable and the outcome is seen to be fully consistent with the totality of shari'a as well as with any of its established principles and rules."[59]

As noted earlier, scholars of Islamic law have divided its elements into two broad spheres—one part that deals with the relationship between the individual and the Creator, and of which most questions are settled, and a second part that looks at the question of an individual's relationship with others. It is in this latter category where there has been argued to be a lacuna between the existing jurisprudence (*fiqh*) and the needs and challenges presented by an ever changing political and social landscape. Within the different Islamic tendencies, there is a struggle between those who believe that all has been revealed through existing primary, secondary, or minor sources, methods, and techniques; and those who believe that we must revisit either the process that gave rise to current Islamic law or reopen the doors to *ijtihad*, which will allow renewal of the sources. As there is no agreed position, just how the interface between civil and political rights, as defined within international law, relates to what are ostensibly "Islamic" restrictions with regard to human rights must be understood within so many caveats.[60]

### *Islamic criminal law and procedure*

It is when we turn to the question of Islamic criminal law and procedure, which preoccupies much of the material that looks at human rights and Islamic law, that the caveats noted above are the most acute. The interface of Islamic criminal law and human rights principles are a site of potential conflict in matters related to substantive law, evidence, and procedure. As there are significant bodies of work that undertake audits on the administration of criminal justice and the application of shari'a, this section will only briefly summarize some of these writings and provide references for additional and more detailed review. There are three forms of offenses that have been extracted from the general treaties of Islamic jurisprudence—*hudud*, *jinayat*, and *ta'zir*—with each case attaching either a fixed, retributive, monetary, or discretionary punishment. It merits note that the Qur'an and sunna, from which Islamic law is extracted, are religious, not legal texts, and

> early Muslim scholars and jurists did not distinguish between the religious, ethical, and legal aspects of Shari'a let alone identify specific legal fields. Consequently, those principles and rules of Shari'a relevant to what is known in modern terminology as criminal law, evidence and procedure can be extracted only from general and extensive treatises of Islamic jurisprudence.[61]

Where this is most evident is on the procedural and practical application of Islamic criminal law. So while a *hudud* offense may come with a fixed penalty, the textual sources for the procedure by which the offense is proclaimed have been characterized as "rudimentary and informal."[62] A historical review of the application of Islamic criminal law suggests that its modern post-Second World War construction may reflect the grafting of a number of both minor and major sources and jurists from a number of different schools (extinct, minor, and major) and approaches (from textualists to contextualists). It is, in short, one of the most underdeveloped areas of Islamic law. It is beyond the scope of this chapter to engage further in this area, and there is ample secondary literature on Islamic criminal law. What is worth noting here, however, is that in reading the commentary on the modern construction of Islamic criminal law with regard to procedure, there is a tendency, as Mayer has argued, for "anachronistic projections of modern principles of criminal justice back in to a legal order in which they were unknown."[63] Similarly, Sayid Reza argued that an inquiry into Islamic criminal procedure has the potential to change criminal procedure to "Islamizing" it, as the current system, arguably, is not grounded in the Qur'an, but rather in state authority.[64] He argues that

> modern-day systems of Islamic criminal law enforce criminal prohibitions and punishments originating from Islamic doctrines that are up to fourteen hundred years old, but operate mostly under codes and practices of procedure that were adopted from European nations in the twentieth century. Thus, states that enforce shari'a criminal prohibitions and punishments today do so mostly according to procedural rules and principles that did not originate to govern Islamic criminal law.[65]

What is evident from the divergent approaches is that there is room for examination of the modern construction of Islamic criminal law, especially where it involves principles related to evidence, and procedure, which has allowed some contextualists to posit ways to "reform" criminal procedure to bring it in line with international criminal law. That said, within this textual lacuna, more recent Muslim state practice differs, and certainly some of the implementation of Islamic criminal law within Muslim states has conflicted with rules and procedures established under international criminal law.

Islamic criminal law meets the sharp end of the norms of international criminal law primarily in cases of *hudud* offenses. It is here where there is little discretion afforded to states with regard to the punishment of these offenses, which are quite severe, and as Mayer has argued, "laws imposing penalties like amputations, cross amputations, and crucifixions would seem to be in obvious violation of Article 7 (of the ICCPR)."[66] While there are six *hudud* offenses, Abdullahi Ahmed An-Na'im suggests that in two of these cases—*sukr* (intoxication) and *ridda* (apostasy)—the Qur'an does not provide specific punitive measures, and therefore, he argues that these two should not be understood as *hudud* offenses (with fixed punishments).[67] The distinction between a *hadd* and *ta'zir* offense is not simply a matter of classification. The punishment for a *hadd*-type offense is fixed and there is no discretion allowed:[68] "[a]ccording to the logic of shari'a as a religious law, once the Qur'an and the sunna speak clearly and definitely, the believer has no choice but to comply."[69]

For scholars who are looking to bridge or "reform" Islamic principles in order to move them closer to conformity with international human rights law, the *hudud* and the ostensibly "religious imperative" read into the penalty for a *hadd*-type offense pose a significant challenge. However, even where the texts suggest a clear penalty for a given offense, contextualist scholars have questioned the definition and scope of *hudud*. While this approach is undertaken by a rather limited number of scholars, their arguments, nonetheless, merit some review as they may provide a way of examining *hudud* punishments without challenging the divine judgment revealed in the texts. Before turning to these arguments, there are two other categories of offense identified by modern writers of Islamic criminal law—that of *jinayat* and *ta'zir*. The penalty for the offense of *jinayat*, or homicide or bodily injury, is exact retaliation (*qiyas*) or monetary compensation (*diya*), depending on the preferences of the victim. *Ta'zir* offenses confer the ruler, and his judges, discretionary power over the penalty for each offense. The discretionary nature of these two offenses contrasts with the, ostensibly, fixed prescriptions attached to *hudud*-like offences.

There are a number of scholars (albeit relatively small) who are endeavoring to pry open the spaces where even the most obvious of compatibility issues between Islamic law and human rights exist. Baderin has indicated that the conflict between the prescriptions for offenses under Islamic criminal law and prohibitions on cruel, inhumane, or degrading treatment under international law can be resolved in one of two ways. The first recognizes the discretionary mechanisms open to the authorities in a non-*hadd* offense. This provides the state with discretion, which could be used to bring whatever punishment is conferred in line with international human rights law. Reza makes a similar argument when he posits that the religious police in some states exceed the authority granted to them in the Qur'an when investigating wrongdoing. The privacy rights of individual Muslims could provide a "key counterweight to enforcing Islamic criminal prosecutions."[70] The emphasis on discretion and leniency in the Qur'an suggests that excessively harsh punishments carried out in the name of shari'a are the result of the state exerting its authority, rather than a Qur'anic mandate.

The second method Baderin articulates endeavors to deal with the more complicated *hadd* offenses. Following on from some of An-Na'im's writing on criminal procedure, Baderin suggests that one potential opening is through procedural devices (for example, extending all reasonable doubt to the accused). In applying a "strict adherence to procedural and evidential requirements for those Qur'anic offences," it may be possible—and, Baderin notes, it has already been applied in a relatively recent case law within Muslim states—"to avert the (hudud) penalty without impugning the Law" through a possible "reconciliation" allowed "indirectly through legal procedural shields available within Islamic law."[71] Reza argues that "[s]everal reports in the Sunna reflect a preference that *hudud* crimes—for all their seriousness, and even if they satisfy the 'manifestness' requirement ... not be prosecuted at all."[72] According to Reza, "[t]he Prophet himself could not disregard *hudud* crimes, since punishing for them is a right of God (*haqq Allah*), and he was God's vice regent on earth; but for that very reason, fellow Muslims should avoid bringing them to his attention."[73] There is, as this inquiry highlights, a presumption of non-prosecution within Islamic criminal procedure that,[74] coupled with other procedural requirements articulated by Baderin and An-Na'im, might allow states to reduce the number of *hudud* punishments administered while staying faithful to the words of God and the Prophet.

Revisiting the public interventions of Islamic law, including the application of shari'a in domestic law and its interface with international human rights law, is not to suggest that the various readings of Islam into the rights discourse have no consequence. Mayer reminds us that factoring culture and context into the interpretation and application of international law requires some consideration as Asian or Islamic "culture-bound" values and norms that have "political usefulness" for "foes of human rights,"[75] and there are challenges in wrestling this concept from political agendas.

The crafting of Islam as the gatekeeper that limits access to a "universalist" reading of human rights is, of course, unique to Muslim states. Yet, both value and interest systems are challenged by the social realities they confront. Indeed, it is only when we examine what is unfolding in the broader political space that we come closer to understanding the legal landscape of any particular state or regional system. The interests (moral, political) of states (Muslim or non-Muslim) sometimes overlap but often are in conflict with the international rights machinery, a machinery that, as I have argued, is in conflict with itself.

*Faith in democracy?*

Read into "democratic" state-building projects in the Middle East by US and European "repertory companies,"[76] so much of the framing around the "role" of religion in the state is, as Elizabeth Hurd rightly notes, "a modern discourse of religion-in-politics."[77] It is a discourse specific to particular places and periods and sanctioned by particular authorities that rely "on a fixed and stable representation of the shifting roles played by that which is named as 'religion' or 'sect' in politics and society."[78]

In the considerable commentary that followed the Arab Spring into the "Islamist winter,"[79] rather than unpacking the complexities of the region's political terrain, the focus of analysis has been on the participation (and gains) of Islamist parties in the political arena. This was particularly true in the commentary on the 2011 electoral success of the Muslim Brotherhood's Freedom and Justice Party (FJP).[80] So much of the analysis focused on the party's (albeit moderate) Islamist agenda, rather than the fact that it was a well-funded, well-organized party that was able to draw upon established networks within civil society in Egypt, which gave it a distinct advantage over the parties that were more recently formed.[81] Framing the Egyptian elections solely in secular/non-secular electoral wins and losses, straw-manned a much more complex story, leaving more substantive analysis that contested—or at the very least, contextualized—the notion that religion served as a political mobilizer either dismissed or simply not engaged. The subsequent removal of the FJP from power, orchestrated by both internal and external interests, was served well by this discourse,[82] one that occupies our imagination in ways that are totalizing.

Many commentators within and outside the Middle East who adopt a militant secularist agenda may well have genuine concerns over the impact of faith-based regimes on human rights. Indeed, forms of Islamic discourse adopted by certain state and non-state actors have had a significant effect on the human rights regime in the region.[83] At its core, however, this secular hegemonic knowledge regime has historically been an extension of colonial interests, and quite unsurprisingly was read, internally, as colonialism in contemporary clothing. Sectarianism (ethnic/religious) was a tool used by successive sovereign powers in the region to exercise and maintain control. That ethnoreligious identity politics continues to weigh heavily in the "colonial present" of the Middle East is without question. However, as Eric Davis reminds us, "The key task is not to identify the existence of sectarian feelings, but to explain why, *at a particular point in time*, such feelings are translated into violent behavior."[84] The answer may well be contained within the movements themselves.

The marginalization of segments of civil society and a sectarian entrepreneurial system that created in and out groups—sometimes based on religious divides, and often on tribal or ethnic affiliations—is a feature of the politics of sectarianism that has taken root in the Middle East. While these divisions are unsurprisingly still present in the current revolutionary moments, the language of rights through which civil society from Tunisia to Bahrain has articulated (and continues to articulate) its challenge to the structural inequalities of the state is also underpinned by broad and inclusive principles of equality and non-discrimination, and guarantees concerning the rule of law. How the political communities that emerge from the fraught political terrain are ordered and governed in the region is, at the time of this writing, uncertain. That said, they are likely to include degrees of legal plurality, including personal autonomy rules that continue to have salience for many faith-based communities. It is a system of governance that is rarely understood in a modern Western context that is premised on notions of the rule of law, and an accompanying legal system.[85] Yet personal laws have survived in the Middle East despite concerted attempts to standardize and/or secularize them. Arab countries engaging with questions concerning personal status laws are likely to be also mindful of the Lebanese example, viewing these as short-term solutions to avoid conflict, while mindful of a need to foster genuine "national" projects of mutual respect and a unitary identity.[86]

Whether there can be faith in democracy remains a genuine, but unresolved debate, as present in Europe—and to some degree, the United States—as it is in the Middle East and other parts of the world. Negotiating the public space for religion is, however, likely to reflect the diversity of societies; and that is, I argue, as it should be. Undoubtedly, states do devise culturally specific and religiously framed arguments—not to assert a space for the voices of otherness—but as a hegemonic technique to subjugate the rights of women, of minorities, and so on. However, as noted earlier, the language of rights and the more formal legal practices that arise in Muslim countries with regard to human rights are more likely to be informed and shaped by the historical social formation and underlying power politics of a state than by Islamic principles.[87] As I have argued elsewhere, "the language of rights and the more formal legal practices that arise in Muslim countries ... draw on a variety of sources which are evolutive and which may, like readings of Islam, not be consistent across Muslim cases."[88] Recognizing this opens up the possibility of creating an analytical framework within which we can better understand how state practices—with regard to human rights in the Muslim world (and ostensibly based on Islamic authority)—intersect and inform modern constitutionalism and international law.

*Conclusion*

That power politics is embedded within the rights-based discourse of states is not, as this chapter has detailed, unique to either the MENA region or, indeed, the Muslim world. However, it is within this region that the question of whether there can be faith in reason hangs the heaviest and where some of the most vibrant and enduring debates about religion and rights emerge. As I have argued, in the push and pull between the hegemony of the language of the "universal" and the voices of diversity, and "where 'enemies' of democracy are imagined to be those who introduce religious arguments in to public reason, the exclusion of significant parts of civil society is likely to follow."[89] The policing of the public square to ensure religion is contained within the private has created zones of exclusion based on an understanding of rights and religion that are read as fixed. As this chapter has detailed, this approach is deeply flawed.

This belief, that faith can never be accommodated in reason, is mapped on to the very core of the human rights discourse, which contrasts an essentialized (universal) "truth" against that which lies at the margins of modernity. Yet when the human rights project speaks for the "other," insisting on a universalizing "truth," it creates a zone of exclusion where difference is produced, reviving a type of Kantian liberalism that "invites us to assume that everyone wishes to be treated like we would like."[90] The only alternative, as Joan Scott has noted:

> is to refuse to oppose equality to difference and insist continually on differences—differences as the condition of individual and collective identities, differ-

> ences as the constant challenge to the fixing of those identities, history as the repeated illustration of the play of differences, differences as the very meaning of equality itself.[91]

Reframing the discourse in this way recognizes that the language of rights can privilege elite human experiences and subjugate the very real "other" human experiences. This suggests that, far from holding "relativity" hostage through a Eurocentric reading of these margins, we must be willing to deconstruct the very notion of a universal truth that displaces/excludes alternative voices. This presses us to ask if there are discourses/narratives/collective imaginaries that question, overcome, and ultimately undermine the categories of "East" and "West." Disrupting the notion of rights as neutral and pre-political opens up a space to question the legal points of departure for both international and Islamic law. Moreover, it also opens a space where we can begin to reframe how we understand and inform the concept of the "universality" of human rights.

Kennedy has argued that re-orientating this rights debate may crack some space for parallel systems to coexist in the wider rights regime,[92] which, I argue, should include rather than preclude faith-based developments. And, as political projects in the Middle East continue to take shape and form, is it not "precisely at these moments of founding and re-founding within a polity, when obligations of justice are extended to previously excluded groups, that religious, philosophical, and extra-rational modes of persuasion are most urgently needed?"[93]

2

# FORMAL EDUCATION SYSTEMS AS ARENAS OF INCLUSION AND EXCLUSION

## COMPARATIVE CASE STUDIES FROM LEBANON AND SYRIA

*Annika Rabo*

As a state apparatus for fostering citizens, formal education constitutes an ideal arena for scrutiny of inclusion and exclusion in a society. Through policies, pedagogical principles, and classroom practices, schools are, after all, where the future generation is prepared for their adult lives. The overarching purpose of this chapter is to contribute to such scrutiny by focusing on the formal education systems in Lebanon and pre-2011 Syria. These two countries exemplify very different approaches to how the future citizen is fostered and who is excluded and included in policies, curricula, and classroom practice. Exclusion must be understood in contrast to inclusion. In educational systems, certain perspectives, subjects, pupils, and so on are excluded because others are included. There is no educational system where everything and everyone is included, but what is included and excluded is an indicator of values propagated by educational authorities. Syria and Lebanon can be characterized as linguistically, religiously, and ethnically heterogeneous, but the two countries have managed this pluralism in very different ways. In Syria, formal education has, until recently, been extremely centralized and similar in form and content all over the country. In Lebanon, the situation has been almost the opposite due to the dominance of private schools. The difference between the homogeneous and centralized Syrian system and the fragmented and heterogeneous Lebanese system, I argue, sheds critical light on state–community relations in a heterogeneous society.

All over the world, education is praised and political leaders extoll its virtues. It is, in fact, possible to claim that the perceived benefit of modern mass education is the only common denominator in world politics. There is enormous concern about the level of education and about its form and content. International agencies and organizations are devoted to the spread, advancement, and comparison of educational systems. Education is serious business indeed. It is deemed both an inalienable human right and an obligation. Since education is so fundamental, it also comes under constant scrutiny and evaluation. Education must become more efficient, more widespread, and better attuned to the demands of society, according to many national and international agencies. Yet just as formal education is often lauded, it is also regularly considered to be in a state of crisis. Schools, some argue, do not form equally informed and knowledgeable citizens. Some experts claim that formal education is an instrument to discipline the dominated classes into submission, while others still stress the weak relationship between what pupils are taught in school and the skills they eventually develop to make careers.[1] In such discussions, the perspective is typically statist and the views and goals of pupils are lacking.

The gap between the expectations of the effects of formal education and its results seems to be ever widening. This is true also for the Arab world, where critique against the educational system has been scalding. Reforms have been called for, planned, and instigated, but critique persists. Much of the critique has focused on old-fashioned pedagogy, but some have drawn attention to the values fostered in the schools. Pupils, according to this view, are not taught to think critically and do not learn to develop responsible and independent decision-making skills. The lack of educational equality between boys and girls in the region has also been noted. Other forms of exclusionary practices in educational policies, curricula, and textbooks have, however, been largely ignored.[2]

Curriculum theory constitutes a general theoretical frame of reference in this text, and I also rely on empirical material from various research projects conducted since the late 1970s.[3] This is a field in education research in which curricula are scrutinized in relation to educational policy as well as the organization and implementation of education. Researchers scrutinize what knowledge is legitimized in curricula and how contents and methods are selected. They also study the roles of different actors within the educational system, as well as the larger political, social, economic, and cultural structures in society. Such concerns draw attention to the tensions between different decision-making levels and different actors, and their importance for how a curriculum is enacted, interpreted, and reproduced, not only on a national level but also among international and regional organizations with an interest in education and development, such as UNESCO, OECD, the EU, and the UNDP. Curriculum theory thus offers a useful frame of reference to analyze and understand how citizenship education, broadly speaking, is organized and governed in specific contexts.[4] In the next part of the chapter, I sketch the development of education from the framework of modernization to the framework of "knowledge societies." The section that follows focuses on inclusion and exclusion in education. The third section, which contains the bulk of the empirical material, looks at the historical trajectories of education in Lebanon and Syria, with a focus on subjects such as history, civics, and religious education. Who and what is included and excluded in the Lebanese and Syrian educational systems is examined, and the educational development for Syrians post-2011 are discussed.

*From modernizing societies to knowledge societies*

Historically, the spread of universal, formal mass education in the West is closely linked to the emergence of nation-states. This is also true in the Arab world and other parts of the world. Two of the salient features of any given modern state are a national educational system and an army, however weak and inefficient they may be. Even in countries with many private educational institutions, like Lebanon, the state still assumes responsibility for education planning. The link between the state structures and mass education is today so strong and obvious that we readily accept it.[5] Already by 1989, Ernest Gellner saw modern education as a mode of production. The definition of the modern state, he argued, is an agency that has the "monopoly of legitimate education,"[6] paraphrasing the well-known Weberian definition where the state is the agency with a legitimate monopoly on violence. Education can also be looked at from another perspective. It is remarkable, John Boli noted in 1989, that despite the great variation in political systems, mass education is very similar and "homogenous in aspiration throughout the world."[7]

Mass education rests on the individual as the central unit, and it remains "surprising how consistently educational systems attempt to build collective society by enhancing individual development."[8] This statement still holds true. Formal schooling and mass education emerged as part of completely new institutional arrangements between society and its members. Children were prized out of their kin-groups and families and were placed in schools to learn how to become loyal members of new collectivities. In this way, we can regard modern mass education as a "ritual construction of modern citizens."[9] Those lacking formal education are regarded as "an anomaly, a violation against the moral order."[10] This highly moral aspect of education also exists in the Arab world. A person cannot be modern and developed if she or he has not been to school. Formal education is the single most important means to becoming modern. To be educated, as we see it today, is a right, but also a duty, and children have become a potential to be tapped for the development of the nation.[11]

Education and development constitutes an enormous sub-field of scholarly and public interest.[12] From the 1950s until the 1990s, mainstream educational research and policies in, and on, the so-called developing world was typically framed within a paradigm of modernization. Modernity and development would only come about through the adoption of rational teaching methods. The developing world, hence, ought to emulate the successful model of the West. A very ambitious example of research in this vein is Joseph Szyliowicz's *Education and Modernization in the Middle East* (1973).[13] The book's analytical starting point is to contrast a stagnant and non-egalitarian Middle East burdened by obsolete traditions with a vibrant, egalitarian West, embracing change and social mobility.[14] In such a perspective, the Middle East thus needed to engage in far-reaching educational reforms to climb the developmental ladder. International comparative statistics showed that, for decades, the Middle East/Arab world had largely lagged behind other regions in implementing universal formal education, and there were dramatic differences in many countries in the region between the attendance of girls and boys.

The perceived failure of education was not unique to debates in and on the Arab world. The calls for educational reforms were, on the contrary, practically universal by the turn of the twenty-first century. Spearheaded by international organizations like UNESCO and OECD, a new educational paradigm suited to *information* or *knowledge societies* was heralded and quickly became hegemonic. New citizens, who needed to be more entrepreneurial and less dependent on the state for education and employment, were called for.[15] The global emphasis on neoliberal politics and new forms of governance even had an impact in countries like Syria, where ideas about "active citizens" who are open to the world fitted the decreasing ability of the state to finance education and to absorb the educated.

This shift to the still-hegemonic educational paradigm is closely linked to processes of globalization and increased interconnections across national borders. Economic development depends on the production of ideas rather than on the production of things. In this promotion of a "knowledge society," the relationship between state and citizens has shifted. Individual (or family) choice of school and education has become essential to economic development. From this perspective, Lebanon's long history of a large private educational sector can be seen as an example to be emulated.

The first Arab Human Development Report in 2002 received great regional and international attention due to its scalding critique of how education in the Arab world was incapable of supporting individual and national development.[16] The report emphasized that education in the region had made strides but was deteriorating and thus in need of restructuring to help the new generation cope with an uncertain future in a flexible way.[17] Interestingly, in the Arab Human Development Report and in other critical texts, a rather narrow vision of the "new citizen" was presented.[18] This citizen did not differ much from the dominant nationalist views propagated in education in the modernization paradigm. The "new citizen" was still perceived to be predominantly Arab, and the nations in which pupils received education were still understood as all Arab in nature. Linguistic, ethnic, and religious pluralism was ignored or even denied. And, as noted by André Elias Mazawi, debates about the so-called knowledge society generally exclude "the poor, refugees, displaced groups, women, disabled, nomadic, rural and agricultural communities, to name but a few."[19] In other words, international and national demands for educational reforms in the Arab world have continued to promote a mono-cultural ideal citizen. Furthermore, there has been limited interest in deliberating how inclusion and exclusion is played out—or even produced—in, and through, education.

### *Inclusion/exclusion and the creation of pluralism and difference*

Inclusive education is a concept commonly used to denote the preparedness to support and give equal educational opportunities to pupils with so-called special needs; that is, pupils with some kind of physical or mental impairment.[20] In this chapter, however, inclusion and exclusion in education will be analyzed against a backdrop of plural societies (that is, societies that are heterogeneous in terms of religious, linguistic, and ethnic affiliations, identities, and/or communities). Such heterogeneity is not always recognized and is seldom perceived as an asset in the Arab world, but ignoring societal heterogeneity also commonly occurs in other parts of the world. Until quite recently, the dominant historical trajectory in Sweden, for example, was based on ideas of the country as linguistically, ethnically, and religiously homogeneous. Only with massive labor immigration in the post-Second World War period (and from the mid-1970s with the arrival of many non-European refugees) was there a shift from social homogeneity to heterogeneity. But heterogeneity—however defined—is not the product of modern immigration. Instead, the idea of a homogenous Swedish people must be recognized as a product of nation-state building. Formal mandatory education constituted a fundamental vehicle to spread such an idea. But in 1997, Sweden by parliamentary declaration became a multicultural society where pluralism—whether historical or recent—would be considered a positive aspect of everyday life.[21]

Inclusion and exclusion are mutually constituted. The inclusion of someone or something is linked to the exclusion of others, or other things. Formal mandatory schooling for the young is a particularly fruitful arena for an analysis of inclusion and exclusion since it is consciously constructed to educate and cultivate the next generation. There are different kinds of educational inclusions/exclusions, or inclusionary/exclusionary processes. One issue concerns access to education. In many countries in the Arab world, access to free or subsidized education is conditioned on citizenship or at least permanent residence. In Syria, for example, Palestinians have had access to public education on par with Syrians.[22] Iraqi children who came to Syria after 2003 were allowed to enter schools, but the children (and grandchildren) of the 100,000 Kurds in the northeast of the country—who had their citizenship revoked in 1962—were denied access to basic education.

Even with the legal right to education, access may be highly differentiated. Critique concerning access to education in the Arab world has typically been articulated in terms of gender rather than, for example, the access for linguistic minorities like Kurds in the Mashreq or Amazigh in the Maghreb. In all countries of this region, basic education is today mandatory and usually available free of charge. Yet in a country like Lebanon, the quality of free education in public schools and fee-based education in private schools is—or is perceived to be—very different. Parents are willing to make many economic sacrifices to send their children to private schools, and there is a highly differentiated market where schools come with different price tags. In private schools, tuition ranges between USD $3,000 and $12,000, but there are many parents who cannot afford these schools fees and instead send their children to what they see as inferior public schools. Thus, in a country like Lebanon, with a highly developed educational market, access to education is very much dependent on the economic means of parents. Education in Lebanon is, in principle, mandatory until the age of sixteen, but the law is not enforced. Dropout rates are high from many public schools.[23]

In pre-2011 Syria, public schools dominated the educational system, yet schools were not equally spread out or of equal quality. Urban schools were generally known to have better-qualified teachers than rural ones, and better-off quarters of the cities were seen to provide schools with a better learning environment than poor quarters. Therefore, although there was equal access to education in principle, the quality of that access depended on where one lived.

In addition to access, inclusion/exclusion can be gauged in terms of exposure. What sort of perspectives of differences and plurality are propagated, available, or contested in schools? Inclusive/exclusive exposure can be assessed through a scrutiny of curricula, including textbooks, and through classroom practices, including both teacher–pupil and pupil–pupil interactions. Exposure can also be assessed through the range and delimitation of plurality. All school subjects can be studied to assess exposure to how religious, linguistic, and ethnic differences, as well as gender, are included or excluded in the curricula. For example, in Sweden in the 1980s there was an effort to stress girls' names in mathematics and science textbooks, to counteract the stereotype that only boys excelled in such subjects. A decade later, the discussion focused on the need to name not only "Marianne" and "Markus" but also "Miriam" and "Muhammed" as examples of children in textbooks. But although all school subjects and all textbooks reflect some notions of inclusion and exclusion, subjects such as religious education, history, geography, social studies, and civics lend themselves more easily to an examination of what and who is included and excluded (that is, how plurality is understood, promoted, or managed). Hence, below I will concentrate on curricula and textbooks in such subjects. As outlined above, all systems of education depend on selection and thus on exclusion, but what and who is included and excluded varies from one system to another. Pupils are not the same. Are differences between pupils ignored, denied, acknowledged, or used in classrooms? All societies are differentiated in some way or another. Are social, ethnic, linguistic, and religious differences ignored, denied, acknowledged, or used in educational policies, curricula, and textbooks? Is the diversity and pluralism in the world ignored, denied, or acknowledged in educational policies, curricula, and textbooks?

These questions can be illustrated by the following examples from outside the Arab world: in the Swedish educational system, diversity in the classroom and in society is almost exclusively associated with immigrants and their children. Multiculturalism is officially acknowledged and is said to encompass all those living in Sweden, but in concrete classroom practice it is typically pupils with an "immigrant background" who are seen to represent diversity. These pupils are often asked about "their religion" and "their culture," and are thus seen to embody particular bounded differences from a taken-for-granted Swedish-ness.[24] French policies, curricula, and classroom practice differ very much from the Swedish. Ethnic, linguistic, religious, and other differences are acknowledged on a global scale and acknowledged, as found in France. However, in schools they are not only ignored but also actively denied. The school is a place in which "mono-cultural" values are instilled. Pupils have to learn to put their differences aside at the school gate to benefit from the rights of the republic.[25]

This reasoning should not be regarded as a normative tool to highlight the idea that "inclusion" is better than "exclusion." Instead, I see it as a way to think better about the complexities in educational systems. When studying education, it is thus important to trace how social homogeneity and pluralism are deployed discursively in policies, curricula, textbooks, and classroom practice, and to be equally critical of the underlying ideas of both. The "multiculturalism" of Sweden and the "mono-culturalism" of France are obviously closely linked to the politics of classifying people. In Swedish schools, "differences" are deployed as personal characteristics, and pupils are not trained to think in a more abstract way: that "differences" are constituted against notions of "sameness." In France, personal experiences of "otherness," be it language- or religion-based, are denied and deemed irrelevant for performing citizenship.

### *Educating the future citizen in Lebanon and Syria: past and present*

Syria and Lebanon differ greatly in terms of educational history and the role of the state in policy-making. Lebanon, unlike Syria, has a long history of extreme educational heterogeneity. National educational policies are absent, weak, or non-enforceable. Foreign schools and institutions of higher learning have been a salient feature of the educational system since the mid-nineteenth century. In addition, local religious organizations started to set up their own schools. At the end of the Ottoman period, all religious groups in Lebanon had their own educational institutions.[26] Public spending on education has been low in Lebanon, and the private sector is larger than the public. In 2011–12, the enrollment in private schools exceeded 600,000 pupils, while the public schools had fewer than 300,000 pupils. About half of these pupils were enrolled in private schools with public subsidies. This policy developed during the French mandate when private schools accepted poor students. Such schools register with the Ministry of Education, and their curricula are generally close to the national curriculum.

Until today, French-language schools or schools that follow the French curriculum still dominate over schools teaching mainly in English or following the British or the American curricula. However, French is losing ground since English is considered a more globally useful language. Many schools offer good instruction in Arabic, English, and French, and trilingual competence is valued.[27] The educational system in Lebanon is thus in most ways dominated by schools in which the main language of instruction is not Arabic, or schools that follow non-Lebanese curricula. Yet in order to enter a national Lebanese university, a Lebanese professional association, or to become a public employee, pupils have to pass the national grade-nine brevet and the grade-twelve baccalaureate. This forces many Lebanese pupils to simultaneously follow two—often grueling—curricula.

In the late Ottoman period, formal education developed at a much slower pace and more modestly in the Syrian provinces compared with the Lebanese. During the French mandate, furthermore, the limited investment in education focused on instruction in French and knowledge about France. In 1943–44, with a population of about three million, "Syria had only thirteen public secondary schools serving less than 5,000 pupils; at least 80 per cent of the population remained illiterate."[28] In the first years of independence, foreign and private schools became more controlled, and there was an effort to develop Arabic as the major language of instruction. These policies were strengthened through the Ba'th Party coup in 1963. Education became state controlled, free of charge, and mandatory for six years.[29] Education—along with mandatory military service for young men—was considered the most important instrument to forge modern and Arab nationalist citizens. Educational policies and educational decision-making was highly centralized, the same textbooks were used all over the country, and teaching followed the same lesson-by-lesson routine. Educated citizens had a right to be employed, but they also had a duty to serve their country. Medical doctors, and civil and agricultural engineers, for example, were asked to serve in state organizations, public enterprises, and administrations for a number of years. Teachers were sent to rural areas to be part of the expansion of education all over the country. This policy of "serving one's country" was not universally popular among the Syrians I knew in the 1970s and 1980s, but many appreciated the right to employment, which, for example, dramatically increased the rate of female labor participation.

In 1990, pupils constituted the single largest "occupational category." A quarter of the total population were in school from grades one to twelve.[30] At the end of the 1990s, muted public debates arose over the poor quality of education in the country. With increasing economic austerity, the educational institutions, whether primary, secondary, or tertiary, could simply not keep pace with the large and still augmenting cohorts of every school year. Already from the end of the 1980s, public employment had become increasingly difficult to obtain. At the turn of the century, the state gave more freedom to the private sector and allowed for profit-making schools until the turn of the century.[31] Even then, the state kept a tight rein on educational policies. Practically all private schools in Syria followed the national curricula and offered the national ninth- and twelfth-grade examinations. The molding of similarity was still very strong in Syrian schools.

### *History and civics in Lebanese education*

In Lebanon, what is excluded and included in curricula, including textbooks and in classroom practice—in school subjects such as history, geography, and religious education—is extremely heterogeneous. In many of the private schools where Arabic is not the main medium of instruction, the books that are used are often produced in, and focus on, other parts of the world. Many Lebanese students therefore may not be very familiar with the history, geography, and so on of the country in which they live. The only common curricula for all public schools (and studied by the pupils in private schools who plan to sit for the Lebanese ninth- and twelfth-grade examinations) is *civics* (called "national education, civil upbringing"). The main purpose of civics is to promote unity and solidarity among the Lebanese, perhaps as a counterweight to *history*, which has proven to be a divisive element in educational policies and in curricula. The development of civics is very interesting compared with the troubled development of history.

The so-called Taif Agreement in 1991, which was designed to end Lebanon's fifteen-year civil war, included provisions for educational reform in the country. One of the decisions was to unify and standardize all history textbooks used in public schools. In order to heal the wounds from the long war and to build a new common ground, a committee comprising representatives of various religious and political groups was set up. The objectives for teaching history were many and simultaneously vague and imprecise, including:

> raising national awareness, developing the national collective memory, recognizing the importance of the Lebanese culture and the contribution of the Lebanese in the broader Arabic civilization, recognizing the impairment that had been caused by internal disputes, identifying the role played by foreign powers, extending appreciation toward religious values (Christianity and Islam) and recognizing the treachery entailed in Zionism.[32]

Not surprisingly, the committee working on the history curricula had great problems since the Taif Agreement had not resolved the historical tension between the Lebanese who claimed that the country was part of the Arab world and those who disagreed it. The committee was hindered in its work, members resigned, and when the new national curriculum was presented to the government for approval in 1996, history was not included.

In 1999, a document that Munir Bashshour describes as "tamed, desensitized" was resubmitted.[33] Finally, in 2000, the government approved a curriculum that stated that Lebanon is a homeland for its entire people. However, the earlier suggestion that it is "Arab in identity" was modified to become "Lebanese identity" and "Arab affiliation." Terms such as "committed to Arab culture" were removed as well.[34] Nevertheless, even with this "tamed" curriculum, it proved impossible to write history textbooks. In 2001, new history books were issued for grades two and three in elementary school. In these books, Arabs were listed among other foreign conquerors that occupied but eventually left Lebanon in previous times. After objections, these pages were removed.

In 2003, more than a decade after the end of the war, Bashshour concluded that the Lebanese could not agree on how to write their history. Efforts to unify the curricula failed. More than a decade after Bashshour's research, this is still true. In public schools, several Arabic textbooks are used with very similar content in order to comply with the policy issued in 1970. There is, in other words, "no history" after the Lebanese civil war.

While history has proven too sensitive a subject to reform and bring up to date in Lebanese public schools, civics has actually developed as a unified school subject with a common curriculum and common textbook all over the country. Civics is taught for one hour every week from grades one to twelve. During the development of the curricula, the Ministry of Education consulted Lebanese, American, and French experts, and representatives from the six largest political and religious groups were involved to ensure that the textbook became acceptable to all. The objectives are very similar to what we find internationally to prepare the youth for the demands of the contemporary "knowledge society." Pupils should be trained for democratic citizenship, which requires deliberating, decision-making, and civic engagement skills. Among the general aims, pupils should "develop social skills as members of a society whose unity is enriched by its diversity," and pupils should be aware of their "brotherhood with others, regardless of gender, color, language, religious, or cultural differences."[35]

History and civics are both school subjects in which the future citizen can be conceived. In the first, she/he is discerned through the way history is produced. "History textbooks highlight quintessential lessons of the past for the future, and by doing so define the future."[36] Civics provides a sort of blueprint for the ideal citizen for the future society. In Lebanon, history has been, and still is, such a sensitive subject that public textbooks have not been revised to include events after the early 1970s. Civics, on the other hand, which has a politically agreed upon curricula and textbooks, instead suffers from extreme blandness. Values extolled are either extremely concrete (do not litter and drive carefully) or very abstract (be peaceful and tolerant).[37] At the same time, the value put on these subjects in Lebanese public schools is not very high. History and civics have fewer hours and fewer credits than science and languages. In the ninth-grade exam, furthermore, civics, history, and geography together add up to a maximum of sixty points, while each other subject individually gives a maximum of sixty points. Civics and history books are studied mainly to pass the exams rather than to deliberate over content.[38]

School choice in Lebanon is related to class, religious affiliation, and language preferences. The school landscape is very complex, ranging from very expensive non-religious international English-medium schools to French government-supported schools, to foreign schools with a non-Lebanese Christian element, and Lebanese schools run by religious establishments of all kinds. The very wealthy class often cuts across religious affiliation, and the reverse is generally true for the poor. In such an educational system, pupils typically socialize with others of a similar background. During an educational conference in 2013, a principal from a well-known Islamic educational philanthropic association voiced concern over how various Lebanese groups viewed each other. She claimed that Lebanese diversity was not regarded as an asset in education or in society. The new civics curricula and the old history books were not helping, she said. This principal is not alone in raising such concerns. The content of history is, for example, one important issue in such debates. Should there be renewed efforts to unify Lebanese history, or should different and competing historical perspectives be presented instead? In the Lebanese case, we see that the very heterogeneity of society and the educational system does not automatically lead to an inclusive view of plurality. In line with the questions raised above, pluralism in society is acknowledged but fraught with tension and associated with political conflicts. In classrooms, hence, pluralism is ignored.

### *Geography, history, religious education, and national upbringing in Syrian education*

Public or semi-public debates over citizenship education in pre-2011 Syria have been, broadly speaking, much more muted than in Lebanon because of the extreme ideological dominance of the ruling Baʿth Party. Curricula in geography, history, and religious education were carefully honed to spread the party message "one nation with an eternal message." Even the elementary school reader drummed such a message into the pupils. "I am a Syrian and my soil is Arab" is the introductory line to a verse in a reader used in elementary school. Various historical heroes are depicted in texts, illustrations, and songs as early Arab nationalists.[39] From the intermediate stage, the mandatory uniforms took on a decidedly military cut. Saluting the flag (in the morning, twice a week), singing, and lauding the current and former President al-Asad was mandatory.

In the 1980s and 1990s, books on the subjects discussed here contained a great deal of text and few illustrations.[40] Geography and history were taught with an emphasis first on the country itself and then on the wider region, with very little information on other regions in the global south.[41] In geography, emphasis was placed on regional advances in agriculture, industry, and trade. History was taught as Arab/Islamic history, and various historical "stages" were repeated in the different school cycles with increasing attention to detail. Very little was taught about the rest of the world, and the history of the global south was practically non-existent. Early Arab/Islamic history was exceedingly important as a point of reference for later "stages." Pupils were taught that Arabs were once strong, independent, and righteous. This message was very common among the essays that pupils wrote for me in the late 1980s. In Syria, the almost 500-year period of the Ottoman Empire was described as a period of darkness, exploitation, and Turkish occupation. The Arab revolt was practically ignored in Syrian textbooks, and the emphasis was put on the spread of Arab nationalism, with Syria as its center and heartland.[42] The Ba'th revolution is obviously extremely important for the modern history of the country, but no mention was made of the differences and conflicts the Syrian party had with the Iraqi Ba'th Party. Interestingly, despite the direct and indirect glorification of the present political leadership, there was little critique of the political system of neighboring countries. Glorification was not done at the expense of others in the region. They were simply ignored, and instead modern regional history was firmly tied to a national trajectory in which Syria stood curiously alone on the scene.[43]

While history as a school subject was stripped of much content and, in general, was taught as a chronicle of important national events, there were other subjects where an ideological message and basic civic values were more directly apparent. Compared with other countries in the region, religious education was not a dominant school subject in post-independence Syria.[44] In Jordanian public schools, for example, the past was very closely associated with Islam. It was taught as a school subject with high moral relevance for the contemporary world, although the texts were often quite abstract. In Jordanian public schools, religious education in Islam is mandatory for all pupils, whether Muslim or not. In Syrian public schools, Christian pupils had religious education in a generic Christianity. In religious education studied by Muslim pupils, Islam was linked to the general advances of Arab civilization. In line with Ba'th ideology, Islam was depicted as a vehicle for Arab expansion and conquest, rather than the other way around. Parallels were also drawn between Islam and Ba'th ideologies. Equality between individuals, social justice, and freedom from political oppression were stressed in the schoolbooks as an Islamic cultural heritage, which the Ba'th Party expressed on behalf of the realization of a unique Arab civilization.[45]

The ideologically most important school subject in intermediate and secondary school, however, was "national upbringing."[46] Under this heading, the Ba'th ideology was taught by teachers who had specialized in the subject. Pupils were instructed in detail about the Ba'th revolution, on the progress of the party, and its general ideas and advances. In the 1980s, the subject changed from, in the official wording, a "subject for national awareness and progressive consciousness," into one where the statements of the party leadership, and particularly President Hafiz al-Asad, were taught as a scientific truth.[47] At the turn of the century, when the Ba'th Party became less politically influential, the emphasis on Hafiz al-Asad—and after 2001, on the son who succeeded him—became even more salient. To flunk in "national upbringing" in pre-2011 Syria was to declare oneself a potentially dangerous opponent to the political system. Until today, pupils who follow the curricula of the Syrian regime cannot fail in this subject—with unchanged content—if they want to pass the ninth- or twelfth-grade examinations.[48] In the Syrian educational system, contrary to the Lebanese, it is the very centralized and homogenous educational system that fosters a denial of pluralism.

*Ignoring, denying, acknowledging, or using pluralism in Lebanon and Syria*

Public education in Lebanon is a case of inclusive curricula in a very non-concrete way, as discussed. There are seventeen recognized religious communities in the country that are crucial for the organization of political life and for the civil identity of the citizens. The religious diversity of the country is acknowledged in documents and curricula, and pupils should learn to respect these differences. These communities, however, are not discerned in teaching material in civics, and they are extremely muted in history. The conflict in Lebanon over the Arab or Phoenician "ethnic" affiliation of the Lebanese, where Arab affiliation is associated with Islam and non-Arab affiliation with Catholic Christianity, is perhaps less salient today.[49] However, it is still perceived to be sensitive and the cause of violent conflicts in the country. Debates about this issue are not brought out directly in textbooks, but are indirectly present through the very avoidance of the topic. Lebanese pupils who study in private schools may learn about Lebanese society and history from other types of school material, often in a non-Arabic medium.

In regime-controlled Syria, religious communities and affiliations are simultaneously acknowledged, accepted, and downplayed.[50] All Syrians regardless of religion are constitutionally equal (and ought to be equally Arab), and religion and state are in many ways separated.[51] But personal status law is based on religious affiliation and is very important for family life. The personal status law of the state is based on the Hanafi legal school from which Druze and Christians have certain exceptions when it comes to marriage, divorce, and inheritance. Both Islam and Christianity are taught as school subjects. Just as in Lebanon, Muslim and Christian pupils are separated for religious education. The religious education textbooks are generic, and the differences between, or historical development of, different Muslim and Christian sects are not discussed or acknowledged. "National upbringing" focuses on the unity of the nation and, as discussed, the glorification of the Ba'th Party, and especially the al-Asad family. There is no civic education where pupils are taught about the diversity of the country. Most Muslim pupils come to learn about Christianity and Christians from an Islamic point of view. Christians know much more about Islam and Muslims because they are exposed to this in public life. Muslims are not treated equally in the educational system. Shi'a Muslims—including Alawites—and the Druze have no place in the instruction in schools. The ethnic and religious variation of the country is completely silenced in history and geography.

Religious pluralism among Syrians is thus accepted and acknowledged on a general Islam–Christianity level but managed through different curricula depending on religion. Some ethnic and linguistic pluralism is acceptable as well, although not brought out in textbooks. Armenians, Assyrians, and Syriacs are recognized as non-Arab Christians, and their use of their mother tongues is accepted in their own schools.[52] Such schools, which followed the national curricula and had extra language instruction, were mainly found in Aleppo and the northeast of the country before 2011. Christians from these communities were typically tolerated as "guests" in the national Arab body and posed no political threat to the regime.[53] The Kurds, however, who constitute the largest non-Arab community in Syria, were not allowed to develop their own language in schools. Many were stripped of their citizenship in the 1960s, and they and subsequent generations were not allowed to attend school. The Kurds were deemed a threatening "foreign" community with possible secessionist claims.[54] Some much smaller Muslim non-Arab communities such as Circassians and Turkmen were much more acceptable and non-threatening to the Ba'th regime, but their presence was also ignored in curricula. Despite the differences in how religious, linguistic, and ethnic diversity is handled in Syrian and Lebanese schools, there is one phenomenon that is remarkable by its absence in both educational systems.

A glaring exclusion in both Lebanese and Syrian curricula is the neglect of migration and mobility—both "forced" and "voluntary"—and the absence of migrants, both "native" and "foreign." The 2002 Arab Human Development Report notes that "migration within, from and to the Arab region is an important demographic feature."[55] Yet this is not at all reflected in the discussion on education. This lacuna is very telling and reflects hegemonic discourses on development and education in the region as a whole. Education is still regarded as bounded by national borders and of concern only for the national citizens actually living there. Nevertheless, exclusion or inclusion of persons and perspectives does not stop at national borders. Half of the Lebanese population, for example, lives outside the country, and every Lebanese pupil has family members who are migrants. Their remittances are crucial for the Lebanese economy, yet this is not discussed in schoolbooks. Nor is there any discussion about the transnational links that are forged when Lebanese migrate for longer or shorter periods, for instance to the Arabian peninsula states. Finally, there is no mention in the curricula or in textbooks of the many labor migrants coming to Lebanon. They are completely invisible.[56] Yet global connections and international influences in the "knowledge society" are highly valued at the rhetorical level. In Lebanon, the importance of mobility and of receiving an education that can be marketable is highlighted in how private schools present themselves to potential customers. After the turn of the century, when Syria allowed more private schools, their international connections were used as a selling point.

Thus, using the lens of curriculum theory, a number of tensions in the educational system in Lebanon and Syria stand out. In both Lebanon and Syria, what policy-makers and/or powerholders perceive to be sensitive issues are avoided in official textbooks. In Lebanon, there is a more open and "plural" struggle over curricula, which is part and parcel of the political mobilization in the country. The result is the fostering of a parochial citizen open to the world, but with few tools to deal with the challenges of the country.

In pre-2011 Syria, the aversion to openly discussing ethnic, linguistic, and religious differences in schools and elsewhere was officially seen as a way to preserve the unity of the country. But it would be a mistake to regard Syrian ideological propaganda as all-encompassing or successful. Pupils and other citizens were never meek victims of state or educational propaganda. The very public silence over religious and ethnic differences instead made many Syrians highly attuned to such differences.[57] In 2015, Zeina Bali interviewed sixteen female and male Syrians aged twenty-five to thirty-five with different religious and ethnic affiliations who had been relocated to Gaziantep. She asked them about their recollections of oppressive experiences in Syrian schools.[58] Her material shows that they developed beliefs contrary to those propagated in school. The essays I collected in Syria and Jordan in the late 1980s demonstrated that the grade-twelve pupils I met had mastered the mandatory ideological lesson. In Jordan, for example, all but one of about 200 pupils started their essays with the Islamic invocation *In the Name of God, the Merciful, the*

*Compassionate*, reflecting the official importance of religious education in schools. In Syria, not a single pupil used this invocation, even in schools situated in quarters where such an invocation would frequently be used outside school. However, mastering the ideological message is not the same as embracing it. From the pupils' point of view, schools are powerful institutions, but pupils also have a life outside school. Politicians, educational planners, and policy-makers tend to place too much emphasis on the ability of education to mold the future generation in a specific direction. Nevertheless, we should not, of course, neglect the potential of education to develop an ethos of civility and conviviality for the future generation.

* * *

In 1988 and 1989, I asked Jordanian and Syrian grade-twelve pupils to write about their own future and the future of their country. Despite individual and national differences, the essays all reflect impressive developmental and educational ambitions for their homeland, the Arab world, and themselves. The essays also reflect a view of Syria as ethnically and linguistically homogenous with little room for cultural differences. A girl in a school situated in a conservative quarter in Damascus wrote:

> Concerning my future I want to be a working cadre in society to raise my Homeland. I hope to study a scientific subject and then apply it practically, like medicine, and I want to work in this field. Concerning my Homeland: I am proud first of all of being an Arab girl and secondly I am proud of being a Syrian. I hope that the name of Syria will become renowned all over the world, especially in foreign countries. They do not believe we have knowledge, and yet it is the opposite. Arabs are the origin of civilization, knowledge and science, and we will return to this situation. God willing we will become the ones who once again will pull the Arabs and the Syrians forward. God has created intelligence equally in all people and anybody who really wants can reach towards knowledge. I hope for success, not only for myself and Syria but for the whole Homeland, and hand in hand we will take whatever responsibility is needed.

In other essays authored by twelfth graders almost three decades ago, a Syrian boy writes poetically about living in the end of the twentieth century "where time is a struggle and where we want all people to understand their role in the theatre of life." He, like so many others, expresses a wish to study medicine, to serve humanity, and aspires to obtaining the Nobel Prize, thus raising the profile of his country. With hindsight, such ambitions are simultaneously preposterous and heartbreaking. Since 2011, the Syrian education system has rapidly deteriorated, and many children and youth inside and outside the country have no—or very limited—access to schooling.[59] At the time of writing (mid-2017), half of Syria's population of about twenty million are displaced, and about half of these are outside the country, mainly in the neighboring countries that have taken the brunt of the people fleeing. By the summer of 2014, Lebanon hosted almost half of the 2.8 million Syrian refugees registered with the UNHCR (United Nations High Commissioner for Refugees) and more than half a million unregistered Syrians.[60] Around 600,000 school-aged Syrians needed educational assistance, and of these, fewer than 100,000 were served by Lebanese public schools. The gap between educational needs and supply was similar in Turkey and Jordan. The situation was slightly better in the Kurdistan Region of Iraq, but there—as in Turkey—the problem was often one of language. Pupils in Lebanon following the Lebanese curricula have not been prepared for the importance of foreign languages in public schools. In Jordan, about 20,000 Syrian pupils had access to some schooling inside camps and about 100,000 had access outside. In both Jordan and Lebanon, the strain on the public school system was of course considerable, even though Syrians received—and still receive—less and more inferior education than the native citizens.

Access to and quality of education are enormous problems for children and youth both inside and outside Syria, but curriculum content is almost equally problematic. In Lebanon and Turkey, various Syrian and non-Syrian organizations have set up their own schools, often with curricula of their own. Inside Syria, in areas outside regime control, new curricula have been introduced. Sometimes this only entailed taking out "national upbringing" and purging regime propaganda in other school subjects, but in areas controlled by jihadist organizations, many subjects disappeared and a new and expanded curriculum for Islamic religious education became mandatory. For Syrians, what and who is included and excluded in education is clearly particularly desperate. Nonetheless, the need to develop education that acknowledges a diversity of perspectives is desperately needed in the whole Arab world. Undertaking such a development will require that policy-makers, curricula experts, and citizens steer the educational ship between the Scylla of fragmentation and the Charybdis of centralization.

3

# THE RULING FAMILY'S HEGEMONY

## INCLUSION AND EXCLUSION IN QATARI SOCIETY

*Islam Hassan*

The official historical narrative surrounding the composition and evolution of Qatari society is an *imaginaire* that contributes to the reproduction of a social and political order based on inclusion and exclusion.[1] The official historical narrative emphasizes the role of Arab tribes in the inhabitation process, the evolution of Qatari governing authority, and the creation of the state while disregarding other sections of society, particularly those of Abd, Hawaleh, and Persian backgrounds.[2] This chapter argues that, ever since coming to power some 165 years ago, the Qatari ruling family has consistently employed a social conservative approach to consolidate its own position, in the process maintaining Qatar's pre-existing social hierarchy.[3] One of the main ways in which the state has sought to achieve this goal has been to narrow the definition of what constitutes a "Qatari." As we will see, the ruling family has promoted Arab tribal social values, culture, traditions, and customs in order to perpetuate a system based on inclusion and exclusion, thereby securing their own position and that of Arab tribal social actors at the apex of the Qatari state.[4] As part of this process, the state has also used juridical means—its constitution, the legal system, and family policies related to marriage and nationality—to cement an ideology and narrative that maintains the existing social order.

Table 3.1: Population Estimate, 1908–77

| *Year* | *Total* | *Foreign* | *Foreign (%)* |
|---|---|---|---|
| 1908 | 26,000–27,000 | 6,000 | 23 |
| 1939 | 28,000 | 11,000 | 39 |
| 1940/5 | 25,000 | – | – |
| 1969 | 80,000 | – | |
| 1970 | 79,000 | – | – |
| | 80,000 | – | – |
| | 111,000 | – | – |
| | 111,100 | – | – |
| | 112,000 | – | – |
| 1971 | 90,000 | – | – |
| | 111,000 | 65,300 | 59 |
| 1972 | 100,000 | – | – |
| | 126,000 | – | – |
| 1973 | 170,000 | – | – |
| 1975 | 92,000 | – | – |
| | 160,000 | – | – |
| | 170,000 | – | – |
| 1976 | 150,000 | – | – |
| | 180,000 | – | – |
| | 202,000 | – | – |
| | 210,000 | – | – |
| 1977 | 200,000 | 150,000 | 75 |

Source: Rosemarie Said Zahlan, *The Creation of Qatar*, London: Croom Helm London, 1979, p. 11.

Like other countries of the Arabian Peninsula and the Middle East, Qatar is home to numerous ethnicities, languages, and cultures. Beginning in the fourth quarter of the seventeenth century, waves of migration from Saudi Arabia to Qatar by tribes escaping drought and famine, and similar waves and patterns, albeit of a smaller scale, from Persia and Africa, contributed to the creation and evolution of Qatar's diverse social structure.[5] As a result, Qatar came to host multiple populations with distinct identities that were highly mobile across Qatar, the whole Arabian Peninsula, and the shores of the

Table 3.2: Tribal Families Living Near the Coasts in Qatar in 1907

| *Tribal Name(s)* | *Number of Members Residing in Doha* | *Number of Members Residing in Known Area* | | *Number of Members Residing in Unknown Area N/A Distributed* |
|---|---|---|---|---|
| Al Thani | 100 | Al Wakra | 70 | 705 |
| Al Binali | 300 | Al Zubarah | 1,450 | N/A |
| Al Swaidi | 80 | N/A | N/A | 320 |
| Al Manaah | 10 | Chemal (Bathlof) | 70 | 320 |
| Al Mussalam | 40 | N/A | N/A | N/A |
| Al Bukuwarrah | 20 | Al Thaaeyn and Fwairat | 250 | 2,300 |
| Al Sada | 280 | Chemal | 170 | N/A |
| Al Kubassah | N/A | Chemal | 700 | N/A |
| Al Buromaih | N/A | Um Al Maa | 98 | 430 |
| Al Muraikhat | N/A | Al Khor | N/A | 2600 |
| Al Sulatta | 650 | | N/A | N/A |
| Bani Hajjar | N/A | Dukhan | N/A | N/A |
| Al Buainain | N/A | Al Wakra | 400 | N/A |
| Al Bufalasah | N/A | Al Wakra | | N/A |
| Al Ammamrah | 20 | Al Wakra | 20 | N/A |
| Al Bani Maqla | 10 | Al Wakra | 40 | N/A |
| Al Dawaswer | N/A | N/A | N/A | 200 |
| Arab Najd | 500 | N/A | N/A | N/A |
| Al Baharnah | 500 | N/A | N/A | N/A |
| Al Khulaifat | N/A | Al Wakra | 170 | 10 |
| Al Muthanhkah | N/A | N/A | N/A | N/A |
| Al Mahandah | N/A | Al Khor | N/A | N/A |
| Al Jalahimah | N/A | Chemal | N/A | N/A |
| Bani Yas | 15 | Al Wakra | 110 | N/A |
| Bdu (Nomads) | 25 | N/A | N/A | 400 |
| Al Abid (Slaves) | 1,000 | Al Wakra | 1,000 | N/A |
| Free Slaves | 2,000 | N/A | N/A | 2,000 |
| Al Huwalah | 2,000 | N/A | N/A | N/A |
| Al Baqaqla | 50 | N/A | N/A | 40 |
| Al Humaidat | N/A | Al Khor | 250 | N/A |

Source: Buthaina Mohammed Al Janahi, "National Identity Formation in Modern Qatar: New Perspective," Qatar: Qatar University, 2014, p. 49.

Persian Gulf, under the loose administrative body that existed at the time.[6] By 1907, the settled population in Qatar was made up of 27,000 mainly tribal and nomadic individuals "consisting of twenty-five major clans, largely concentrated in Doha and Wakrah," in addition to Abid and Persians that comprised up to 23 percent of the population and continued to increase in size over the following decades.[7] Although none of Qatar's inhabitants are indigenous to the country, having arrived during previous waves of migration, the

Table 3.3: Tribal Families Living Near the Coasts in Qatar in 1907

| | *Ajamis* | *Huwala* | *Arab Tribes* |
|---|---|---|---|
| Purported origins | Persian | Original Sunni Arabs who moved from the Arabian shore to Persia and returned between the 1930s and 1950s | Qatari tribes tracing their origins to the Arabian Peninsula |
| Families and clan | Al-Ansari | Al-Ansari | Al Thani |
| | Al-Fardan | Al Darwish | Al Attiya |
| | Mustafawi | Al-Hammadi | Al Buainain* |
| | | Al Jaber | Al-Humaidi |
| | | Al Jaidah | Al-Kaabi |
| | | Al-Malki | Al Khater |
| | | Al Muftah | Al-Kubaisi |
| | | Al Jassim | Al-Kuwari |
| | | Al Ahmed | Al-Maadeed |
| | | | Al-Malki |
| | | | Al-Jahni |
| | | | Al-Marri |
| | | | Al-Mohannadi* |
| | | | Al Mahmood |
| | | | Al Mana |
| | | | Al-Mannai |
| | | | Al Misned* |
| | | | Al-Muraikhi |
| | | | Al-Noaimi |
| | | | Al-Sulaiti* |
| | | | Al-Suwaidi |

* Originally from Bahrain.
Source: Mehran Kamrava, "State–Business Relations and Clientelism in Qatar," *Journal of Arabian Studies*, 7, 1 (2017), p. 6.

Arab tribes claim to be the main settlers while Abid and Persians are considered "foreigners."

Qatari society was made up of three main elements: a small number of Bedouins, villagers who worked in fishing or trade, and merchant townspeople living in Doha and Al Wakrah.[8] The Bedouins, who were very few in

Table 3.4: Hadar (Urban Population): Major Professions

| *Tribal Name(s)* | *Type of Activity/ Craft Practiced* | *Tribal Name(s)* | *Type of Activity/ Craft Practiced* |
|---|---|---|---|
| Al Bin Ali | Pearling and trading | Al Sada | Diving, hunting, grazing |
| Al Baharnah | Pearl trading, Goldsmith, Blacksmith, Shipbuilding, Copper tools | Al Ammamrah | Diving, hunting, maritime |
| Al Huwala | All types of trading, diving, some handcrafts | Al Mussalam | Pearl trading, diving |
| Al Maadhed | Pearl trading | Al Bufalasah | Diving, hunting, maritime |
| Al Bukuwarrah | Diving, hunting, grazing | Al Baqaqla | Modest profession: serving in house of sheikhs and water transportation |
| Al Sulatta | Pearl trading, diving, fishing, grazing | Al Dawaswer | Diving, hunting |
| Al Mahandah | Pearl trading, diving, fishing, grazing | Al Mudhahkah | Grazing |
| Al Khulaifat | Pearl trading, diving, grazing | Arab Najd | Trading, some crafts |
| Al Sudan | Pearl trading, diving, grazing | Abd (slaves) | Diving, fishing, guarding |
| Al Kubassah | Pearl trading, diving, grazing | Abd (free slaves) | Diving, fishing, domestic services, guarding |
| Al Manaah | Pearl trading, diving, grazing | Iranians | Trading, diving, handcrafts, fishing |

Source: Al Janahi, "National Identity Formation in Modern Qatar: New Perspective," p. 53.

number, were all of Arab tribal origin, while the villagers and merchant townspeople were a mixture of Arabs, Persians, and Abid. At that time, the Qatari economy was mainly dependent on pearl fishing, and to a lesser extent, on camel breeding.[9] According to John Gordon Lorimer, "Qatar's meager resources in 1907 consisted of 1,430 camels, 250 horses, and 817 pearl boats."[10] Table 3.3 shows how Abid and Persians contributed to the economic activities of Qatar through pearl fishing, trade, and handicrafts. Their economic contribution played an important role in supporting the government, which relied on the taxes it derived from pearl boats and custom duties for running the sheikhdom.[11]

However, this situation changed dramatically following the discovery of oil in Qatar and the ensuing flow of petrodollars into the country. Whereas the ruling family had previously depended on the population for income generation, the population now became heavily dependent on the state for jobs and contracts.[12] At the same time, Qatar found itself confronted by new geopolitical and economic realities, which, together with competition over oil resources, led to political changes and intensified the efforts to maintain the stratification that characterizes Qatari society.

Max Weber's complex stratification model perfectly elucidates the hierarchal system in Qatari society, which is not exclusively stratified based on an individual's relationship to modes of production, as Karl Marx suggests, but on the interplay of three stratification systems.[13] These systems include:

> a caste system based on ethnicity, race, religious sect, purity of Arab blood, and tribal lineage that impacts an individual's position in the Qatari social hierarchy; a class system that is determined by economic wealth; and a party system based on the relationship of the individual's tribe to the ruling family.[14]

The interplay of these three stratification systems inevitably places the ruling family at the apex of the hierarchal pyramid, followed by loyal Arab Sunni tribes, and other tribes and families depending on their ethnicity, race, religious sect, purity of Arab blood, tribal lineage, economic wealth, and allegiance to the ruling family.

The state's national identity narrative has merged the social and political hierarchies in Qatari society in the sense that social class determines a person's position in the political hierarchy and vice versa. As this narrative enabled the Arab tribes to consolidate their position within Qatari society, they soon rallied around and conceded allegiance to the ruling Al Thani tribe. Thus, according to Zahlan, during the early stages of state formation, tribal loyalty provided "the necessary elements to transfer this loyalty to the state and ruler of Qatar. Although the concept of a nation is new, the underlying acceptance of such a concept has its roots firmly in the past."[15] Crystal claims that there were three new ruling bargains:

> The first group to be placated was the ruling family. They had the highest historical expectations. With oil, Sheikhs tried to buy [public] support using three mechanisms—allowances, land, and state jobs. Finally the rulers took a similar approach with merchants, giving selected merchants profitable access to state contracts and legal protection from foreign competition. The ruler also tried to develop new allies in the national population using social programs and state employment.[16]

However, the emir's offerings to the members of the ruling family were not enough to keep peace within the ruling family and other Arab tribes. Hence the emir began offering members of the ruling family powerful positions in the government and encouraged them to become involved in the private sector in order to boost their income.[17] The state distributed influential government positions and government contracts based on ethnicity, purity of Arab blood, and relationship to the ruling family.

There is little, if any, research on the role played by the Qatari state in establishing and reproducing the social and political order based on social inclusion and exclusion. The current chapter addresses this gap in the literature by investigating the official historical narrative of the state, as well as the policies it uses to maintain and further perpetuate the existing social hierarchy. The chapter starts by first defining "state" and "conservative social stratification," before going on to highlight how the state has deliberately restricted the criteria for what defines a "Qatari" in order to maintain a system of social inclusion and exclusion based on ethnicity through the institution of marriage and nationality law.

### *The state and conservative social stratification*

Social scientists have failed to reach a consensus on the definition of a "state," with available definitions varying depending on the field of social science from which they originate. For example, the definition of a "state" varies depending on whether the field is international relations or sociology.[18] In this chapter, the concept of "state" is examined through Adham Saouli's conception of the state as an integral part of the social field. He claims that the social field, or "the arena in which social interaction is bounded and takes place," has four main structures: material structure, cultural structure, political structure, and institutions.[19]

Saouli claims that institutions "evolve out of interactions among social powers" and are "devised by one or more social powers to consolidate power, regulate power relations, or install constraints against the monopoly of power."[20] Furthermore, "a social power could be a leader, tribe, political party, clan, ruling family, monarchy, sectarian elite, or an economic social force. These forms of social power are represented by a minority elite, which seeks to articulate the interests of a larger group."[21] He adds that social powers are the result of the existing material and cultural structures, which are the social and economic foundations of the state, as well as human behavior that follows specific trends and patterns.[22] As part of the interactions between different structures, institutions tend to "shape ... political behavior by setting certain standards and norms on social actors."[23] Accordingly, institutions "shape the political struggle" that results from politicization and attempts to revise and reproduce the cultural and material structures.[24]

When focusing on the young Qatari state, one can see that it has been in a continuous process of constructing and exerting a Gramscian hegemony over society. However, it is important to note that Gramsci's definition of a "state" differs from Saouli's. For Gramsci, the "State is the entire complex of practical and theoretical activities with which the ruling class not only justifies and maintains its dominance, but manages to win the active consent of those over whom it rules."[25] Although Gramsci's definition of the state differs from Saouli's, Gramscian hegemony is still applicable when deploying Saouli's definition of the state. Gramsci argues that human society has two major superstructural levels: civil society and the state.[26] These two levels "correspond on the one hand to the function of 'hegemony' which the dominant group exercises throughout society and on the other hand to that of 'direct domination' or command exercised throughout the State and 'juridical' government."[27] The dominant group uses intellectuals as "deputies" to construct a social hegemony architecture. This architecture is fortified by two fundamental underpinnings. The first is "spontaneous" consent from the populace to the ideology propagated by the dominant group—in this case, the Qatari ruling family. This consent results from the "historical" prestige that the ruling family enjoys due to its status and position in society. The second underpinning is the "apparatus of state coercive power which 'legally' enforces discipline on those groups who do not 'consent' either actively or passively."[28]

The behavior of Qatari state institutions is best understood through the lens of "social conservatism."[29] Lyle A. Scruggs and James P. Allan argue that "Social policy in conservative welfare regimes has a primary goal of preserving traditional status differences in society."[30] Through such policies, the political institutions of the social field fortify the existing social hierarchy. The authors use the example of Bismarck's Germany to exemplify how those who developed the welfare state reinforced the state's role as a centralized authority in accentuating "traditional" roles with regard to the social structure and the family.[31] Thus the privileged position of the state in conservative welfare regimes is protected when status differences are maintained in the social field.[32]

The Qatari ruling family has used its hegemony over civil society—schools, media, mosques, etc.—to impose an exclusionary historical narrative that highlights the contribution of Arab tribes to state-building while disregarding the contributions of the various other communities that share the same territory. This historical narrative in turn serves as the basis of the ruling family's ideology.[33] This ideology has been met with consent from the Qataris of Arab tribal origins, for obvious reasons, and interestingly also from Abid, Huwalah, and, to a certain extent, Persians. Abid and Huwalah tend to either embrace Arab heritage or at a minimum hide their own heritage, as discussed later in the chapter. Persian Qataris, on the other hand, avoid contesting the state as doing so would risk harming their business interests. Mehran Kamrava discusses this behavior in his article "State–Business Relations and Clientelism in Qatar", which I take the liberty to quote in length:

> Many of the Ajami and Huwala families have grown wealthier over time, at the same time remaining loyal to the Al Thani. Today, among the most renowned business families in Qatar, the Ajamis and the Huwala tend to be over-represented relative to the size of their overall community in the country. Table II lists some of Qatar's most famous business families. Of a total of fourteen families, half happen to belong to either the Ajamis or the Huwala. Among them, the Al-Fardan family, who in Qatar are viewed as Ajamis, and the Al Darwish and Al Jaidah, both of whom are Huwala, are generally perceived to be among Qatar's most influential and wealthiest business families. In the process of ascending to their positions of wealth and affluence, these families have become among the most loyal clients of the ruling Al Thani. Given their comparatively less secure position in Qatari society, they have been among the most loyal supporters of the state.[34]

Huwalah and Persian Qataris recognized the hegemony of the Arab tribes and consequently chose to abandon politics for business. Since the ruling family remains at the center of politics and business in the country, Huwalah and Persian Qataris are among the most loyal to the ruling family. This consent from the different actors of Qatari society has in turn strengthened the hegemony of the Arab tribes. This hegemony was then cemented by juridical structures, such as constitutional articles, laws, and policies, which protect this social hegemony from class contestation. The interplay of social hegemony and juridical structures maintains the ruling family and its Arab tribal allies at the apex of the social hierarchy, and hence political hierarchy.[35]

### *Narrowing national identity*

"National identity" refers to the way a single community views itself and is based on five main features: a historic territory, or homeland; common myths and historical memories; a common, mass public culture; common legal rights and duties for all members; and a common economy with territorial mobility for members.[36]

Qatar, like Kuwait, recognizes the right of individuals to become Qatari citizens if their fathers resided in the country before 1930.[37] However, being a citizen of the state does not necessarily mean that an individual satisfies the features of official Qatari national identity, as a citizen is an individual that enjoys the political, social, and economic rights outlined in the constitution and laws of the state, while a "national" is not only a citizen but an individual that possesses the dominant characteristics of the "nation." Thus a Qatari of Persian or Abd origins, or a naturalized citizen, may enjoy equal political, social, and economic rights but may not necessarily be perceived as a representative of Qatari national identity.

This fits with Anthony D. Smith's claim that national identity differs from any conception of the state.[38] This chapter accordingly makes a clear distinction between a "citizen" and a "national." Based on a citizen's satisfaction of the five features of Qatari national identity, his or her national identity is evaluated, and thus he or she is perceived as belonging to a specific social class, and either granted or restricted access to influential political positions and lucrative economic contracts. However, this is not to say that Persians, Huwalah, and Abid have never been represented in important political positions. In fact, "in February 2015, for example, there was ... one Ajami (Ali Sharif al-Emadi, Minister of Finance) and two Huwalas serving in the cabinet (Muhammad al-Hammadi, Minister of Education and Higher Education; and Hussa Al Jaber as the Minister of Communication and Information Technology)."[39] Instead, the argument made here is that Qataris of Arab tribal origins predominate at the highest political echelons of the state.

### *Historic territory, common myth, and historical memories*

The Qatari state reinforces its Arab and tribal identity through an official historical narrative, its constitution, and its official symbols. Its historical narrative is ostensibly biased toward the Arab tribes in that it emphasizes the inhabitation process and patterns of movement of Arab tribes to Qatar, without highlighting the role played by those of Abid, Ajam, and Hawaleh origins.[40] This is important, as out of the 27,000 inhabitants in 1907, slaves and free slaves comprised up to 18.5 percent of the population, and Hawaleh counted up to 7.4 percent, in addition to the Persians who have also historically inhabited the region. Thus the inhabitation process of a major section of Qatari society is disregarded in the official Qatari narrative. Moreover, the official narrative also fails to account for the social engagement and struggle between Abid, Persians, Hawaleh, and Arab inhabitants. This is critical because most of these social actors, according to Table 3.1, took part in trade and pearl fishing, which were the cornerstone of the Qatari economy at the time. Therefore, although Qatari culture is not solely of Arab tribal origin, it has traditionally been propagated as such, making it an *imaginaire* that does not necessarily reflect reality.

Since the discovery of oil in the country, the state has reproduced this culture by ensuring that those of Arab tribal origin dominate the oil-based economy.[41] Thus, by fostering and enforcing a dominant cultural structure and controlling the material structure of the state, Arab tribal social actors have dominated other social actors in the political field. Political institutions capitalized on this, as the tribe became the prime determinant of an individual's inclusion as a national of the state.[42] This has helped to reproduce the tribal identity and dominant culture that continues to manifest itself in the lifestyle of Qataris. Although tribal allegiance is currently of lesser social importance relative to the period before the discovery of oil, it still influences an "individual's status, possibilities of marriage partners, business opportunities, land rights, and heritage."[43]

As is also the case in Yemen, one can argue that Qatar's Arab tribes have played an equivalent role to political parties or civic society organizations in the West.[44] Ali Al Shawi argues that there are several tribes in Qatar that play party-like roles in the Qatari political arena.[45] The state tends to appoint members of these families to important governmental and military positions in order to gain their allegiance by allowing them to participate in political life.[46] This is also a manifestation of the domination of Arab tribal social actors, which in turn leads to the reproduction of the dominant culture and ensures the domination of the ruling family and other Arab tribal social actors in the Qatari political system. The placement of the Al Thani tribe at the top of the social pyramid, followed by other tribes ranked on the basis of their origin, ethnicity, and allegiance to the monarchy, is a direct result of the official Qatari narrative.

Article 1 of Qatar's Constitution states that Qatar is an Arab state and that the people of Qatar are "part of the Arab Nation."[47] In addition, *Qatar: Year Book 2009*, which was published by Qatar Ministry of Foreign Affairs, states that:

> The people of Qatar are the descendants of Arabian lines of kinship due to the close proximity of the country to the Arabian Peninsula and to the deep-rooted cultural background they share with the people of Arabia. As a result of such factors, the present composition of the Qatari people was formed by a major migration wave from the neighboring regions of Najd, al-Ihsa and the Omani mainland in different periods in the 17th and 18th centuries. Tribal migration to Qatar went on until the early 19th century.[48]

This official account is very important, especially when considering the statistics presented earlier on the composition of Qatari society. One should also consider the Qatari families of Persian origins, who migrated to Qatar and were naturalized as other Arab tribes with the creation of statehood and the issuance of Law no. 2 of year 1961 on Qatari nationality. However, the official description of the Qatari population and tribal migration disregards these different groups, even though they are legally equal to other Arab tribes in terms of citizenship rights.

The Arab states of the Persian Gulf use the heritage industry to reinforce their official national identity narratives, and thus consolidate their legitimacy, and Qatar is no exception.[49] Museums across the Arabian Peninsula have always neglected and excluded certain segments of the social fabric from a given state's national identity, most notably Persians, Abid, and Huwalah.[50] In 2015, Msheireb Properties, a subsidiary of the semi-private Qatar Foundation for Education, Science, and Community Development, opened the Bin Jelmood House, a museum that narrates the history of the Abid and their contribution to Qatari culture. The museum narrates how the Abid arrived in Qatar, their contribution to the Qatari economy, their interactions with their Qatari masters, and aspects of their cultural traditions—particularly dances like *laywa* and the *Zar-bori* spirit possession rituals, which the museum claims that slaves "practiced in private." The museum's narration of the role of Abid in Qatar ends with the abolition of slavery in Qatar by Sheikh Ali bin Abdulla bin Jassim Al-Thani, ruler of Qatar, in 1952. However, the integration of Abid into Qatari society after the abolition of slavery is absent in this narrative, which consequently ignores the contribution made by those of slave origin to Qatari history after their emancipation. People of Abid origin are present in almost all Qatari tribes that granted their tribal name to their slaves after abolition, as well as families such as the Al Abdullah family, which was formed from unrelated slaves.[51] The neglect of the role played by emancipated slaves in Qatari society is endorsed by both Arabs and freed slaves. Arab tribes attach a great deal of value to the purity of their Arab blood, which places them at the top of the social pyramid. Recognizing the integration of freed slaves of different ethnicities into these tribes would dilute their claims of Arab purity and thus superiority. Freed slaves, on the other hand, have chosen not to challenge the official narrative in order to avoid damaging their position in society, thus contributing to the nourishment of a culture of neglect of slavery heritage in Qatar.

*Public culture*

The Qatari Constitution recognizes Islam as the official religion of the state, shari'a law as the main source of legislation, and Arabic as the official language of the state.[52] In addition, Article 2 of Law no. 38 of year 2005 on the acquisition of Qatari nationality requires a good knowledge of the Arabic language in order for any non-Qatari to acquire Qatari nationality.[53] This is especially significant in the case of slaves that adhered to religions other than Islam, as they had to convert to Islam in order to be integrated into Qatari society.

The official narrative in the Bin Jelmood House states that "because those enslaved were non-Muslim, their acceptance of Islam was an important element of social integration"; thus their "integration into Gulf society was also made easier by learning to speak the same language and practicing the same religion as the host society."[54] And as far as the conditions for the slaves' integration into Qatari society are concerned:

The extent to which enslaved people could become part of their new society depended on:

- The ethnicity of the enslaved person.
- The degree of contrast between their home society and their new surroundings.
- Their master's religion: If a master was Muslim, enslaved people would often accept Islam and could sometimes be manumitted as a result.
- Their placement: Those operating as individuals or in small groups had greater opportunities for integration than those in large groups.
- The prospect of living or working alongside their masters.
- The ability to learn new languages and absorb new beliefs and traditions: In particular children often forgot their original language and place of birth..[55]

Hence the official narrative simply removes the role played by slaves, and their culture, from Qatari national identity, as slaves had to abandon their own cultural traditions in order to be manumitted and integrated into the society.

An important aspect of the Qatari identity narrative is the specific version of Islam that prevails in the country, namely state-sponsored Wahhabism, as manifested in the decision to name the state mosque after Imam Mohamed Ibn Abd Al-Wahhab.[56] In the ceremonial inauguration of the mosque, the emir of Qatar, His Highness Sheikh Tamim bin Hamad Al Thani, stated:

> We named the mosque after the great reformer and a renowned reviver Imam Muhammad Ibn Abdul Wahhab in honor of the Muslim scholars, who still carry his thought and call for revival to serve Islam and Muslims. ...
>
> His walk all through life in the path of light spread throughout the Arabian Peninsula, guides people to the right path according to the Holy Quran and *Sunnah*, removes confusion from the minds and deviations that confounded souls. ...
>
> We, as we meet today to open this mosque and name it after Imam Muhammad bin Abdul Wahhab, are honoring scholars who still carry his thought and his message to serve Islam and Muslims. I'm honored along with you to open this mosque and I pray to Almighty Allah to help us now and in the future to keep this mosque a platform to light and a torch of guidance.[57]

Thus the state sponsors and endorses the Wahhabi religious school, although it should be noted that Qataris who identify as Wahhabis practice a much more liberal form of Wahhabism than that practiced in the Kingdom of Saudi Arabia.[58] Yet the official narrative does not necessarily reflect Qataris' religious beliefs, but rather what the state promotes in order to create an "us" and "them," thereby excluding sections of society that follow other religious schools or sects, such as Persian Qataris, from the definition of Qatari national identity. By doing so, the state is able to influence an individual's social status and maintain a static social order, as it is unlikely that these groups will convert, and in the event that they do convert, other factors, such as original beliefs or ethnic identity, will serve to restrict any movement along the social-class spectrum.

Tribal identity is also reinforced by the state as an integral part of Qatari national identity. In 2007, for example, the state changed the national day from 3 September, which celebrated Qatar's independence from the British Empire, to 18 December in order to commemorate Sheikh Jassim bin Mohamed Al Thani's unification of the Qatari tribes in 1878.[59] The national day is celebrated with "military parades, conscious displays of the Qatari flag and 'national' symbols."[60] An integral part of the celebrations is the erection of tents by different tribes that host the emir to demonstrate their Arab tribal identity through folklore and renew their allegiance to the ruling family. As well as the state, therefore, Arab tribal social actors also propagate the official narrative of Qatari national identity.

One can also see how, in 2006, "*Souk al-Farsi*, or the Iranian Souq for the background of its merchants, was redone in traditional Gulfi style and renamed Souq Wakif" as an attempt by the state to replace any symbol of Persian culture with an Arab "Khaleeji" culture.[61] A consultant to the Qatar Museum Authority claimed that the authorities had asked for any events that involved Persians, whether domestically or regionally, to be expunged from a timeline of Qatari history.[62] With regard to the Msheireb Museums, in the Bin Jelmood house, the narration states that, as mentioned earlier, "When the master was asleep, [the Abid] would sneak out of the house to the *tanbura* or *laywa* performance."[63] This narration suggests that only Abid performed these dances and only in the private sphere. Yet, on the contrary, in a video played in the Mohammed bin Jassim House, another museum of the Msheireb Museums complex, a Qatari man recalls his childhood memories of living in Doha. He says that at Eid and Ramadan, children would go out on to the streets and perform the *laywa* dance.[64] Abid dances therefore melded into Qatari culture and were performed by Qataris as well. The difference in people's lived memories and the official historical narrative of the state reflects an attempt by the state to present a censored history that serves a contemporary agenda. Rather than homogenizing Qatari identity to include all Qataris of different cultures, the state excludes segments of Qatari society, particularly those of Persian and Abid origins, from the official version of Qatar's national identity.

According to Smith, the other fundamental features of a national identity include "common legal rights and duties for all members" and a "common economy with territorial mobility for members."[65] In the case of Qatar, all Qatari citizens are granted equal legal rights regardless of their background.

The state in Qatar, dominated by the Al Thani tribe, has sought to gain legitimacy by emphasizing how the Al Thani tribe, along with a number of other tribes that share the same fundamental features, fits into the Qatari national identity narrative.[66] Hukoomi, Qatar's official website, for example, describes Sheikh Jassim bin Mohamed Al Thani as the "founder" of Qatar and asserts that the people of Qatar perceived him as an "imam."[67] The state promotes this discourse in an attempt to show how the ruling family shares the same historic territory, common myths, and historical memories.[68]

The state's social conservative approach, which is based on a restrictive definition of Qatari national identity, has generally gone unchallenged, thus maintaining the existing social hierarchy and further perpetuating an identity and political system based on inclusion and exclusion. This failure to challenge the established hierarchy limits vertical social mobility and keeps the ruling family and its court's tribal allies at the top of the social pyramid. In addition to public consent, the apparatus of state coercive power, represented in its family policies and legal system, has also served to maintain the existing social hierarchy.

### *Family policies and legal system*

#### Family policies

Qatar's political institutions define the family as a central institution of the social field.[69] In analyzing Qatar's family policies, it is important to consider the "multiplicity of policies rather than a single, monolithic, comprehensive legislative act."[70] Sheila B. Kamerman and Alfred J. Kahn claim that: "'Family policy' encompasses families and policies, and includes both the policy field or domain (specific laws, regulations, and activities ... designed to affect families) and family and child well-being—or family impact—as a criterion for assessing the outcomes of relevant governmental and non-governmental policies."[71]

Family policies can vary from providing cash-transfers; parenting policies; child-care policies; laws of inheritance, adoption, guardianship, foster care, marriage, separation, divorce, custody, and child support; family planning and abortion laws; personal social service programs; housing allowances and policies; and maternal or family and child health services.[72] They can be further divided into two main categories: explicit family policies and implicit family policies. Chiara Saraceno notes that:

> Explicit family policies are deliberately designed to achieve specific objectives with regard to individuals within families and/or the whole family. Implicit family policies include actions taken in various policy domains for non-family-related goals, but which nevertheless have important consequences for children and families.[73]

The following analysis focuses on the implicit family policies imposed by the Qatari state to influence "how families are organized and behave," which in turn leads to the reproduction of the social order.[74]

## The Qatari legal system

This chapter defines the Qatari legal system as the Qatari Constitution and the Law Code, which serve as the basis on which individuals living in the Qatari territories are governed. The Constitution was drafted by the political elite and then endorsed by a public referendum in 2003.[75] With regard to the Law Code, there is no parliament with legislative power in Qatar, and no law can be "issued unless ratified by the Emir" according to Article 67 of the Constitution.[76] Although Article 76 of the Constitution grants legislative powers to the Shura Council, at the time of writing, it has not been implemented. Thus the legal system can in many ways be seen as a manifesto of the state's agenda. This section claims that the constitutional articles and laws presented below serve as implicit family policies, since they indirectly influence the shape and formation of the family as an institution.

### The Constitution of the state of Qatar

Like many other constitutions, the Qatari Constitution emphasizes the importance of the family as an integral institution of the country's social and political structure. Article 21 states that: "The family is the basis of the society. A Qatari family is founded on religion, ethics, and patriotism. The law shall regulate adequate means to protect the family, support its structure, strengthen its ties, and protect maternity, childhood, and old age."[77] Thus the Qatari state claims responsibility for imposing laws and policies that intervene in the family institution to protect its formation.

In addition, according to Article 24, "the State shall foster, preserve and help disseminate sciences, arts, cultural and national heritage, and encourage scientific research."[78] This article reflects the Qatari state's social conservative approach to national identity, as it effectively gives the state the right to "preserve" its cultural and national heritage, including tribalism and its associated values.

### The Qatari Family Law

Law no. 22 of year 2006, the "Family Law" of the state of Qatar, is based on Islamic shari'a law.[79] The law covers all aspects of the marriage institution, including: the engagement for marriage provisions; marriage conclusion; capacity of spouses; marriages forbidden on the grounds of consanguinity, affinity, and fosterage; marriages temporarily forbidden; guardianship in marriage; matching, or *kafa'a*, in marriage; marriage witnesses; dowry provisions; dowry, trousseau, and possessions' disputes; types of marriages; stipulations associated with concluding a marriage; the rights of husband and wife; maintenance; marital support; relatives' support; foundling child support; proof of parentage by the marriage bed; proof of parentage by admission; denying parentage by testimony; denying parentage by mutual cursing, or *li'aan*; and parentage claims. This outline conveys the ways through which the state intervenes and defines regulations in all aspects of the marriage institution. It should, however, be noted that these regulations are not exclusive to Qatar, as they are commonly applied in other countries as well, such as Egypt.[80]

By regulating the marriage institution, the Qatari state indirectly influences the shape and formation of the family as an institution. Articles 26 to 30 of the Qatari Family Law, for instance, recognize "the father, the agnate grandfather, the son, the full brother, paternal half-brother, the full uncle, and then the paternal uncle" as the bride's guardians.[81] A marriage cannot be concluded if the father does not approve, and in the case of his death, the next legal guardian in the order highlighted above has to approve the marriage.[82] If the first guardian rejects the marriage proposal, the judge can conclude the marriage if another guardian approves.[83] Ultimately, the bride's father has to consent to a marriage in order for it to be concluded, and in the case of his death, one of the guardians has to approve of the marriage. Under no circumstances can the bride be married without the approval of her father or legal guardian.

It is revealing to analyze Articles 31 to 35, which are related to *kafa'a*, or competence between potential spouses, in light of the aforementioned article. The Family Law recognizes *kafa'a* as a "condition for enforceability focusing on piety and good manners at the time of contracting."[84] Although the law suggests piety and good manners as standards for *kafa'a*, it still retains individual subjectivity and personal judgment, as it does not provide a definite basis on which *kafa'a* should be judged, unlike other issues such as guardianship. In fact, a fatwa, or an Islamic ruling, published on Islamweb, a website directed by Qatar's Ministry of Endowment and Islamic Affairs, claims that *kafa'a* can be judged upon lineage and ethnic origin, yet the same fatwa also suggests that *kafa'a* should not be based on ethnicity and lineage.[85]

Bernard Lewis claims that the function of *kafa'a* in shari'a law is to "ensure that a man should be at least the social equal of the woman he marries ... Its aim is to protect the honor of respectable families, by enabling them, if they wish, to stop unsuitable marriages."[86] Building on this, one can claim that

Qatari Family Law, through the guardianship articles, grants the father or legal guardian the right to reject a marriage proposal if they believe that the husband is of unequal social status, even if the woman accepts the social difference. Additionally, the Family Law's *kafa'a* articles give rights to the woman and her father or legal guardian to reject or revoke a marriage within one year, as long as the wife did not give birth or is pregnant, based on social equality. This is important because it gives the father the opportunity to rethink his decision if he accepted the marriage of his daughter to a husband of a lower social class. Moreover, if the father dies within one year of the marriage and the woman is not pregnant and did not give birth, the law gives the next legal guardian in line the power to revoke the marriage if he rejected the marriage proposal while the father was alive. As such, Qatar's Family Law helps to maintain traditional social values, which further perpetuates a system of social exclusion based on ethnicity.

As the law draws on shari'a, it is not unique to Qatar. Although this is correct, one has to consider that there has been a debate in Islamic jurisprudence over this issue. According to Islamweb itself, it is religiously unacceptable to intervene between a wife and a husband to divorce them, even on a *kafa'a* claim.[87]

## Marriage to foreigners

In 1961, the state of Qatar issued Law Decree no. 2, which regulates Qatari nationality; though the law was later repealed, one of its articles is revealing of the state's efforts to regulate social life and thus merits further discussion. Article 12 stated that: "A Qatari woman who is married to a foreigner may acquire her husband's nationality if the Law of her husband's country permits, otherwise she may retain her Qatari nationality for one year following the date of the marriage contract."[88]

This article would consequently have given the state the right to denaturalize a Qatari woman if she married a foreign national, thereby demonstrating the state's intention to establish barriers to prevent Qatari females from marrying non-Qatari males. Although the law was later repealed, that it was promulgated in the first place is likely to have had a social impact in questioning a Qatari female's right to call herself a Qatari in the event she married a non-Qatari, thus affecting the social status of those who take this step.

Similarly, Law no. 38 of year 2005 on the acquisition of Qatari nationality, which was given constitutional validity, sets out a series of stipulations relating to the children of a Qatari mother and a foreign father.[89] Article 2 states that:

> Any non-Qatari may acquire Qatari nationality, by decree of the Emir, provided that:
>
> 1. On the application date for Qatari nationality he has been a regular resident in Qatar for not less than twenty-five consecutive years. This provision shall not be prejudiced by the applicant being absent from Qatar for not more than two months in a single calendar year, provided the applicant has the intention of returning. These periods of absence shall be deducted from the actual cumulative residence period. Should the applicant leave Qatar following the submission of the nationality application, and remain absent from Qatar for longer than six months, the Interior Minister reserves the right to disregard his previous residence, and discount his application.
> 2. He has a lawful means of income.
> 3. He is of good repute and has not been convicted of any offense impugning his honor or integrity.
> 4. Has a good knowledge of the Arabic language.
>
> In the application of the Qatari nationality rules, in pursuance of the provisions of this Article, priority shall be given to those applicants who have a Qatari mother.
>
> Those born to a naturalized Qatari father in Qatar or outside Qatar shall be deemed to be a naturalized Qatari.
>
> Those born in Qatar to unknown parents shall also be deemed to be a naturalized Qatari. Foundlings shall be considered as born in Qatar unless proven otherwise.[90]

Although this law gives priority to children of Qatari mothers in claiming nationality rights, Ghada Al-Subaey claims that children of a Qatari mother still struggle to attain this status, as bureaucratic constraints make it very hard for such children to claim Qatari nationality.[91] The father of these children must have "lived in Qatar for 25 years, have a legal source of living, good reputation and knows Arabic."[92] If these conditions are satisfied, the children can apply for citizenship after reaching the age of eighteen; however, they do not receive Qatari nationality automatically and must apply and wait for a committee's decision.[93] A *laqit* (an abandoned child of unknown parentage), on the other hand, is automatically eligible for Qatari citizenship as long as it can be proved that he or she was born in Qatar; thus a *laqit*, who might not be of Qatari origins, actually has more of a priority than children of a Qatari mother when claiming Qatari nationality.[94]

Qatar also influences people's choices as far as marriage is concerned via Law Decree no. 21 of year 1989, which has since been amended by Law no. 11 of 1994 and Law no. 8 of 2005. The law mandates gaining approval from the interior minister for any marriage between a Qatari citizen and a foreigner,[95] thus providing another example of the state intervening in its citizens' personal lives in order to maintain the existing social order built on ethnicity and religion.

Article 1 of the law prevents a wide range of individuals from marrying foreigners, including: ministers and deputy ministers; heads of boards of institutions, public bodies, and their deputies; diplomatic staff and consular corps; officers, non-commissioned officers, and members of the armed forces, police, and other security agencies; and students on scholarship who are studying abroad, whether supported by the state or studying at their own expense.[96] This law is not applicable if the marriage partner is a national of the Gulf Cooperation Council (GCC) states, a cousin, or born to a Qatari mother.[97] Although preventing certain people who hold official positions from marrying partners of different nationalities is common in some countries, placing restrictions on civil servants, members of armed forces, police, and students abroad clearly reflects the state's efforts to resist intermarriages between Qataris and people of non-Arab ethnicities, origins, and cultures.

Article 2 requires a social reason for Qataris to marry a non-Qatari partner but without defining what a "social reason" is. This law was intentionally crafted in an ambiguous way in order to give the state more power in maintaining the existing social order.

The articles discussed above reveal how the state has sought to use these laws to establish barriers preventing Qatari citizens from marrying foreigners, thus intervening in Qataris' marriage choices and limiting intermarriages between Qataris of different ethnic and cultural backgrounds. This is important when considering the effect of marriages between spouses of different nationalities, as this kind of marriage influences the prevailing system of social inclusion and exclusion, especially in the case of women. For example, if a foreigner who does not hold the same ethnicity and values of Qatari society marries an Arab Qatari female, this would affect her "Arabness" and that of her family and offspring. Besides the likelihood of her father or legal guardian rejecting such a marriage using the guardianship and *kafa'a* rights granted by the Family Law, if this marriage were to take place, it would lower her social class and status and that of her family.

## *Conclusion*

Rather than creating a homogenous Qatari identity that would include Qataris of different backgrounds, the Qatari state has consistently promoted a historical narrative on the composition and evolution of Qatari society that solely emphasizes the role of Arab tribes in the inhabitation process, the evolution of Qatar's governing authority, and the creation of Qatari statehood. This official narrative disregards a major section of Qatar's society, particularly those of Abid, Huwalah, and Persian backgrounds, even though these sections of society played an important role in the economy of Qatar before the discovery of oil in the country.

Arab tribal social actors have gained a dominant position in Qatar's social and political structure at the expense of other social actors, especially those of an Abid, Huwalah, and Persian background. Together with the state, they have enforced a dominant narrative that fails to acknowledge other actors as genuine Qataris with the aim of supporting their domination over the material structure of the state. This domination has perpetuated the system of social inclusion and exclusion in Qatari society.

In adopting a social conservative approach, the Qatari state has maintained and deepened the existing social hierarchy and the system of inclusion and exclusion on which it is based. The state has used two methods to achieve this goal. The first has been to restrict the criteria that define Qatari national identity, limiting the definition of homeland, common myths, and historical memories to being of an Arab tribal origin and practicing the Sunni Wahhabi version of Islam. By doing so, the state has systematically hindered the possibilities for vertical social mobility and secured the position of the monarchy—and its Arab tribal allies—at the top of the social pyramid. This has in turn served to limit the distribution of power among the different social actors, thus affecting pluralism in Qatari society. Power remains undispersed, as non-Arab tribal social actors lack effective means of representation. Given their reluctance to challenge the prevailing system, marginalized social actors either hide their origins to avoid damaging their social status, particularly in the case of Abid and Huwalah; or they yield to this narrative in order to avoid harming their position in the economy, particularly in the case of Persian Qataris who are overrepresented in the Qatari business community and are often awarded lucrative state contracts.

Besides public consent, the state also relies on its juridical structures to maintain the dominant position of Arab tribes in the social and political hierarchy. As we have seen, this narrowing of Qatari national identity is reflected in the country's Constitution, its legal system, and its national symbols, as well as the official history promoted by the Qatari government. Through these tools, the state has perpetuated a system of social inclusion and exclusion, a system that also extends to citizens' private lives insofar as marriage choices are concerned. This, in turn, influences the social perception of social hierarchy and the system of inclusion and exclusion in Qatari society.

However, the state-sponsored historical narrative does not reflect people's lived memories, which are passed down from one generation to the next. These realities have been lived within a diverse society formed by those of Arab, Persian, Abid, and Huwalah descent who have lived in the country for more than a century of Qatar's short existence. Yet, by successfully ensuring that there is little public resistance to this narrative, and by relying on juridical structures that maintain the existing social hierarchy, Arab tribes have exerted their hegemony over the state, thus limiting other social actors' representation in the state and preventing the recognition of pluralism in Qatari society. Whether the state's *imaginaire* will eclipse people's lived realities or not is something only time can reveal.

4

# THE SHI'I STATE AND THE SOCIOECONOMIC CHALLENGES OF THE SUNNI COMMUNITIES IN IRAN

## HISTORICAL AND CONTEMPORARY PERSPECTIVES

*Afshin Shahi* and *Ehsan Abdoh-Tabrizi*

Although there has been a substantial amount of research into Iran's role as a major sectarian player in the international politics of the Middle East, there is hardly any literature on the politics of the Shi'i–Sunni divide in modern Iran. Since the establishment of the Iranian Islamic Republic in 1979, Iran has been perceived as one of the forces behind the resurgence of Shi'i politics in the region, which has in turn inflamed sectarian tensions. Yet, very little attention has been given to the large Sunni population in Iran. This gap in the literature is partly due to the paucity of English-language information on the political and socioeconomic challenges faced by Iran's ethnic Sunni minorities.

Iran's Sunni population is neither monolithic nor a united community. Sunni Iranians are geographically divided all around the country and comprise many ethnic, linguistic, and tribal groups, making Sunnism their only common sociocultural element. This begs the question of whether we can even refer to the Sunni population of Iran as a "Sunni community." And even if the category of "community" is acceptable, there is a more fundamental question to be answered: given obvious linguistic, ethnic, cultural, and geographic diversities, do Sunni Iranians constitute a religious minority? Can we class these diverse groups—many of whom are located in different parts of the country—as a cohesive minority only because they share Sunni Islam?

Anglo-American academics have published a wealth of studies on Iran's many ethnicities—particularly the Kurds—and non-Muslim religious minorities, but to this day, a general comprehensive study on Sunni Iranians has not been produced. Minority studies in Iran have focused on ethnic identity and have treated religious identity as of lesser import. Simultaneously, the studies of Iran's religious minorities have focused on Iran's non-Islamic minorities and have entirely disregarded Sunni Iranians. It is interesting to note that while the constitution of the Islamic Republic of Iran recognizes the four main schools of Sunni Islam, it does not name them among Iran's recognized religious minorities.[1] In fact, the word "Sunni" is not even mentioned in the constitution, and Iranian authorities and even Sunni Iranian activists tend to avoid using the term "minority" for Sunni Iranians, instead using the historical term *ahl-ison'nat* (those of Sunni orientation).[2] All this indicates that ethnic identity in Iran always takes precedence over religious/sectarian identity. However, as stated by Lois Beck, the factors that shape communal and individual perceptions of identity in Iran are multiple and evolving.[3] Thus, language, sect (Sunni, Shi'i, and Sufi Islam), ethnic, and other cultural features, national-minority awareness, and tribal affiliation all shape the identity of Iran's numerous communities.[4]

Communal identity is not fixed in time and space. Various factors such as the internal politics of the state and the external regional environment can have an impact on the ways in which minority communities perceive their own status in relation to the majority. Communal identity is dynamic, fluid, and unremittingly influenced by multiple factors.

The Iranian Revolution, which brought Shi'i Islam to the forefront of politics, created an environment that made Sunni communities more conscious of their sectarian "otherness." In the words of Stéphane Dudoignon, the rise of Shi'i political Islam, and the foundation of the Islamic Republic under Ayatollah Khomeini and the Shi'i clergy leadership, led to the emergence of "a nascent sense of solidarity within the henceforth self-conscious Sunnite community of Iran."[5] This awakening of sectarian consciousness has been amplified by four decades of the Islamic Republic's rule. It remains to be seen how Sunni Iranians will be affected by the rise of violent sectarianism in the Middle East, particularly in Syria where a proxy war with a sectarian tone is currently being fought between Iran and Saudi Arabia.

There are a number of academic works in English, Persian, and French dealing with ethnic groups such as the Kurds and Baluchs in Iran, but their main focus is often on ethnicity rather than sect. To our knowledge, this is the first study of the socioeconomic challenges faced by Sunni Iranians across the country. Given the lack of directly related academic literature on this topic, this study has benefited from a wide range of primary sources in Persian.

The chapter starts by mapping the Sunni population in Iran. Before addressing the socioeconomic challenges of this section of Iranian society, it is important to highlight the geographic, cultural, and linguistic detachments among them. This will be followed by a brief historical overview of the evolution of Iran's Shi'i–Sunni divide. Iran was a Sunni majority country up until the sixteenth century when the country went through one of the most significant socio-religious transitions in Islamic history. Although this radical top-down social engineering policy transformed the religious landscape of the country, it could not religiously homogenize all social groups. Accordingly, most communities managed to maintain their Sunni identity for centuries thereafter.

A clearer historical insight into the relationship between the Shi'i state and the Sunni communities can help us better understand the current situation. Following a brief discussion of the sociopolitical realties of the Sunni population in the Safavid and Qajar periods, the chapter provides an overview of developments in the Pahlavi era. The Pahlavi shahs embarked on a radical process of nation-state building, which was centralist and Persian-centric. Reza Shah, the founder of the dynasty, used heavy-handed measures to modernize the country, and some of his policies had serious implications for ethnic groups living at the periphery of Iranian society. Although Pahlavi policies had no sectarian foundation, the Sunni communities, which belonged to various marginalized ethnic groups, were nonetheless affected by these modernization policies.

This chapter gives more attention to the Sunni communities after the formation of the Islamic Republic, which brought Shi'i clergy to the forefront of Iranian politics. It will examine the socioeconomic conditions of the Sunni population in the four decades of the Islamic Republic. Although the Islamic Republic championed wealth distribution to the impoverished margins of the country, the Sunni majority provinces faced years of economic marginalization and underdevelopment, often fused with sectarian discrimination. The Shi'i-centric political model that emerged in post-revolutionary Iran exacerbated the socioeconomic conditions of the Sunni majority provinces such as Sistan-Baluchistan. This has paved the way to insurgency and political violence, which has been dealt with by the repressive policies of the state.

*Mapping the Sunni population of Iran*

There are three distinct ethnicities that constitute double minorities on both ethnic and sectarian grounds and form the majority of Iran's Sunni communities: the Baluchi (populating Iran's southeastern region, mainly the province of Sistan-Baluchistan), Kurds (located in the northwestern provinces of Kurdistan, Kermanshah, Ilām, Eastern and Western Azerbaijan, and Ardebil), and Turkmens (located in various regions of Golestān and Northern Khorasan provinces). Apart from these three main Sunni ethnicities, there is a considerable number of Sunni Iranians, including Taleshis, situated in the northwestern edge of Gilān province and the Caspian Sea, and Persian-speaking Sunnis of the Khorasan and Fars provinces.[6] The inner Sunni regions of Fars, most notably the Lār district, are close to Iran's Persian Gulf coasts, where, historically, a long-standing flow of migration has taken place between Iranian and Arabian shores. A considerable number of Iranians (both Arabic and Persian speakers) of these southern coastal communities are Sunni and continue to have "a double belonging status."[7] This status is anything but unusual, as before the 1920s Baluch, Kurds, Turkmens, and other borderland nomads of Iran were in a similar position. The Kurds were effectively divided between both the Ottoman and Iranian Empires, and the Baluchi and Turkmens were also territorially locked between the ailing Qajar Iran, the growing British Raj, and an aggressive tsarist Russia.[8] These geopolitical factors had important consequences for these Sunni ethnic groups: division of their historical land between neighboring states, double belonging, and—in the case of the nomadic Turkmens and Baluch—statelessness. More importantly, it meant that nomadic border-landers were able to move between borders with relative impunity. This situation changed after the First World War, as the rise of modern nation-states in Turkey, Iran, Iraq, and the menacing presence of the Soviet Union led to tighter border controls. However, while the freedom of movement available to Iranian border-landers, including those of Sunni ethnicity, was significantly reduced, it never came to a total end, and Iran's border inhabitants can still move between Iran and its neighbors, which has clear economic, political, and security implications for the state.

Most of the aforementioned groups live on Iran's border areas with Iraq, Turkey, Turkmenistan, Afghanistan, and Pakistan; with the exception of Iraq, which was created in 1923, all are nominally Sunni-majority nations. There are other small pockets of Sunni Iranians who live on borderlands, including the nearly unknown Sunni Azari Turks, who are locally referred to as Küresünlī, and who live in isolated and thinly populated villages in the Eastern Azerbaijan province.[9] While most Sunni Iranians still live in their historical place of habitat, modern development and urbanization patterns have caused the relocation of some Sunni Iranians to more central areas of the country such as the cosmopolitan city of Tehran.

Iran and Afghanistan have long historical links, and Afghan laborers were active in Iran decades before the Soviet invasion of Afghanistan.[10] Since the Soviet invasion, Iran has also been the unwilling host to millions of Afghan refugees. These Afghanis have not been granted any rights, and face growing discrimination and hostility, but are among some of the most important work forces in Iran with many cases of marriage between them and Iranian citizens, not only in border regions but also in Tehran.[11] At least half of the Afghan migrants are Sunni Tajiks and Pashtuns.[12] Despite attempts to repatriate them, their presence seems irreversible and continues to add to Iran's social, cultural, and religious complexity.

### *Sunni Iranians in the pre-Pahlavi period*

Shi'i communities have a long history in Iran; indeed, there is a widespread belief that there is an organic historical tie between Iran and Shi'ism.[13] However, it is well established that before the rise of the messianic Shi'i Safavid Sufi order in the late fifteenth century, most Iranians were of Sunni orientation.[14] The Safavid dynasty changed all that by making Shi'ism Iran's official sect.[15] Initially, the Safavid policy of mass conversion was conducted through violent campaigns—leading to a long-lasting religious and political war with the Sunni Ottoman Empire—before later turning to discursive and administrative policies in order to achieve the same goal.[16] Through these measures, the Safavids converted the formerly Sunni-majority Iranian population to Shi'ism and carved a unique status for themselves as the guardians of Shi'i Islam. The severity of the Safavid policy of top-down conversion lessened over time but was never abandoned entirely. During their 200-year rule, the

Safavids eventually converted most of Iran proper to Shi'i Islam. However, they did not succeed in converting the territories located on the margins of their empire. This was most evident in Iran's Afghan territory, where, despite much cultural and linguistic commonality, Safavid Shi'ism did not take hold.

After the fall of the Safavids, a state of total chaos and war engulfed Iran until the last year of the eighteenth century, when the Qajar tribe finally defeated other tribal contenders and seized the throne. During Qajar rule, official control over Iran's Sunni-populated regions—all of which were borderlands—was minimal in some areas and non-existent in others. The Shi'i-Sunni division had little if any role in this situation, as Iran's state and society had failed to unify after the fall of the Safavid dynasty in 1722. The Qajar dynasty did not possess the religious legitimacy that the Safavid enjoyed and was never able to reinstate central control, maintain reliable armed forces, or create a strong economy.[17] The weakness of the Qajar dynasty highlighted a longer-term problem of governance in Iran, where, as Homa Katouzian describes it, power had no source of legitimacy, with "the ultimate test of 'legitimacy'" residing in the ability to seize and maintain power.[18]

The inability of the Qajar dynasty to maintain and exercise its power led to a semi-permanent state of banditry, tribalism, and instability in Iran, described in Persian as the state of "molūk al-tavāyefi" (rule of tribes), synonymous to chaos. There is no doubt that Shi'ism played an important role in keeping the realm together, but Shi'ism and Shi'i solidarity was not strong enough to overcome the problems of arbitrary rule. Many Shi'i-dominated areas were under the control of rulers who would withhold tribute and obedience as soon as Qajar ineptitude exceeded a certain level, and they would even rebel if a suitable opportunity for doing so presented itself. Thus the state of rebellion and disobedience in Iran's Sunni regions was not the exception but the norm.

During the Safavid era, Iran's Sunni-populated regions remained disputed borderlands between Iran and its rival Sunni neighbors, the Ottomans, the Uzbek Khanates of Transoxiana, and the Mughal Empire of India. In the nineteenth century, Iran's eastern territories and its relations with its traditional eastern neighbors were fundamentally reshaped by "the Great Game," with the aggressive expansion of tsarist Russia in Central Asia and the British domination of India.[19] Russia's ambitions toward Iran and India, and British machinations to counter them, led to the drastic diminishment of Iran's territories and its status as a regional power, with Iran losing vast parts of its eastern possessions, which were predominantly Sunni-populated.[20]

The Qajar shahs did try in vain to reclaim the former possessions of the Safavids in these areas, which led to conflict with Britain over Iran's Afghan possessions and long-lasting blood feuds with Sunni Turkmens and Baluch.[21] Yet the dynamics of Shi'i Iran's relations with its Sunni neighbors and subjects thoroughly changed as a result, and the Sunni–Shi'i divide played a minor role in this outcome. The old Ottoman–Iranian feud had run its course, as the two now had greater concerns. Rarely, if ever, during their many attempts to secure Iran's former possessions in Transoxiana and Afghanistan, or crushing the numerous rebellions of Turkmens and Baluch, did Qajar rulers justify their actions in religious terms. Their claim was entirely based on reestablishing Iran's traditional authority in these regions, and the state's prerogative of tribute, tax, and garrisoning key areas. The Shi'i–Sunni divide may have entrenched the animosity between the Qajar rulers and the rebellious Sunni Turkmens and Baluchs, but it was not the pivotal cause of their conflicts. On the whole, these feuds resulted from the seemingly endless conflict with an arbitrary state, which treated the stalwart and unrelenting Turkmen and Baluch tribesmen as unsavory "savages."[22] The Sunni–Shi'i aspect of animosity further intensified these conflicts, which occasionally became horrifically violent, even by the standards of the time.[23]

The weak Qajar state often had to struggle against unruly tribes who were nominally Shi'i. Thus, various tribes and clans feuded with one another, and their Shi'i orientation did not lead to political harmony. Tribal loyalties and clan lineage were the most decisive factors in the identity of many Iranians, often taking precedence over religion among Iran's vast and varied tribal and nomadic populations, Shi'i and Sunni alike.

The case of Sunni Turkmens is highly instructive in this regard. The nineteenth-century Turkmens who moved between Iran's northeastern borders were devoted Sunnis, but Sunni Islam was only one of the decisive characteristics of Turkmen identity. The eighteenth- and nineteenth-century Turkmen tribes of Iran used three conditions to identify proper "Turkmen-ness:" ancestry, the ability to speak the Turkmen dialect, and being of Hanafi Sunni persuasion.[24] As one component was not enough without the others, the Turkmens' strong sense of tribalism did not allow a sense of solidarity based on Sunni Islam.

Turkmen tribes usually warred with each other, which in turn caused long-lasting blood feuds.[25] These feuds even spread within the various Turkmen tribes themselves, which were usually divided into two or more main clans.[26] The same situation prevailed among the Sunni Baluchi tribes, who were in a state of perpetual warfare with each other. When faced with the possibility of being attacked by the central state, the feuding Baluchi tribes were quick to ally themselves with the state forces at the expense of their Baluchi rivals.[27] All this demonstrates the absence of any sense of national consciousness among the tribal-minded Baluchi and Turkmens. Another conclusion is that a common Sunni orientation was unable to build a sense of solidarity and unity among the Turkmen and Baluchi tribesmen—at least before the mid-twentieth century.

Unlike the Safavids, the Qajar shahs had little incentive to promulgate the Shi'i faith. Although they upheld the shari'a according to Twelver Imami Shi'ism, and as Shi'i rulers, they were duty-bound to defend the "true faith," they did not embark upon religious campaigns or forced conversions. While the relationship between the Qajar state and Iran's eastern Sunni Turkmens and Baluchi was usually violent, there were few cases of sectarian violence in Iran. The worst of these occurred during the chaos of the First World War, yet it was caused by a Muslim–Christian binary rather than Shi'i–Sunni division and was limited to the northeastern province of Azerbaijan.[28] This was at a time when the neutral but helpless Iran had become a minor frontline between imperial Russia and Britain, and the sectarian violence was probably triggered by the Ottoman-initiated Armenian genocide.[29]

### *The Pahlavi state's economic policies and Sunni Iranians: uneven development and ethnic inequality*

Economically, many regions of Iran, including the Baluch, Kurdish, and Turkmen regions, were locally integrated on tribal, ethnic, and communal lines, with economic relations being conducted largely on a subsistence basis.[30] This was probably due to few urban centers and a general lack of stability, which did not encourage trade and production. Rural and pastoral nomadism was the dominant form of life in most of these tribal areas. In the isolated areas of Baluchistan, the desolate and harsh natural environment and pastoral nomadism created a warlike mentality and a pillage economy.[31] The only economic relationship between these areas and the state was the taxes and tributes they paid to the central government when the latter was strong enough to enforce them.

Yet this situation did not mean that there was no inter-regional trade in Iran's Sunni-populated borderlands. Iran's Turkmen region—which by the end of the nineteenth century had become Iran's frontier with the Russian Empire—had a lucrative trade with Russian merchants in foodstuffs and other goods through the port of Gomishtappeh.[32] Similarly, Iran's Persian Gulf

Sunni population had long-standing trade relations with their brethren across the water, trade that continues today.[33]

The rise of Reza Shah, and his reestablishment of order through force of arms, may well have been a form of salvation for many urban and trading Iranians, but it also meant an unprecedented level of social and economic control by the state. The state used its newly increased power to demand revenues such as taxation and customs, and the political and regional elites of the Qajar era, many of whom had not paid any tax for decades, were soon struggling under the heavy pressure of Reza Shah's treasury.[34] The state's force was of such intensity, and was so humiliating, that it drove a former prime minister of the constitutional era and grand landholder to suicide.[35]

The state's political and economic power reached all sections of Iranian society, and Sunni Iranians were no exception. In the 1920s, the state's forceful policies over trade and customs became so extreme on Iran's Persian Gulf shores that many Sunni residents left for the Arabian side of the shore in order to escape it.[36] However, nowhere was the power of the new order felt more keenly than among Iran's tribal populations, which included the majority of the country's Sunni communities. After defeating tribal forces in the Turkmen, Kurdish, and Baluchi regions, government institutions—such as the police, postal service, tax offices, and state schools—were established, and communications and roads were greatly expanded, all of which served the central government in its efforts to entrench and expand its control over these regions.[37]

Sunni Turkmens were hit particularly hard, as the state's restructuring of the regional economy, coupled with security considerations toward the Soviet Union, halted the thriving indigenous trade with Russia and practically destroyed the successful trade port of Gomishtappeh.[38] Urbanization also served as a tool for government control, with new cities being established for this purpose. The most important among them were Bandar Shah (today's Bandar Turkmen) in the Turkmen region, and Zahedan, which became the capital of the new province of Sistan-Baluchistan. Both cities were mere villages before government resources turned them into provincial focal points. Zahedan and Bandar Shah had the potential for profitable trade given their proximity to Iran's borders, and both were incorporated into Iran's general railroad system. In all this, the indigenous Turkmen and Baluchi played little role despite forming the majority of the population.

In 1940, Bandar Turkmen was still a small city divided into two: there was a modern side built around a train station with new streets and a few other government-sponsored buildings, where nearly all its inhabitants and state employees were Persian-speakers and Azeri Turks;[39] the other side of the city, which housed the majority of the population, was entirely Turkmen. Almost no Turkmen worked for the train station or any other government institution; their main occupations were traditional animal husbandry and carpet-weaving.[40]

Zahedan was in a similar situation. From the 1930s to the 1950s, the majority of state employees (teachers, civil servants, and law enforcement personnel) were non-Baluch; they were mostly local Persian-speaking Shi'i Sistanies and Khorasanies, while trade was in the hands of Yazdi tradesmen and Indian Sikh merchants,[41] and the majority of state schoolteachers were Khorasani Persian speakers.[42] In both cities, the indigenous ethnic population played little role in the economy other than as manual laborers.

Reza Shah's rule had other negative economic effects for ethnic Sunni Iranians, as it sought to destroy, or at least amend, the old socioeconomic order in favor of government control regardless of the hardships it caused for tribal and ethnic populations. The general policy of tribal settlement was brutal, and it severely weakened tribal organizations.[43] Many Kurdish tribes were forced to migrate and settle in fixed locations, while the rebellious tribes were transferred from their ancestral lands to other provinces.[44] Forced land-grabs, relocating Kurdish leaders to Tehran, and other measures were used to ensure the subjugation of Kurdish tribes.[45]

In areas where the local Kurdish leaders had not opposed the state's authority, the tribal organization was left alone, but various state policies and tactics undermined tribal lifestyle, tribal solidarity, and local economic practices. Indeed, had Reza Shah not been forced to abdicate in 1941, he would have completely destroyed Kurdish tribal organization.[46] The Baluchi tribal elite were not treated as harshly, as they cooperated with the Pahlavi state when it was in their interests to do so. Similar to other ethnic groups and tribal populations, Iran's Baluchistan also experienced a period of excessive militarization, and it seems that Reza Shah intended to eliminate Baluchi tribal chiefs as well.[47] However, the regime formed a lasting client–patron relationship with one group of Baluchi tribal leaders, known as *sardārs*, which, along with the state's military presence, kept Baluchistan secure and under state control.[48]

The modern state's accommodation with the Baluchi *sardār* system was primarily a matter of priorities and resources. Other than reestablishing its authority, the central government had little incentive to undertake massive restructuring in Baluchistan. Most of the land was impoverished and had little prospect of being a source of revenue in the short or medium term. Reza Shah's government was always short of funds for its various development projects, and massive changes in Baluchistan risked much for an uncertain return—the *sardārs* who led the nomadic Baluchs in distant areas could have engaged government forces in long and bitter campaigns. It made far more sense from an economic perspective to buy the loyalty of the *sardārs* by allocating them modest amounts of funds and other privileges in order to keep the peace.[49] The government's policy of co-opting local tribal chiefs varied according to Baluchistan's political and geographical situation.

According to Philip Salzman, the Baluchi chiefs of the relatively fertile and agricultural southern lands, known as *hokoms*, were completely displaced by the state, a process made easier due to the non-nomadic rural lifestyle of those inhabiting these areas.[50] By contrast, establishing direct centralized administration in the distant border regions and nomadic areas was extremely difficult without the *sardārs*' cooperation.[51] As a result, the Baluchs maintained their borderless status and their ability to move between Iran and the British Raj's Baluchistan (and future Pakistan), while the Kurds and Turkmens either lost that ability or had it severely constrained. Iran's Turkmen population suffered acutely as state policies were carried out with utter harshness and brutality.

The Pahlavi state was able to implement these policies by massively expanding Iran's road network along with other technological advancements, which made Turkmen regions easy to access.[52] Turkmen regions were among Iran's most fertile areas, which made the state more determined and brutal. The militarization of the region, the constriction of freedom of movement, political and civil suppression, heavy taxation, and state institutionalization and Persianization policies meant that Turkmens were forced to abandon their nomadic life while the state appropriated their fertile lands for mass agricultural purposes.[53] These land appropriations were nothing more than legal theft by the new arbitrary ruler of Iran, with most of these lands becoming part of Reza Shah's royal properties.[54]

Thus, the rise of the modern nation-state was a grim period for most Sunni Iranians. Their predicament may have been more bearable if the state's policies had provided them with economic opportunities and advantages, yet Reza Shah's policies of centralization and tribal settlement aggressively targeted and harmed their traditional economy and entire way of life. These policies were implemented in the most brutal, arbitrary way and without meaningful support or relief for the heavy burdens of such a transition, which both victimized and humiliated Iran's Sunni ethnicities and tribal population.[55] Their grievances made the Pahlavi regime's other achievements in health, education, and infrastructure seem trivial to entire generations of Turkmens, Kurds, and Baluch.

The Pahlavi regime's heavy-handed policies somewhat diminished after the fall of Reza Shah; however, political tension between the state and Iran's ethnic minorities nonetheless continued during the rule of his successor Mohammad Reza Shah. This tension resulted in open animosity and hostility in northern Kurdish regions, with the city of Mahabad as its focal point. Kurdish ethno-nationalism, which was particularly powerful there, led to the emergence of separatist movements that were often formed with the help of the Soviets. In 1946, one such movement made a bid for power via the creation of the Mahabad Republic, but this was defeated after the Soviet evacuation of Iran a year later.[56] Due to the continued hostility between the Iranian state and Kurdish ethno-nationalists, who enjoyed considerable popular support, many observers believe that Mohammad Reza Shah deliberately withheld funds from Kurdistan's development projects.

In Reza Shah's era, the state attempted to strengthen its position in Turkmen and Kurdish regions by settling other, more reliable ethnicities in troubled regions. Thousands of Persian-speaking Hazara were settled in Turkmen regions, while in Kurdistan, the habitats of rebellious Kurdish tribes were given to Shi'i Turkic-speaking groups.[57] The Pahlavi state had embarked on other policies of social engineering to form its ideal nation, and the attempt to change the demography of Kurdish and Turkmen regions was probably aimed at assimilating these ethnicities in the new Persianized Iranian state. Similar inner migration took place in the Khuzestan province, where Persian-speaking groups increased in number to the disadvantage of Iranian Arabs.[58] Naturally, this policy created ever more resentment among Kurds, Baluchs, and Turkmens.

During Mohammad Reza Shah's rule, the economic situation facing Sunni Iranians continued to deteriorate as a result of the government's policies. With an increase in Iran's oil revenue, and the stability and economic planning brought about by the shah's dominance, from 1960 to 1978 Iran had a thriving, vibrant, and expanding economy. The Pahlavi regime was successful in achieving most of its economic and social objectives: between 1960 and 1977, Iran's real growth rate was nearly 9.6 percent, a much higher figure than other developing countries.[59] However, these great strides belied a number of fundamental weaknesses. Most notably, the modernization of Iran's economy was uneven, and its economic growth was unbalanced, weakening it as a whole. These two factors had negative effects in many areas of Iran, and particularly in the provincial areas that contained the majority of Iran's Sunni ethnic groups. These fundamental problems were infused in the economic policy of the Pahlavi regime, which favored centralism, urbanism, and industrialization. These factors, along with the regime's chauvinistic tendencies, marginalized many non-central areas, including the Turkmen, Kurdish, and Baluchi regions.

The uneven modernization and imbalanced growth brought about by the Pahlavi regime's policies proved particularly damaging to Iran's Sunni Turkmen, Kurdish, and Baluchi ethnicities. In 1960, the share of agriculture in Iran's GDP was about 30 percent, but by 1977 this figure had declined to less than 10 percent. The annual growth rate of agriculture, moreover, was much less than the respective figures for the industrial and service sectors.[60] This was hardly favorable to the 57.1 percent of the Baluchi workforce who labored in the agricultural sector. Although the number of Kurds and Turkmen employed in agriculture was not as high as the Baluch, it was still significant.[61] Thus most Sunni ethnic Iranians worked in the agricultural sector, and the government's policy shrunk this sector without providing substitute employment in other areas, as the majority of industries were in Persian-speaking Iran proper and in cities such as Tehran, Esfahan, and Shiraz.

Pahlavi development policies allocated the lion's share of resources and funds to urbanized areas, particularly cities such as Tehran. Smaller cities and rural areas, which included most Kurdish, Turkmen, and Baluchi regions, were at the bottom of the government's development budget. In 1974, after years of growing oil revenue, only 4 percent of Iran's villages had access to electricity and piped drinking water.[62] Similar disadvantages extended to social welfare. Nearly all Iranians benefited from the regime's modernization of the health and education sectors and the commensurate decline in infant mortality, malnutrition, endemic diseases, and illiteracy. But again, these services, particularly education, were better provided in urban areas closer to the center.[63]

While the extent and level of the Pahlavi regime's chauvinist nationalism declined over time—from its peak in Reza Shah's era up until the more relaxed period of Mohammad Reza Shah's rule—this economic policy remained relatively intact. The economic modernization model adopted in Reza Shah's era was a centralized order economy, which gave priority to urban development and industrialization at the expense of regional and rural development and agriculture. This policy remained unchanged during the Pahlavi era, and to a certain extent became institutionalized, with the non-central, rural areas of Iran and non-Persian ethnicities given less priority in the national budget and development programs. This was, of course, uneven, as Azeri Turks were historically infused in the Iranian state and continued to have considerable political representation and economic advantage in the Pahlavi system. The Sunni Turkmen,

Kurdish, and Baluchi ethnicities were probably the worst off among other Iranian ethnicities due to many reasons other than their sect. The lack of a pluralistic model of development, political animosity between the state and ethnonational Kurdish movements, and Baluchistan's traditional society and general impoverishment were the main drivers for this economic inequality.

From the 1960s onwards, Pahlavi economic policy was controlled by Western-educated technocrats who encouraged the regime to implement a centralized policy of urbanization and industrialization. Although the budget allocations given to the Kurdish and Baluchi regions were increased when rising oil revenue made doing so possible, the state did not make policy changes to tackle the problem of impoverishment and extreme inequality in these regions. Iran's Baluchi regions had the highest rate of illiteracy, and until 1965 no single Baluchi student was enrolled in any institution of higher education. The situation slowly began to change in the late 1970s as the number of Baluchi in universities began to rise and the state began to establish the first institutions of higher education in Baluchistan. By 1978, two universities in Zahedan and one university in Chabahar had begun operating in Baluchi regions.[64]

However, these improvements did not change the prevailing economic situation of the early Pahlavi period, as their pace was too slow to overcome the already existing gap. The construction of a dam in Mahabad, which provided piped water, electricity, and other necessities for northern Kurdish regions, lasted from 1966 to 1974. These areas had great potential for development and industrial agriculture, but the lack of roads and irrigation kept agriculture at a primitive level, leading to increased poverty.[65] The agriculture and development of Sistan-Baluchistan faced similar problems, and even political influence at the highest level failed to persuade the shah and his technocrats to change the regime's economic course.

Amir Asadollah Alam was a close confidant of the shah, whom he served as prime minister and court minister for decades. Alam came from an old family of hereditary local rulers in the Sistan region with ties to many Baluchi tribal leaders, and was perhaps the most important decision-maker in Iran's Baluchistan. Yet despite this, Alam was unable to persuade the shah to adopt a coherent development and agricultural policy for the Sistan-Baluchistan province. Alam had a sense of belonging to these regions, but in the late 1970s his discussions with technocrat colleagues came to nothing as they felt that investments in the region would not yield sufficiently high profits.[66] The shah was equally indifferent to these regions and only saw the necessity of development when local tensions reached a point of crisis.

In 1972, the Baluchi nationalist uprising in Pakistan threatened to expand to Iran's Baluchistan. The shah took extreme measures to deal with this potential crisis, including massive growth in Baluchistan budgets for both military and development projects, particularly the installations at Chabahar port.[67] However, a couple of years later, when the crisis had been dealt with through a combination of diplomatic and military means, the shah all but forgot his development plans for Baluchistan and usual business was resumed once again.

The most important development program in Baluchistan was the geopolitically important port of Chabahar, which had great potential but remains incomplete to this day. Due to a lack of government planning and investment, Baluchistan's agriculture regressed to an even more dismal position. In the 1970s, reports from impartial observers suggested a depressing state of affairs. Lack of water, tribal feuds, and lack of modern planning and investment plagued the local agricultural sector and entrenched impoverishment, forcing many Baluchi to seek employment in Oman and other Arab sheikhdoms. Other reports indicate a rapid increase in opium abuse among the local population, which turned into a much more serious problem in later decades.[68] All of this confirms Akbar Aghajanian's argument that the Pahlavi regime's uneven development policies and superficial integration of ethnic communities actually promoted the impoverishment and underdevelopment of these areas:[69]

> Political centralization, domination of Persian language and culture, and centralization of early industrialization contributed much to the development of the interethnic inequality at early stage of the Iranian modernization. In the new era, the 1960s–70s, the existing gap was further widened by centralized and urban-biased economic growth. This was possible only because of the government's unique access to the increasing oil revenues, which were generated with very little help from the domestic means of production.[70]

Aghajanian claims that this underdevelopment was a product of the particular nature of Iranian modernization, which had harmful consequences for all non-Persian ethnic groups, including the Shi'i Azeri Turks and Arabs.

### *The Pahlavi regime's religious neutrality and Iran's thriving middle class*

Both Pahlavi rulers were reluctant to adopt a pluralistic development model that could create bridges between the core and the periphery of Iranian society. As a consequence, there was no major improvement in the economic situation of the Sunni communities during the Pahlavi era. Yet despite all its faults and shortcomings, the Pahlavi state did not seek to establish a homogenous society based on Shi'ism. The main religious policy of the first Pahlavi shah was both anti-Shi'i and anti-clerical.[71] The second Pahlavi monarch, Mohmmad Reza Shah, was less repressive toward the Shi'i clergy, but he too prioritized Westernized progress, modernization, and the creation of a secular state, which led to his clash with Khomeini and his religious followers. Sunni Iranians had their objections to the regime's secular policies, but, to a certain extent, they benefited from the Pahlavi government's religious tolerance. This was important because, during the Pahlavi era, the government remained the most important source of employment, particularly in the 1960s and 1970s when oil revenues and various state programs led to an extremely active public sector.[72]

Pahlavi reforms also created a new middle class, made up of a mixture of educated Iranians, intelligentsia, politicians, women, state-employed civil servants, modern businessmen, technocrats, doctors, and so forth. Their common link was that, directly or indirectly, they owed their inception and existence to Pahlavi reforms, and their economic, political, and cultural characteristics were distinctively different from Iran's traditional middle class, which was mainly formed around traditional institutions such as the bazaar. Although this new middle class owed its existence to the Pahlavi dynasty, there was no automatic sense of loyalty to the state.[73] Most of the sociopolitical forces that challenged the Pahlavi dynasty, and contributed to the 1979 revolution, came from this class.

All of the above were part of the wide-ranging changes of the Pahlavi era, which altered the very fabric of Iranian society and provided opportunities for many Iranians, including those Sunni Iranians who were not bound by their ethnicities. As mentioned earlier, there was no institutional discrimination against Sunni Iranians, and those Sunni Iranians who complied with the Pahlavi regime's Persian-centric political order were able to rise to influential positions in the system. The regime's religious neutrality ensured that Sunni Iranians could be employed and promoted in government institutions and the public sector.

Many Sunni Iranians, Kurds in particular, migrated to Tehran and other major cities in search of better opportunities. Many of the Sunni Iranians who attained influential political positions, or those who became part of Iran's middle class, became religiously and ethnically desensitized.[74] Many of them became Persian-centric, and their achievements were attributed to their personal qualities rather than representing the Sunni Iranian community as a whole—successes that were not shared with the ethnic Sunni Turkmens, Kurds, and Baluchs who had justified grievances. Mowlavi Abdul-Hamid Esmā'īl'zehī (b. 1947), one of the most important Sunni religious leaders of today's Iran, summarizes the situation in the following way:

> The monarchist system wanted to stay in power at all costs. It was irreligious, laicist and secular and did not involve itself with religion. The Sunni society of Iran was not in desirable shape ... They neither had educated figures to lead them in social and political matters, nor noted religious leaders. ... the Sunni regions were on the margins of the country, and Sunnis did not have any social and political position. Sometimes certain individuals could reach offices within parliament and government. But they were not people's representatives. The system would appoint and promote those small numbers of loyal individuals for its own needs. On the other hand, the Sunnis could be employed, particularly in the armed forces, without much discrimination and they could reach high ranks. They could also be employed in the civil service ... As far as I know, the employment forms of these agencies did not ask if one was Shi'i or Sunni. They were against religious discrimination ... from this angle, the situation of Iranian Sunnis was relatively positive.[75]

### *Sunni Iranians and the Islamic Republic*

Nearly forty years have now passed since the revolution of 1979 and the foundation of the Islamic Republic. During this period, the Iranian economy has gone through different transitional phases, and to a certain extent, the economic conditions of the rural community, including the Sunni ethnic communities, have improved over recent decades. One of the many initiatives of the Islamic Republic's promise of social justice and economic equality included an ambitious program of providing electricity to rural and provincial households, which was largely successful, increasing rural households' electrical access from 16.2 percent in 1977 to 98.3 percent in 2004. Furthermore, there was a radical improvement in access to piped water among rural households, increasing from 11.7 percent to 89 percent.[76] However, the economic marginalization of Iran's ethnic minorities has continued, and the fundamental economic problems of the Pahlavi era have persisted under the Islamic Republic.

One of the main indicators of the continued economic marginalization of Sunni ethnic communities is the high unemployment rate in the Sunni provinces. The existing data suggests that unemployment in the provinces of Iran's ethnic communities (both Shi'i and Sunni) is worse than the more central and Persian-speaking provinces. In 2009, West Azerbaijan, East Azerbaijan, and

Zanjan provinces (Turkish Azeri/absolute majority Shi'i), Khuzestan (relative majority of Arabs and absolute majority Shi'i), Kurdistan, and Sistan-Baluchistan (Sunni majority) provinces had two digit numbers for their unemployment rates.[77] The Golestan province, which contains Iran's Turkmen region, is the only province with an unemployment rate of less than 10 percent. However, according to local estimates, Turkmens form less than 35 percent of Golestan's 1.8 million population, and Persian speakers (of various ethnicities) are in a relative majority of 40 to 45 percent. The huge numbers of immigrants, including the high numbers of Sunni Baluchi (about 4 percent of the population), makes Golestan one of the most diverse provinces of Iran, both ethnically and religiously.[78]

Sources close to the Islamic Republic consider Golestan to be a success story of social assimilation and relative economic prosperity. This is partly true, as unlike the Baluchi and Kurdish regions, Iran's Turkmen regions are not haunted by armed insurgency and daily ethnic and religious tension. However, Iran's Turkmen regions were among the first areas to experience armed conflict in the immediate aftermath of the 1979 revolution, and the memory of that brief but bloody period still lingers. The relatively small proportion of the Turkmen population and their comparatively smaller terrain have made them easier to manage, politically and security wise. Their region has always been part of non-ethnic Persian-majority provinces, which is a construct of history but enforced by state policy in both the Pahlavi and Islamic Republic eras. The economy of the Turkmen region is in much better shape due to its favorable geographic and economic position. State policies have also resulted in a considerably higher level of development in their province. However, there are still some signs of economic inequality in Turkmen areas. One major area where Turkmens are an absolute majority is the Bandar Turkmen (formerly Bandar Shah) district which suffers from high unemployment rates despite great economic potential.[79] Unemployment decreased from 24.3 percent in 1966 to 19.6 percent in 1996, but the average rate of unemployment remains high in this area. Furthermore, the local Turkmen carpet-weaving industry has failed to compete with its rivals in recent decades. Additionally, the port of Bandar Turkmen has failed to play an important role in trade with Central Asia and Russia, despite its access to the national railway system.[80] Although the economic situation facing the Turkmen is not entirely clear, relative inequality, the Islamic Republic's discrimination against Sunnis, and strong ethnic rivalry in Golestan are dangerous ingredients that have the potential to contribute to a sense of victimization among the Turkmens.

The sense of victimization is much stronger and more justified in other Sunni ethnic provinces. Migration due to poverty and underdevelopment persists in Iran's Kurdish and Baluchi regions. A major problem is the lack of specific policies to promote the local economy of these regions. The Pahlavi-era policy of industrial growth has not been uniformly implemented in these regions, nor has it been successful where it has been implemented. Many Kurdish Iranians claim that the existing industrial units in their region cannot provide high levels of employment, and with agriculture suffering from mismanagement and drought, many Kurds have been forced to become involved in illegal economic activity, particularly the smuggling of goods.[81]

A similar situation persists in Iran's Baluchi regions, where the Pahlavi-era policy of industrial growth was disowned and abandoned in the early period of the revolution due to Sistan-Baluchistan regional situation. Though the policy was relaunched and received considerable state sponsorship during the reconstruction period in the 1990s, it failed to transform the troubled economy of Sistan-Baluchistan, with unemployment rising and the "informal economy" becoming the main economic occupation of the population. If anything, from the 1990s to the 2000s, the job-creation ability of the regional industries in Sistan-Baluchistan slowly began to decline.[82]

Certain projects in Baluchistan, such as the Bāft textile factory in Iranshahr that were joint ventures with multinational companies and depended on foreign investment, suffered from the turbulence generated by the revolution. The construction of this factory began in 1974 with the aim of providing local employment, expanding urbanization, and rivaling Pakistani textile production. The construction of the factory was delayed by the revolution, and various problems also emerged due to mismanagement and the withdrawal of international partners. To this day, the factory has not reached its full production capacity and is continuously being passed from public to private sector.[83] Similarly, Chabahr port and its free trade zone faced similar delays and problems, and the port is still not functioning as originally intended. As a result of these problems, many local workers have moved to other parts of Iran and the Gulf Arab sheikhdoms in search of a better life.[84]

## Religious discrimination

Similar to the previous regime, the Islamic Republic has been reluctant to embrace sociocultural pluralism in Iran. Over the last four decades, the Islamic Republic has had limited success in transforming the economic problems of ethnic Sunni provinces, which have existed since the Pahlavi era. The existing gap has widened due to the growth of the population and economic mismanagement. The official statistics suggest that the provinces populated by Sunni ethnic Iranians—particularly the Kurdish and Baluchi regions—have the highest rate of unemployment, which breeds numerous socioeconomic problems.[85] While discrimination against non-Persian minorities has continued, the Islamic Republic has made the situation even worse by discriminating against the Sunnis and other religious minorities. The sectarian intolerance of the new political system was immediately demonstrated after the revolution, as the constitution of the Islamic Republic officially outlawed the president from being a non-Shiʿi. This was in addition to the position of the supreme leader, which was exclusive to a Shiʿi clergyman. Apart from the constitutional restrictions, unspoken practices of discrimination and the exclusion of Sunni Iranians became widespread within state institutions. Since the revolution, few if any Sunnis have been able to join the Islamic Republic's hierarchy and political elite or rise to influential positions within the state's bureaucracy or military. This practice was also maintained at the local level: since 1979, no Sunni Iranian has served as provincial governor (*ostāndār*) or even as city governor (*farmāndār*). The moderate and reformist factions of the Islamic Republic tried to challenge this practice during the Khatami and Rohani presidencies, but their efforts were lukewarm and faced strong resistance from the Shiʿi clerical establishment and hardline factions.

This anti-Sunni discrimination at the local level has created considerable resentment among local Baluch and Kurdish Iranians. Apart from its symbolic and political consequences, the policy has also greatly intensified the sense of inequality at the local level. The state openly encourages Shiʿi-favoritism and anti-Sunni bias in Iran's huge public sector, which has real effects on economic opportunities for Sunni Iranians. The complaints made by Sunni Baluchs about unequal allocation of local specialist posts in the Sistan-Baluchistan province have been largely disregarded by Islamic Republic's authorities.[86] In the early 1960s, for instance, nearly all teachers in the Sistan-Baluchistan province were from the neighboring provinces of Khorasan and Kerman.[87] At the time, the number of educated Baluchs who could teach in Persian was extremely low, and hence the situation was understandable. However, despite the current availability of thousands of university-educated Baluch, more or less the same situation persists in many Baluchi areas such as Chabahar, where non-locals constitute 80 percent of the educational staff.[88]

Iranian Baluchi members of parliament have also been vocal against what they consider to be intolerable discrimination and disrespect toward Sunni

Baluch. They point out that Baluchi human resources and potential are not put to use by the Islamic Republic's authorities, which in turn serves to promote Baluchi resentment and illegal economic activities.[89] Iran's human rights activists, exiled opposition, and Baluchi nationalists have made the same allegations in their campaign against the Islamic Republic. Mohammad Hassan Hossein'bor, a prominent Baluchi nationalist, describes the situation as nothing less than "economic discrimination." Hossein'bor argues that Baluchistan's mineral wealth and the economic capacity of its coastal area would have resolved the issue of poverty if the Baluch had control of their resource management, or if they were independent or autonomous.[90]

There are indications that the Islamic Republic has also continued the Pahlavi policy of demographic engineering in Sistan-Baluchistan with the aim of increasing the Shi'i non-Baluchi population in Baluchi regions through state-sponsored migration.[91] This is most notable in Chabahar port, which has the greatest potential for growth and development in the Baluchi regions, but in which many Baluchs feel they have been sidelined by the state.[92]

## Informal economy and armed insurgency

One consequence of the economic marginalization of provincial ethnic Sunni Iranians has been the sharp growth of the so-called "informal economy" and illegal economic activities. The seed for this was planted in the Pahlavi era, but, under the Islamic Republic, the extent of the informal economy has increased and now includes the smuggling of various goods and the growth of drug trafficking in Iran's Baluchi regions.

These activities are illegal and are harshly penalized as such by the authorities, yet the heavy-handed policies of the state have had limited success in halting them. In Kurdish and Baluchi regions, certain social groups and "professions" have emerged to sustain the informal economy. The main activity of these groups is the smuggling of goods. In Baluchistan, the smugglers are called Badūk and in Kurdistan they are known as Kūl'bars (Kūl'barān in plural); both groups are usually composed of young people with few prospects in the formal economy. The smugglers pass the border between Iran and Iraq's Kurdistan and Iran and Pakistan's Baluchistan, transporting goods between the two countries. They usually travel on foot and carry whatever they can. With no other source of employment, there has been a substantial rise in such activity in recent decades.

In August 2014, Iran's police chief warned that those operators who disregard police warnings would be shot.[93] Kurdish Iranian human rights groups and Iran's labor campaigners estimate that, in 2014 alone, at least twenty-seven Kurdish Kūl'bars were shot dead and another twenty-eight were injured by Iranian police and border guards, with another six dead due to exposure to the harsh natural conditions of the area.[94] This booming illegal trade, which came in the immediate aftermath of the fall of Saddam Hussein, is estimated to be worth billions of dollars.[95] In some areas, officials have all but given up trying to fight such activities. The Kurdish city of Bā'neh has gained a reputation throughout Iran of being a cut-price shopping destination, with dealers coming from as far as Tehran to buy consumer goods. While trade with neighboring Iraqi Kurdistan has benefited local Bā'neh businessmen, and created wealth at the micro level, it has generated little prosperity for the wider province of Kurdistan.[96]

In Baluchistan, the Badūk are not reported to have suffered from similar fatalities, but the state campaign against illegal smuggling of goods is equally problematic. The subject of smuggling and drug-trafficking has a clear religious angle in Baluchistan. The Islamic Republic's police and security agencies acknowledge that Sunni Baluchi clergymen, known as Molavies, have condemned the use of drugs and have issued religious fatvā against drug dealing, which has had positive effects in discouraging Baluchi involvement in the drug trade.[97] However, the Molavies' attitude to goods smuggling is entirely different and runs counter to the Islamic Republic's law and policy, as the Sunni Baluchs clergy do not consider such an activity unlawful. To the contrary, they consider the appropriation of smuggled goods by the authorities to be against shari'a law and that the goods should be returned to their rightful owners—meaning the smugglers.[98] This has been a constant source of bickering between Shi'i authorities and Sunni Baluchs leaders. During a meeting between President Rafsanjani and a delegation of Molavies, the president cited the latter's refusal to ban smuggling as partial justification for withholding provincial government posts from Sunni Baluchs.[99]

In recent years, and particularly during the oil boom under Mahmoud Ahmadinejad's presidency, the smuggling of fuel products (petrol and gasoil in particular) was added to the long list of criminal economic activity in Iran's borderlands. Naturally, this business is much more lucrative in the eastern borders with Pakistan and Afghanistan, which, unlike Iraq, do not have an oil industry. For many Baluchs, this has become a common occupation, with authorities estimating that between three and ten million liters of oil products were traded everyday day in 2013; they also claim that 67 percent of Sistan-Baluchistan vehicles are exclusively engaged in this business.[100] The Baluch are not the only group to smuggle fuel, as at least fifty foreign nationals (mostly Afghani) were killed during Iranian police campaigns against this business in 2010–11.[101]

Baluchi activity in this trade has caused considerable mortality and civil upheaval in Iran's Baluchi regions. In November 2013, Iranian police and coastal guards shot dead two Baluchi sailors in Sīrīk while they were trying to confiscate a boat, leading to public anger and demonstrations in the city.[102] A similar situation occurred in Iranshahr in May 2015, which caused the death of a Baluchi driver. The ensuing public anger led to attacks on the local police station and the burning of a police car.[103]

Since the 1990s, the Islamic Republic has tried to counter illegal smuggling by creating border markets in both Baluchi and Kurdish regions.[104] In more recent years, they have even tried to expand this to the energy sector and to create border markets for fuel products.[105] Yet despite these efforts, the smuggling of goods and fuels continues to be a major economic activity in Iran's Sunni borderlands. Financial experts and the Islamic Republic itself admit that the smuggling of goods is a twenty-billion-dollar business in Iran and is widely spread in all border provinces and on Iran's Persian Gulf coast. There are also rumors that the Islamic Revolutionary Guards are highly active in these operations, particularly in the ports.[106]

The illegal trade of goods and weapons has been taking place in Iran's Baluchi regions since the early years of the Pahlavi era, but the drug trade is more recent. From its inception, the Islamic Republic adopted a zero-tolerance policy on the use, production, and distribution of narcotics. In the early days, taking or dealing drugs was treated as an anti-revolutionary crime that could result in the death penalty.[107] The global drug trade had a major impact on the southeastern region, as Sistan-Baluchistan became the transit route for the flourishing poppy fields of Afghanistan and Pakistan. For decades, the state pursued its own "war on drugs" with considerable public and international support. According to the 2014 UNODC World Drug Report, Iran accounted for 74 percent of the world's opium seizures and 25 percent of the world's heroin and morphine seizures in 2012.[108] The desolate and impoverished economy of the Baluchi regions and high unemployment rates have made the Sunni Baluchs more than willing to risk involvement in the highly lucrative drug trafficking business.

The widespread drug trafficking in the region has spread stereotypes about Baluchistan as a lawless land, rendering the word "Baluch" synonymous with "drug dealer." The sociopolitical impact has been dire too, as it has led to the securitization of Sistan-Baluchistan. Furthermore, the drug war has created high mortality rates among the Baluchi population, as well as Iran's security and law enforcement forces. In 1998, Iranian sources estimated that over 2,500 members of the police and security forces had been killed and over 5,000 wounded in the war against drug traffickers over the past twenty years.[109] Even though the state annually spends half a billion dollars on border control, there are over 100,000 drug-related prisoners and between one to three million drug addicts, which suggests that Iran's war on drugs has failed to achieve its goal.[110] At the same time, hundreds of people have been executed each year on drug-related charges, a considerable number of whom were Sunni Baluchs. There are no official data on the percentage of Sunni Baluchs drug-related executions, but it is undoubtedly high given the significance of Sistan-Baluchistan in the global drug trade. Mohammad Hassan Hossein'bor claims that Baluchs form less than 10 percent of Iran's population while comprising half of the national execution rate.[111] All of this only adds to the already strong sense of resentment and victimization among Iran's Sunni Baluchs populations.

This criminalization of economic activities in Baluchistan, along with state discrimination against Sunni Iranians, played a role in the rise of the Jundollah organization, a Sunni Baluchs armed militancy that operated in Iran's Baluchi regions from 2005 until the capture and execution of the movement's founder, Abdul Malik Rigi, in 2010. During this period, Rigi and his followers wreaked havoc in the region, causing hundreds of civilian and military casualties through sensational and violent operations. The official stance of the Islamic Republic presented Rigi as a career criminal and religious fundamentalist financed by drug money and the imperialist United States. It is true that Jundollah was partially financed by the drug business, a common phenomenon in jihadi extremist groups in Pakistan and Afghanistan,[112] and there are also credible reports indicating that the administration of George W. Bush did flirt with the idea of sponsoring Jundollah.[113]

There are also some less convincing reports by the somewhat sensationalist Pakistani journalist, the late Saleem Shahzad, that Rigi spent some time in a religious Pakistani school known for producing Islamic extremists.[114] However, a semi-official report on his life suggests another motivation for his activities. The report states that Rigi was born in a typically poor Baluchi family and was expelled from his high school because of poor performance and delinquency. Thus, as a teenager, he began buying and selling commercial goods such as illegal CDs and other contraband, and specifically profited from trading alcohol, which is also illegal in the Islamic Republic of Iran. The report claims that Rigi and his friends became involved in a robbery and were apprehended by Iranian CID police (Agāhī), during which time Rigi was treated brutally by the police. Rigi's move to Pakistan and his presumed radicalization took place sometime after this episode.[115] This report demonstrates the correlation of events, revealing Rigi to be the construct of his environment, which provided little opportunity and choice other than illegal economic activity, crime, and the eventual clash with Shi'i Persian-speaking security forces. Perhaps it is possible to argue that, without this, Rigi and many other Sunni Baluchs of Iran would have taken a different path. This and other conjectures outline the dire need to fundamentally improve Baluchi's socioeconomic situation if there is to be any hope of the security situation ever improving. The Islamic Republic's authorities are aware of this necessity, and even the hardline factions pay lip service to it. Only months after the capture and execution of Rigi, the Islamic Republic's police commander in chief, General Esmā'īl Ahmadī-Moghadam, conceded that without fundamental economic changes in Baluchistan, the region's security challenges and drug-related crimes will not be resolved.[116]

While the Baluchs insurgency and Jundollah's successors have lost the exuberance and agility of Rigi, they still engage authorities in bloody clashes, and the environmental factors that helped to create Rigi, still persist. In 2015, a UN human rights monitor reported that Iran had experienced the highest rate of executions in the Islamic Republic in some twenty-five years, most of which were drug-related crimes. The same report warned that the Islamic Republic of Iran executes more individuals per capita than any other country in the world.[117] In February 2016, Hassan Rohani's vice president, Shahīn'dokht Molāverdī, who has a reputation for being blunt, created controversy when she noted that the entire male population of one Baluchi village had been killed or executed for unspecified crimes, and that their relations were all involved in smuggling operations.[118]

Unemployment and economic criminalization of Sunni borderlands is not limited to the Kurdish and Baluchi regions. The Sunni Turks of the Azerbaijan provinces, known as Küresünlī, are also involved in illegal trade and border smuggling. In 2011, one of the rare media reports about them covered the execution of three Küresünlī, two of whom were Shi'i Azeris, for drug trafficking.[119] If the Islamic Republic's policy-makers do not initiate fundamental change, which seems unlikely, the Sunni Iranians' sense of victimization and resentment will inevitably grow to increasingly dangerous levels.

*Conclusion*

Although Iran is one of the most diverse nations in the region, the state has been reluctant to adopt a pluralistic approach to sociopolitical and economic development. Since the beginning of the modern nation-building project in Iran, the Persian-centric policies of the state have undermined the evolution of a pluralistic national consciousness that could empower and integrate the marginalized communities living on the periphery of Iranian society. The revolution and the emergence of the Shi'i supremacist discourse deepened the existing divisions between the center and the Sunni communities in the borderlands. Creating a bridge between the periphery and the core will be difficult unless the state recognizes cultural pluralism in order to implement effective and inclusive development policies across the country. The public policies of both the Pahlavi regime and the Islamic Republic have not been informed by pluralism, and the marginalized communities in the Sunni provinces have not benefited from economic development.

Although the Pahlavi dynasty implemented a major program of sociopolitical reform in the country, the Sunni majority provinces did not benefit from the economic leap of the 1960s and 1970s. And while the previous regime did not enforce any overtly sectarian policy, its Persian-centric and centralist approach did little to transform the harsh socioeconomic realties of the Sunni majority provinces.

The 1979 revolution and the formation of the Islamic Republic in Iran only exacerbated the situation for the Sunni Iranians. The Islamic Republic based its ideology on the redistribution of wealth and the empowerment of the impoverished segments of society. However, the ethnic Sunni Iranians who lived in some of the most impoverished regions of the country received very little attention from the new order in Tehran.

Although some deprived regions have experienced considerable economic development since the revolution, the fundamental economic challenges in the Sunni majority provinces have remained largely unchanged. Informal economic activities, including smuggling and drug trafficking, have become the most lucrative and common occupation for many Sunni Iranians given the lack of viable alternatives. The heavy-handed policies adopted by the state to counter the informal economy have further helped to deepen Sunni grievances and the sense of victimization. The economic challenges, coupled with the state's Shi'i supremacist discourse, have sharpened the existing Shi'i–Sunni divide in Iran. The lack of economic regeneration and the state's indifference are perceived by Sunni Iranians as both sectarian marginalization and discrimination.

The poverty, the sense of victimization, the lack of alternatives for socioeconomic development, and the heavy-handed policies of the state against the informal economy have contributed to the rise of insurgent organizations such Jundollah in Sistan-Baluchistan—groups that adopted violent tactics in their efforts to champion the rights of the Sunni minority. Although the state had the ability to suppress such groups in the short term, the preconditions for the emergence of other insurgency groups are still there, and constitute a major security impediment to the state.

# PART 2

# FRONTIERS OF IDENTITY

5

# INCLUSION AND EXCLUSION IN THE ARAB CITY

## DISCOURSES ON IDENTITY AND URBANISM IN THE MIDDLE EAST

*Nezar AlSayyad*

The urban world underwent a massive transformation at the end of the twentieth century and at the beginning of the twenty-first. The transnationalization of capital, the internationalization of labor, a steady increase in global trading and communication, and fierce competition between multinational corporations has led nations and their governments to attempt to position themselves globally.[1] No region has escaped these changes, and many countries in the Arab Middle East have been particularly affected by them. In this chapter, I hope to show how the construction of the Middle East as a concept has affected the evolution of its urbanism. In doing so, I illustrate the fluidity of identity under both colonial and modern conditions, but also discuss how old ethnic conflicts and religious rivalries in the age of globalization continue different forms of exclusion that shape the contemporary Arab Middle Eastern city.

In a globally compressed world constituted of national societies that are becoming increasingly aware of their ethnic and racial roots, the conditions for the identification of individual and collective selves have become increasingly complex.[2] Of course, any analyst of such trends must take into account the distinctive cultural and unequal conditions under which the notion of the "global" was constructed.[3] It also becomes difficult to comprehend globalization without recognizing the historical specificity of "traditional" cultures, their colonization, and their emergence as nation-states. At the heart of all these issues is the question of identity. In few places is this more evident than in the Middle East, where the problematic dialectic of traditional/modern is often invoked. All societies are of course constructed in relation to one another, and they are produced, represented, and perceived through the ideologies and narratives of situated discourse.[4] For example, the definition of the "Middle East" as a category is very much dependent on the existence of a "West." Both terms are mainly defined by difference, constructed in opposition to the other, and produced in a variety of postcolonial and anti-colonial discourses—although neither constitutes a monolithic, preexisting, real subject itself.[5]

### *From colonialism to independence*

In studying the relationship between the West and the Middle East, and its effect on the corresponding identity of people and architecture, three historic phases may be discerned: the colonial period, the era of independence and nation-state building, and the most recent phase, globalization. These phases appear to have been accompanied by three respective urban forms: the hybrid, the modern or pseudo-modern, and the postmodern. Any attempt at a historical periodization of modernity in the Arab Middle East, because of its diverse sub-regions, will always be an abstract exercise with major limitations. Indeed, generalizations about the varied countries of the Middle East—a fragile geopolitical entity whose existence as a single cultural region should always be called into question—may only be justified in the pursuit of other general themes related to the region.[6]

Before the era of colonialism, and in most of the Arab Middle East, many urban communities lived in traditional settlements in a preindustrial condition. The vernacular forms of their habitats were shaped as much by sociocultural concerns as by the surrounding natural environment. They also reflected, possibly at the subconscious level, the identity of their inhabitants.

Around the middle of the nineteenth century, the world witnessed the rise of modern industrial capitalism and the emergence of organized political dominance represented by colonialism. The paradigm shift from the traditional to the colonial created a relationship of unequal cultural and socioeconomic exchange. In analyzing issues of identity in the Middle East, one must always take this into account and acknowledge the processes by which the identities of its peoples were violated, ignored, distorted, or stereotyped as a result of this experience. In urban planning, in particular, the colonization process affected the overall model by which patterns of development were determined. This was the era when modernist ideas flowed from the countries of Europe to the Middle East. In the 1950s and 1960s, when many Arab Middle East countries launched their wars of liberation and independence, the colonists responded with the age-old urban strategy of destroying the cores of some traditional towns. The goal was to break the subversive influence of the rebels who resided there. But, ultimately, the colonial era produced a hybrid urban condition, which borrowed as much from the culture of the colonized as it did from that of the colonizers.

When the people of the Middle East started to rebel against this colonial world order, they had little conceptual language to employ in their drive to establish sovereignty. Often, they were forced to use the terms of the existing order, with all its physical baggage and ideological constructs, like that of the nation-state. Groups of people living in one region under a colonial power but frequently of different religions, languages, ethnicities, and traditions—as in the case of Iraq and Sudan—sharing little more than a colonial history, had to band together to achieve freedom and independence. In pursuit of these larger goals, the new political and governing bodies had little choice but to highlight what few commonalities existed and to suppress differences. A national identity based on short-term political interest and the ideology of struggle thus emerged as the driving force behind many nationalist movements in the Middle East.

The second phase of independence struggles and nationalism did not fundamentally change the built environments of the Arab Middle East. Yet, during the era of colonialism, important and irreversible decisions were made that affected the production of the built environment. In Egypt and much of the Arabian peninsula, for example, new building codes requiring setbacks (based on Western norms) forced the traditional courtyard house out of existence. Meanwhile, new construction often took the form of banal single-family dwellings that were unsuited to the local climate. In such societies, where privacy was cherished, major adaptations were frequently required to produce these new forms. And in some countries, entire systems of construction were abandoned because they did not suit the modern era. As a result, the urban system fell grossly out of balance, and the urban environment of many Arab Middle Eastern countries became pseudo-modernized.[7]

The obsession with modernity that accompanied the early years of nationalism and independence, and that preoccupied most governments in the Middle East including the most conservative ones, also resulted in the transformation of cities to reflect imported patterns of urban development. Indeed, these became the main frame of reference for members of the urban middle class who stepped in after independence to run the various bureaucracies of these new nation-states. In some senses, it meant simply continuing the same practices that had marked the earlier colonial era, but with a local face.

### *National identity in the Arab Middle East*

Globalization may be considered the third phase in the relationship between the Middle East and the West. Interestingly, this phase has also been marked by a new search for identity. Once independence became a reality, the glue that bound together the various groups no longer held. The long ethnic wars in Sudan, the US occupation of Iraq, and the civil wars in Syria, Libya, and Yemen have exposed these very weaknesses. Such conflicts between various groups within these countries are testament to the true associations of their native populations, where ethnic origin or religious affiliation have been, or have reemerged, as the prime definers of collective identity.[8]

Once independence was achieved and the dust from the anti-colonial struggle had settled, the problems of national and community harmony began to surface. And even where these issues were resolved, religious and political fundamentalisms began to flourish. To understand the impact of these forces on urbanism, closer attention must be paid to the difficulties associated with defining national identity. The primary elements of national identity—race, language, religion, history, territory, and tradition—have always been essential but unequal components in its formation. After the two world wars, the physical and political territories of the new nations of the Middle East were expected to be homogenous entities with a common culture. But the reality was otherwise, as these nation-states were largely put together by international deals that displayed little interest in the will of their inhabitants. Again, Iraq is a case in point.

National identity as perceived by a government is inherently tied to the image it wishes to project in the international arena. Some Arab Middle

Eastern governments resorted to using local and foreign architects to help them create such new national styles. While many of these post-independence projects continued the modernist schema, others retreated to older traditional forms—and sometimes to newly invented ones that they claimed to be based on specific historical precedents. This can clearly be observed in the cacophony of building styles adopted by these governments in the construction of state and institutional buildings.

Of course, identity cannot be based on some myth from pre-colonial times. Many Middle Eastern nations have resorted to a past in which identity may coalesce as a solace against the perceived dominator, often forgetting that respect for the past must also include accepting and coming to terms with the architectural and urban legacy of colonization itself. The problems of national identity are also complicated by the extensive economic exchanges that characterize the world today. Not only do Middle Eastern nations have to mediate between pre-colonial and colonial legacies, between the traditional and the modern, they must also deal with the effects of globalization and the so-called "New World Order."[9]

### *Globalization and the Arab Middle East*

"Globalization" here refers to the process by which the world is becoming a single economic entity characterized by information exchange, interconnected modes of production, and flows of labor and capital within a predominately capitalist world system. Part of this trend has been the considerable migration from the former colonies in the Middle East and North Africa to the lands of their former colonizers in Europe, and the corresponding infiltration of these ethnic subcultures into mainstream European societies. Such demographic change has often been the cause of social conflict, as these local subcultures, often Muslim, have resorted to ethnic, racial, or religious allegiances to keep from being swallowed up by the majority culture.[10]

Current attempts at multiculturalism in Europe—and the struggles, often failed, of many European governments to cope with their minority Muslim populations, usually from Middle Eastern countries—may be interpreted as an effort to embrace difference as a fundamental constituent of national identity. In Europe, the national identity of the former colonial powers is being discussed and reassessed, often in an attempt to become more inclusive. Meanwhile, the national identity of the formerly colonized nations of the Middle East and North Africa (as in much of Eastern Europe and South Asia) is moving in the opposite direction, often becoming more exclusive and more directly linked to national origin or religious association. Indeed, the twentieth century has witnessed the return of states in which belonging to a particular religious or ethnic group is a prerequisite for the enjoyment of full citizenship rights or status.[11]

We must remember, however, that national identity is always subject to processes of transformation and flux. While the contradictory forces of globalization may be playing havoc with traditional loyalties and values, and challenging older ideologies and practices, a single "world culture" inclusive of Middle Eastern traditions remains a distant prospect. Thus, as Benjamin Barber pointed out in his appropriately titled book *Jihad vs. McWorld* (1995), Middle Eastern and Islamic nations want the veil, but they also want the World Wide Web and Coca Cola.[12] Timothy Mitchell, on the other hand, has argued that jihad is not antithetical to the development of McWorld, and that McWorld is really McJihad, a necessary combination of a variety of social logics and economic forces, often driven by and benefiting from the advances in communication technology that led to the emergence, particularly in the Middle East, of current jihadist movements like al-Qa'ida.[13] Here, some Middle Eastern countries have evolved their own local appropriations of Western practices without ever embracing their logic.

I have argued elsewhere that people usually exhibit two conflicting sentiments toward tradition, culture, and the past. The first is to resort to culture and tradition out of fear of change—change that in and of itself may be inevitable. But protectionism against the unknown or the unfamiliar can, and often does, turn into fundamentalism. Some may simplistically argue that this position offers an explanation for the attitudes of some Middle Eastern nations and their people toward the West. However, I believe that the matter is more complex than that, and requires a more global perspective.

The second sentiment, characterized by interest in the culture of the mysterious "other" (an idea that generated the initial interest of European Orientalists in the Middle East), emerges from a totally different feeling—that is, the desire to have the choice to merge with the "other" and share in a wider, or a different, collective consciousness.[14] Interestingly, this sentiment is as clearly present today among groups of Middle Easterners living in the West who have become thoroughly Westernized and are no longer interested in or comfortable with their Middle Eastern heritage as it is among groups of Europeans and Americans who are residents and lovers of particular Middle Eastern countries. The tremendous movement of citizens across borders and the rise of protected ethnic minorities demonstrate that the two sentiments, both legitimate, are not necessarily contradictory. In fact, they may occur simultaneously or, alternatively, be based on time and place.[15] I would argue that the interplay between these two sentiments shapes much of the attitudes of many First and Third World peoples, particularly those in the Middle East. It is here that much work and analysis need to be done to unpack the complexities of the relationships between the "Middle East" and the "West."

The globalizing changes that the Middle East has undergone in the last couple of decades, particularly in its confrontation with the West following the 9/11 attacks in the United States, have opened up new experiences of modernity. One may thus ask: will today's exclusive malls in Cairo, Beirut, Dubai, and Doha—where the *musalla* that shoppers can use to pray in is only a few meters away from a Victoria's Secret store displaying its lingerie on semi-naked mannequins—offer a new and unique Middle Eastern modernity?[16] Or, more simply, will the niqab and the miniskirt comfortably coexist in the larger urban space of the Middle East, as they often do in its luxury private and domestic spaces? Finally, will the attempt to reconcile "McWorld" and jihad lead to a new and different alternative modernity? Or will we see a retreat to traditionalism without an abandonment of the fundamental premises of modernity—a retreat to a sort of "medieval modernity" that deals with the new parameters of survival in an ever-changing and globalizing world?[17]

### *Assimilation, integration, and segregation: on inclusion and exclusion*

An assimilationist tendency has emerged in many countries in the West that receive immigrants and refugees as a method to avoid conflict and to turn a foreigner into a citizen. The relative success of these societies has often depended on the different forms of inclusion they have sought to achieve. These forms may be theorized to range from ambivalent tolerance, to recognition and reciprocity, to full-scale assimilation.

My central issue, the idea of 'urban inclusiveness', as it is practiced in contemporary cities across the globe, begs a fundamental question about the meaning of the terms "include" and "exclude." The *Oxford English Dictionary* defines the verb "to include" as encompassing a range of action words: to shut in, to close in, to confine, to enclose, to contain, to comprise, to place in a class or category, to bring to a close.[18] All of these actions suggest that there is a doer who carries out the dichotomous task of delineating the boundaries and/or the contents of what is to be allowed inside and what is to be left outside. It is a black-and-white landscape with no room for gray. The verb "to exclude" is similarly defined by actions: to bar; to keep out what is already outside; to reject from consideration, notice, or use; to not admit; to expel; to debar; to leave no room for.[19] These actions again imply that a deciding agent determines the fate of the subject. Both definitions thus imply a clear boundary between an inside and an outside realm, which necessitates a clear and final placement without the possibility of one foot in each. However, the definition of exclusion also implies that its subjects are left or pushed out when they would prefer to be let or kept in.

In analyzing Arab Middle Eastern cities in terms of inclusion and exclusion, one must thus inquire: who is being included and who is being excluded, and who is doing the excluding? Of course, we already know the answer: under different circumstances and for different reasons, hegemonic or dominant groups are typically the ones engaged in these practices. However, I believe that anyone interested in a true study of urban inclusion and exclusion must go further and probe the underlying assumption that inclusion leads to good outcomes. Good for whom? And why? In the end, one must pose this question: has the practice of exclusion always resulted in an unjust city? Or, seen from the opposite perspective: did the pursuit of inclusion result in a better life for those who would have otherwise been excluded? Put bluntly, I would like to propose that inclusion may not always result in better urban harmony. After all, one must recognize that inclusion is a culturally determined and culturally relative concept.

As demonstrated in the above examination of these terms, there is an implicit bias in wording that imputes a more positive connotation and greater acceptability to the "in" (as in "include") than to the "ex" (as in "exclude"), which seems automatically to carry a negative value. When one invokes the term "include," there is an assumption that everyone wants to be included, which at times is not the case. In fact, despite the implicit supposition that no one ever wants to be excluded, there are some groups who voluntarily elect to self-exclude. This leads to another imperative question: why and under what circumstances do certain groups engage in self-exclusion? It is useful here to look at some examples of how this particular phenomenon has been articulated in the Middle East. Such a discourse is relatively new in the context of the region. In fact, it has not yet taken strong hold there either in terms of urban governance or national politics. As such, the Middle East may be an appropriate geography in which to investigate the culturally relative nature of the inclusion–exclusion continuum.

## *Identity discourses: on different forms of inclusion and assimilation*

Critical to any discussion of urban inclusivity are the sometimes divergent and at other times complementary notions of identity and difference that frequently define the reasons and expectations for acts of inclusion and exclusion in cities. Etymology reveals that the term "identity" is derived from the Latin root *idem*, meaning "sameness;" it is also related to the Latin *identidem*, meaning "over and over again, repeatedly."[20] Meanwhile, "difference" is defined as the "condition, quality, or fact of being different, or not the same in quality or in essence." In other words, "the relation of non-agreement or non-identity between two or more things, disagreement."[21] From these definitions, one may gather that repression or elimination of difference is a condition for certain forms of collective identity.

National identity in the non-Western or colonized world was not usually a homegrown concept. As I have previously described this condition:

> Groups of people living in one region under a colonial power, possibly having only one common colonial history for some hundred years, but belonging to different religions, languages, cultures, traditions, and races, had no other option but to band together to achieve this new, supposedly better stage of "freedom and independence."[22]

These were the ideals of the Western "Enlightenment"—the world of the colonizer—and the subordinated populations appropriated these ideals in order to free themselves from colonial dominance. However, once independence was achieved, the glue that bound these various groups together no longer existed.

Kathryn Woodward has termed this situation the "crisis of identity," a breakdown of hegemonic sameness into different sub-identities of religion, race, ethnicity, and so on. But while "identity" may have been rooted in "sameness," it has also always been about difference.[23] Here, it is important to recognize that ethnicity, race, religion, and territory have always been essential but unequal elements in the formation of national identity, and to some extent urban identity.

In this regard, Vanessa Watson has argued that certain fundamental and irreconcilable differences between people in specific nations may not allow for consensus or resolution to emerge, and that the result instead is typically a divided or fragmented national population.[24] She suggests that the concept of identity is "often a product of hybridization, fusion and cultural innovation," which is "frequently self-generated and self-constructed."[25] These "deep differences," as she calls them, require us to accept the limits of consensus-driven politics and institute difference as a mechanism of governance. Hence, countries with ethnically mixed populations, like Malaysia or Singapore, may find it more practical to enforce a paradigm of national citizenship to assimilate mixed populations into a single national identity despite these deep differences, as was the case in the United States at the beginning of the twentieth century. However, in the United States today, the melting pot mentality has already given way to the emergence of a culture that valorizes hyphenated identities, even if they challenge national identity. The current surge of the Tea Party movement and the wave that resulted in the election of Donald Trump is an indication that these matters are far from settled, even in the world's only superpower—a nation that was made by immigrants.

The history of assimilation suggests that it has usually been pursued under very specific conditions by nation-states interested in ensuring the creation of a larger national image to which all its citizens, despite their ethnic differences, may belong. This history also indicates that empires—particularly, for example, the Ottoman Empire—have seldom felt the need for this exercise, perhaps because they were held together by force. However, new nation-states, and nation-states where ethnic, religious, or even linguistic conflicts exist between constituent groups, have often resorted to an assimilation discourse to create a national narrative, and hence a "national citizen"—a citizen without racial, ethnic, or religious variation.

The idea of a "national citizen" based on sameness as a prerequisite for national identity has, however, come under attack. As a cause, one might point to the rise of hybrid cultures as a result of new patterns of migration across the globe, particularly to the countries of the Global North. In its place, the concept of difference emerged at the end of the twentieth century as a fundamental constituent of national identity. It is out of these interpretations of national identity that the aforementioned gradation of inclusion—from ambivalent tolerance, to recognition and reciprocity, to assimilation—has emerged and manifested itself in national ideologies and practices.

If in the United States assimilation and inclusion are based on a multicultural paradigm, in parts of Southeast Asia, such as Singapore or Malaysia, one form of inclusion operates through the "logic of proportionality." This means inclusion in all aspects of urban life in recognition/reciprocity of/to each group's size within the entire urban polity. In the case of Europe, inclusion has been executed only as a form of assimilation, as a dominant majority typically demands that minorities assimilate and thereby give up the right to non-secular lifestyles. This has been most evident in the ongoing debate over the veil and the creation of

Islamic schools in France and the UK, in both of which cases the minority's reaction has often been one of resistance and refusal to submit.

*Inclusion/exclusion: reflections on the Arab Middle East*

In the Middle East in general, minority groups seem to have a more acute sense of themselves as minorities. One might cite the case of Jews in Morocco or Coptic Christians in Egypt. Here, the minority group comes to accept some degree of assimilation as a form of submission to the hegemony of the majority. Thus, the overall practices by which identity is constituted by accepting difference are often limited to the national scale, and may not permeate down to the urban realm. In Southeast Asia and Europe, national ideologies typically filter down to the local level, but, in the Middle East, there may be a complete erasure of a dialogue of difference at the urban scale. For example, some Coptic women have started to veil in the streets of Cairo. Their choice is not one made from religious conviction or as a result of state or municipal regulation; it is simply a measure of convenience that affords them protection and allows them to avoid standing out. It therefore embodies a survival tactic within a hegemony of sameness, mandated by a necessity for public engagement in everyday urban practices.

One of the most interesting forms of assimilation may come to us from the Middle East and involves a process through which minority groups are expected to submit to the hegemony of a larger majority to simply maintain their independence. It is possible to understand how this process works by looking at the history of segregation in relation to the theoretical construct of the traditional Islamic city. Indeed, this framing allows us to arrive at an entirely different understanding of inclusion, based on different attitudes toward recognition and reciprocity on the one hand and toward assimilation and submission on the other.

Segregation was an operative principal in the traditional Islamic city, and it gave the urban context several interesting attributes. First, it allowed minorities to maintain a certain position in society that they would not otherwise have had. Second, it gave them certain rights and the autonomy to control certain parts of the economy. Third, it gave them a space within the city that they could claim as theirs, without giving up their right to visit the rest of the city. Ironically, however, by virtue of the spatial consolidation of these minority groups, certain internal groups (either clergy or guilds) often acquired and exercised a special hegemony within their particular spatial enclave.

As Ira Lapidus has noted, "From ancient times through the early Islamic era strong local communities were the basic building block of Middle Eastern societies. They were reinforced at the beginning of the Islamic era by Arab immigrants who were organized into tightly knit families and clans aligned by tribes."[26] He describes in particular how the ethnically and religiously mixed population in the Islamic capital, Baghdad, was grouped into quarters and districts. He also points out that although regional populations in the Middle East typically varied a great deal in ethnic composition and social structure, in the urban realm, clans, gangs, and other local groups often consolidated into separate quarters, which remained basic to the structure of society. In fact, according to Lapidus, in a world where one was only considered safe when among kin, the tightly knit urban communities often sought comfort and protection through solidarity. There was some separation of individuals by families or communities, but no ghetto-like isolation existed. Lapidus goes further to suggest that even among Muslims, different ethnic or racial groups lived apart. In particular, "Certain neighborhoods were favored by the wealthy because of their proximity to the citadel and public affairs, and gave these districts an 'upper' class character, but no class came to dominate a district."[27]

Although the professional corporations or guilds provided the basis of urban society in many places in the Arab Middle East, in many quarters solidarity was based on sectarian-religious affiliation and the leadership of a sheikh rather than race or family relations. Social and administrative roles were often assigned to individual quarters, further unifying the quarter community around these shared responsibilities.[28] However, social life did not depend on quarters alone, because bazaars were important places where "the concerns of the whole city were carried on by the people of the quarters who came, separated from their families, differentiated from their communal roles."[29]

Despite the seductiveness of such a unified view of the traditional Islamic city, it is important to recognize that "the large Islamic empire was not a monolithic entity. It encompassed different people with different original cultures, different economic systems, different national heritages and characters, different climatic and geographical conditions and different strategic defense requirements."[30] In redefining the typical Islamic city in terms of its elements, Albert Hourani challenges Max Weber's definition, which had previously pitted it against a Western standard. He further cautions against the danger and difficulty of any consideration of the Islamic city that sought to cast it as a physical typology.[31] Thus, although the picture of the Islamic city is one where everything was confined, walled, and gated, it does not follow that this level of physical segregation resulted in urban exclusion. Perhaps the example of the Jewish quarter in traditional Islamic cities (often called the *mellah*) could serve to illustrate this point further.

### *The Jewish quarter as a case of inclusive/exclusive space/place*

Judaism developed and spread in a unique urban context. This has allowed some to argue that a historic Jewish tradition of self-segregation was always driven by urban necessity. The community clustered around the synagogue because it was an essential structure for their worship. It was also the most convenient way to observe the Sabbath, at which a certain concentration of Jews was necessary to meet the requirement of *minion* (ten men for regular prayers, three times a day, every day). Because of dietary laws, Jews also needed access to a kosher butcher.

In Europe, the Jewish quarter was typically an enforced ghetto. For example, Jews in Venice during the early fifteenth century were confined to it to protect gentiles from them. The ghetto can thus be interpreted as a punitive space. But its existence also resulted in the evolution of a rich, uniquely Jewish cultural life out of a need to forge a world apart. One reflection of these conditions is that Yiddish came to be spoken prominently in European cities where Jews were excluded.

The experience of Islamic cities with minority Jewish populations was more diverse and multicultural. There was, for example, no strategy of theological Puritanism toward Jews. In Islam, Jews are accepted as a "people of the book," rather than being seen as fundamentally other. Thus, one of the major differences between European and Islamic urban experience for Jews was that the gates of the European ghetto were locked from the outside at the discretion of the gentiles. By contrast, the *mellah* was locked from the inside at night—as were the gates of the other quarters of a typical Islamic city. These gates might also be locked during the Sabbath and on religious holidays at the discretion of its inhabitants.

Despite the apparent isolation or exclusion of Jews into walled quarters in the Islamic world, these spaces were thus very porous, and strong social and economic ties existed between Muslims and Jews within the larger urban community. What architecturally looks like exclusion therefore was far more complicated in social terms. Indeed, one has to look at the history of who was being "excluded" and why to truly understand the difference in social reality between the Jewish quarters of Europe and the Middle East. It is thus interesting that many a Muslim ruler greatly valued Jews because they were useful for furthering his own prosperity. In fact, an Ottoman sultan once commented that Ferdinand and Isabel's expulsion of the Jews from Spain had delivered guaranteed wealth into the hands of their enemies.[32] For this reason, some Muslim rulers sought to protect Jews from urban unrest and theft by outside tribes—Jews were often victims of such attacks because they traditionally dealt in portable capital and goods rather than investments in agriculture and land. Hence, they sometimes relocated the Jewish community so that it was next to the Kasbah.[33]

In hindsight, the concentration of the Jewish population into the *mellah* may have benefited both Jews and Muslims in various ways. First, it often gave the ruler or sultan access to Jewish communities, and hence to goods and services uniquely provided by them—a relationship that gave Jews a good deal of political leverage. Second, this arrangement empowered Jews by enabling them to lead a relatively autonomous existence. Thus, in return for paying taxes, they were afforded representation by their own *shieykh al-yahud*, who had the power to jail people and police the community, and hence to use this leverage with the ruler. Third, while physically segregated, they were still integrated into the larger urban economy and community. Jews thus worked in the courts and the souqs, and they functioned commercially inside the medina. Fourth, non-Jews were regularly allowed to visit Jewish space and participate in activities there that were prohibited elsewhere by Islamic law. North African Jewish quarters, for example, accommodated prostitution, alcohol production and consumption, and gambling. The area inside the walls of the *mellah* could thus provide an important area of escape for the entire urban population.[34]

The Jewish quarter is but one example of physical separation as an attempt to achieve a strange form of urban inclusion. But the presence and long survival of the ethnic quarter indicates that:

> the city was never "free," or rather that its freedoms came through the bounding and containing of the Other. In this sense, such spaces of exception are the "constitutive *inside*" of cities. They are the forms of exceptionalism that constitute the grid of the normal. They lie not at the extra-territorial periphery of city-space but are instead the very modalities of statehood, subjectivity and space that produce the city.[35]

*On identity and urbanism in the Arab Middle East*

So, where does this leave us with regard to the connection between urban identity and urban segregation in an increasingly globalizing Arab Middle

East? First, one may argue that even as many different nations converge into a "world culture," it is a culture marked by the management of diversity, rather than by the replication of uniformity. This so-called world culture, an idea made possible during the heyday of modernization, remains essentially a culture of dominant groups, in which the persistent diversity of the constituent local culture—as is the case with many Middle Eastern societies—is often a product of globalization itself. The second point involves the connection between this placeless global culture and the urban places in which daily life occurs. Indeed, this global culture is created by the rapid interconnectedness of local, national, and foreign communities through flows of information. In this sense, its logic is largely uncontrolled by any specific local or ethnic society, but its impacts shape the lives of everyone in these societies.[36] Nowhere can this be better observed than in the Middle East. Here, its impact on urbanism will mean that cultural experience—even in supposedly "traditional" locales or ethnic areas that are notoriously resistant to change—may become less place-rooted and more information-based. The placelessness of this global culture and the constant movement of Arab and Middle Eastern refugees to many different places around the world today are already undermining well-established citizenship norms, including notions of residential segregation along ethnic or religious lines. These movements may eventually undermine the idea of nations whose citizens only belong to one ethnicity or one religion and enforce a future where cultural diversity is no longer a choice but a necessity. This project will require different outlets for the construction of the multiple and increasingly complex identities of the Arab and Middle Eastern peoples in both their home countries and their host counties.

Finally, and despite the world's preoccupation with globalization, history in general demonstrates a movement toward cultural differentiation—and not homogenization. Thus, it is increasingly possible for each individual to belong to many cultures, and for people to have multiple cultural identities. In this sense, identity is always under construction and in constant evolution. If hybridity is accepted as an inherent constituent of national identity, this means that any particular form of urbanism can only be accepted as a reflection of a specific transitional stage in the life of any society.[37] Indeed, globalization has made the issues of identity and representation in urbanism increasingly cumbersome, and has cast doubt on urbanism's ability to fully represent the peoples, nations, and cultures within which it exists. But despite these trends, urbanism will likely become an arena where one may observe how local and ethnic cultures mediate global domination. Here again the countries of the Middle East will be prime sites for such observations. As the nations of a globalizing Middle East become more conscious of their religious and ethnic roots, they are likely to seek forms and norms that represent these sub-identities.

Whether the different nations that constitute the Arab Middle East will be able to deal with their increasingly diverse ethnic, religious, and sectarian communities remains to be seen. But one thing that is certain is that they need to develop a new political culture and commensurate spatial articulations beyond the slogans of traditionalism, religious revival, and anti-modernity.

6

# MILLET ETHNICITY

## ISLAMIZED ARMENIANS AND ARMENIAN IDENTITY

*James Barry*

Armenian ethnic identity in the Middle East is formulated around language, religion, descent, and the concept of a diaspora–homeland relationship. The historical leadership of the Armenians, who have experienced diaspora and lack of self-rule for the better part of a millennium, has been concentrated in the Armenian Apostolic Church, a non-Chalcedonic Orthodox denomination. A synonymous relationship exists between Armenians and Christianity, which until recently (accurate at the time of writing) remained largely uncontested in the Middle East and elsewhere. Historically, Armenians who converted to another religion were outcast and no longer considered Armenian. However, in recent decades, the "rediscovery" of Armenian Muslims has raised a central question for Armenians in Armenia and the diaspora: can a Muslim truly be Armenian? This is further complicated by another related but more sensitive question: can an Armenian also be a Turk?

The roots of these questions lie in the ethnicization of Middle Eastern religious identities inherited from the millet system of the Ottoman Empire by modern nation-states (as well as minority nationalisms). This system, whereby political representation was segmented along the lines of religious confession, endures today in the Ottoman successor states of the Middle East. In this chapter, I will look at the relationship between the modern millet system, ethnicity, and national identity in Turkey with reference to the construction of Turkish Muslim and Armenian Christian identities, and the consequences this has for Muslims of Armenian descent. After examining the millet construction of ethnicity, I will move on to provide a general background of the role of Christianity in Armenian identity and the way Islam has been described historically in Armenian sources. Through this, I will make it clear that Armenians have traditionally viewed Christianity as synonymous with Armenian-ness (*hayut'iwn*), while Islam is portrayed as the religion of the oppressor, and conversion to Islam is interpreted as abandoning or forfeiting Armenian identity. From there, I will examine two modern case studies that challenge the Armenian relationship with Islam: the Hopa Hemshin and the "Islamized" Armenians. The Hopa Hemshin are an Armenian-speaking Muslim community in northeastern Turkey who identify as a Turkish tribe despite being descended from Armenian converts. The "Islamized," "hidden," or "crypto" Armenians are the descendants of Armenians who converted to Islam during times of persecution in the early twentieth century and maintain a memory of their Armenian origins. Among different factions within the Armenian communities of the Middle East, the interest and corresponding resistance in recognizing these two groups has raised an important question to which I turn later in the chapter: are Armenian attitudes toward Islam changing?

### *Millet ethnicity*

The definition of Turks as outlined by Mustafa Kemal Atatürk was territorial, meaning that anyone born within the borders of modern Turkey was, in effect, a "Turk."[1] In practice, the Turkish identity promoted by the Kemalist state has strong ethnic and religious connotations, and a denial of difference between citizens has been promoted as a strategy to manufacture homogeneity and equality while maintaining a contradictory policy of ethnic Turkish, Sunni Muslim hegemony. While the Republic of Turkey has not been positioned by its rulers as a successor state of the Ottoman Empire, but rather as the savior of Turkish people, many continuities remain despite the alleged secular modernism of the new state. Among these was the millet system: according to Akturk, the Islamic millet became the Turkish millet after 1923, and it is revealing that "millet" is still "the most widely used Turkish word for nation."[2] Under the Ottoman millet system, there were several Christian millets divided into national churches—Armenian, Greek, and Syriac. However, there was only one Muslim millet representing all Muslims of the empire regardless of ethnic and sectarian differences. In practice, the leader of this millet was an ethnic Turkish Sunni, the Ottoman sultan, who legitimized his leadership by proclaiming himself the caliph. After the collapse of the Ottoman Empire, the millet system continued. This was in part due to the Treaty of Lausanne in 1923, in which the European powers recognized the borders of the Republic of Turkey. The treaty required Turkey to recognize and respect the rights of religious minorities. Who these minorities actually were was left up to Ankara to decide. The Kemalist government defined three—Jews, Greek Orthodox, and Armenian Gregorian—which was a continuation of the three original non-Muslim millets from the early Ottoman period. Furthermore, the Muslim millet transformed into the Turkish nation, remaining ethnically Turkish and Sunni, and aiming to absorb other ethnic Muslim minorities (such as Kurds, Circassians, and Laz) and non-Sunni groups, the largest of which are the Alevis. The continuity between the Ottoman millets and modern Turkish conceptions of ethnicity is the reason why, as is explained below, the Hopa Hemshin identify as Turks and deny their Armenian origins, and Islamized Armenians often seek to change their names from Turkish Muslim to Armenian Christian names upon baptism.

Turkey is by no means the only country that has continued the millet system in the former Ottoman Empire, as similar arrangements exist in Lebanon, Syria, Egypt, and Israel/Palestine. As one scholar has argued, the successor states and great powers that colonized the former Ottoman territories "largely froze ethnic cleavages in the Middle East" by reinterpreting the millet system into new legal codes.[3] In Turkey, a secular prime minister replaced the sultanate-caliphate, and a Directorate of Religious Affairs was established as a government body that has defined religion in Turkey as Islam, and specifically Hanafi Sunni.[4]

The minority status of religious minorities is categorized in both religious and ethnic terms. This has allowed the Armenians to foster a sense of separateness based on common conceptions of Armenian identity and Armenian-ness. Although the definition of who is an Armenian varies from country to country—and indeed from person to person—there are a number of salient features that are of particular concern to ethnic nationalists and the Armenian Apostolic Church. These are the identity anchors of religion (Christianity), language (Armenian), homeland (an ambiguously defined Historic Armenia), and descent (preferably from two Armenian parents). It is of course difficult, if not impossible, to demonstrate an uninterrupted continuity in Armenian identity from the establishment of the Armenian Church to the present day. These three themes have been salient among (traditionally clerical) Armenian elites who have utilized each for the purposes of binding disparate Armenian communities together over the centuries. Nevertheless, modern Armenian national identity as it is known today gradually emerged from the seventeenth century onward, as diaspora merchant communities throughout Europe and Asia began to fund intellectual activities in art and literature, as well as printing in the Armenian language.[5] The Mkhitarists, an Armenian Catholic order founded by an Armenian monk from the Ottoman Empire, were highly influential in the development of a vernacular Armenian language as well as a modern Armenian historiography. By the late eighteenth century, publications calling for national liberation were being published by Armenian merchant communities. These journals and pamphlets further developed a modern vernacular standard and built solidarity between the Armenian communities of the Ottoman and Persian Empires by reporting on events within the homeland.[6] These efforts were cultivated by individuals such as Israel Ori (1658–1711) and Joseph Emin (1726–1809), both of whom campaigned for an independent Armenia, and external developments in the Ottoman, Russian, and Persian Empires, all led to the rise of an Armenian national awakening, known as the *zartonk*, in the nineteenth century. In the Ottoman Empire, an increasing ethnic and civic awareness among the Armenians sparked the formulation of Armenian political parties that advocated for the rights of their people in a loosely defined homeland, which centered on Eastern Anatolia. These movements solidified the definition of Armenians as an ethnic kinship bonded by religion, language, and a homeland.

The two case studies in this chapter, the Hopa Hemshin and the "Islamized" Armenians, both possess some aspects of the criteria developed by the Armenian national movement, but not all. The Hopa Hemshin have Armenian descent, speak Armenian, and live in the Armenian homeland, but are Muslim. The Islamized Armenians have partial Armenian descent, live in the Armenian homeland, rarely know the Armenian language, and are liminal Muslims, with some seeking a return to Christianity. Before looking at these two case studies more specifically, however, I will first establish the role of Christianity in Armenian identity, and the consequent relationship between Armenians and Islam. In order to understand why Armenians have traditionally rejected Muslims of Armenian descent, such as the Hemshin and the Islamized Armenians, it is important to understand the historical role of the Armenian Apostolic Church in defining who is an Armenian and who is not.

### *The synonymy of Armenian-ness and Christianity*

Armenians claim to be the oldest Christian nation. Armenian tradition holds that the church was founded by two disciples of Jesus, Thaddeus and Bartholomew, which is why the national church refers to itself as "Apostolic." Armenia only became a Christian nation after the conversion of King Trdat in 301 by Gregory the Illuminator, who is revered as the patron saint and first catholicos (patriarch) of the Armenian Church. These traditions are largely mythological, in the sense that the primary function of these stories is to look into the past in order to find explanations for the origins of the present. Scholars are generally skeptical of the assertion that Armenians converted to Christianity as a nation in 301, arguing that it is more likely that Christianity became the state religion in Armenia only after Constantine's conversion of Rome in around 314.[7] Furthermore, this conversion is unlikely to have been sudden, and given the monastic nature of Armenian Christianity at the time, likely took centuries to permeate the peasantry of the countryside. The traditions are based on the histories of Armenian chroniclers working several centuries after the dates of which they were writing, particularly Moses of Khoren and his *History of the Armenians*. These traditions present neat explanations for the origins of the Armenian nation and describe their uniqueness.

There are a number of other aspects of the Armenian Apostolic Church that make it unique from all others and therefore foster its separateness. First, the Armenian Church is non-Chalcedonic, meaning that it rejects the notion that Christ had two separate natures—one divine, the other human—a doctrine that separates it from both the Roman Catholic Church and the Byzantine Orthodox Churches.[8] This doctrinal circumstance seems to have come about through inertia rather than from an ecclesiastical position: political upheavals prevented the Armenian clergy from attending the Council of Chalcedon in 451, and their failure to ratify the council became a *fait accompli* that reinforced the church's independence from the Greek and Latin Churches. Furthermore, the Armenian Church has its own liturgy, written in Classical Armenian, and maintains its own traditions and hierarchy, all of which played an important role in developing the exclusivity of the national church. The development of a writing system and liturgical form of Armenian allowed the Armenian clergy to distance their congregations from the Greek and Semitic Christian influences that surrounded them, in addition to the Mazdeism of the Persian realm in which many of them lived. By the eighth century, the Catholicos John of Odzun finally compiled the doctrinal positions and organizational structures that now form the core of the Armenian Apostolic Church.[9]

The Armenian Church defines itself as a national church, solely serving the needs of the Armenian nation. For this reason, it does not seek converts and only baptizes people of Armenian descent. The church, and later nationalists, have built upon the myth that all Armenians are descended from one person, Hayk, the grandson of Noah of the biblical flood. From Hayk, they take the name for themselves (*hay*), their language (*hayeren*), and their country (*hayastan*).[10] The concept of a premodern Armenian nation stems from the meaning applied to the term "nation" before the nineteenth century, where, rather than referring to a "sovereign people," a nation was "a cultural group of common descent."[11] Just as the Israelites claimed to be descended from Patriarch Abraham's grandson Jacob, so too did the Armenian chroniclers claim that the ancestry of all Armenians could be traced to Hayk. These traditions have led Anthony Smith to define Armenians as an *ethnie*, a form of the nation that pre-dates the nation-state. Smith, alongside John Hutchinson, defines an *ethnie* as a group of people who share a common proper name, a myth of a common ancestry, historical memories, elements of a common culture (such as language), a symbolic link to a homeland, and a sense of solidarity.[12] More specifically, he placed the Armenian *ethnie* in a category that he termed "vertical" or "demotic," meaning that, alongside the Jews and the Irish, Armenians are defined by territorial dispersion as well as a lack of sovereignty over their homeland, and are bonded by a shared heritage and culture, including a distinct language and religion, as well as an obligation of shared defense of identity.[13] This is based on the observation that, for many centuries, Armenians lacked a kingdom of their own, and the church took over as a national government under occupation.

In reality, the supposed national church is also a myth, both historically and in the present. Armenian Christianity is pluricentric and at times violently fragmented, with four patriarchates: Etchmiadzin (near Yerevan), Constantinople (Istanbul), Sis in Cilicia (now Antelias in Lebanon), and Jerusalem. Each patriarchate developed to serve its own political needs. Etchmiadzin is commonly referred to as the home of the "Mother Church," and the catholicos of Etchmiadzin is viewed as the most senior patriarch, holding the title Catholicos of All Armenians (*Amenayn Hayots' Kat'oghikos*). However, this has not always been the case, and the Etchmiadzin patriarchate has proven to be the most mobile of them all, having moved from city to city throughout its history in order to suit the political needs of the church and its rulers. Jerusalem is one of the oldest but is presently the least politically significant of the patriarchates, although its geographic location is significant, as is its relative independence. Istanbul was previously the most powerful, having been the governing body for the Armenian millet during Ottoman times, but the Istanbul patriarchate lost its status in the wake of the Armenian genocide, and its present authority is limited to the Armenians of Turkey. Sis emerged to serve the medieval Armenian Diaspora Kingdom of Cilicia, along the Mediterranean coast of modern Turkey, but the Sis catholicos was exiled from Turkey in the early republican period and relocated to Antelias in Lebanon, which is why it is often referred to as the Antelias patriarchate. Antelias and Etchmiadzin split from one another during the Cold War, as Antelias came to represent anti-communist Armenian political groups who rejected the catholicos of Etchmiadzin as a Soviet puppet. The division between these churches has been healed in the post-Soviet era, but Antelias remains separate politically and is dominant in the Middle East.

In addition to the tensions between the patriarchates, there has been a historical animosity between Armenians from Western (Ottoman) and Eastern (Persian/Russian) Armenia.[14] A similar tension exists today between Western Armenian and Eastern Armenian speakers, which in most instances (excluding Iranian Armenians) corresponds to the tension between the diaspora and its post-Soviet homeland. Additionally, despite its claims as a unified national church, the pluricentric Armenian Apostolic Church has had to contend with challenges from Catholicism and Protestantism. The rivalry between Armenian Apostolic (Orthodox) and Armenian Catholics is centuries old, whereas the Protestant challenge emerged only after the founding of American missionary schools in the nineteenth-century Middle East. The extent of this division is as such that until today, some members of the Armenian Apostolic Church do not recognize Armenian Catholics and Protestants as Armenians, but rather as "traitors."[15]

However, this is not to move away from the fact that in the minds of many Armenians, both in the Middle East and elsewhere, a unitary singular church and identity exists, and this contributes to the salient assertion that Armenianness and Christianity are synonymous. This is supported by the relative synonymy of "Armenian" and "Christian" in the Middle East. For example, in

Iran the Persian words *armanī* (Armenian) and *masīḥī* (Christian) are used interchangeably to mean "Christian," and a similar association has existed historically in Turkey (although it has been affected by the acrimony between Armenia and Turkey in recent decades). This was reinforced by the millet system in the Ottoman Empire, which placed the patriarch of Constantinople as the head of a semi-autonomous Armenian nation, and a similar arrangement in Safavid Iran between the shah and the archbishop of New Julfa in Isfahan. In modern times, the millet system has continued, albeit in a modern form, where the law courts and governance of religious minority communities are separate. The historical association between Christianity and Armenian identity is exploited by the Armenian Apostolic Church, which still views itself as a government for Armenians in the Middle East.

In this context, Armenians developed an insular view of the world that was hostile not only to Islam—which in their minds was an occupying and persecuting religion—but also to other forms of Christianity, especially Catholicism. While this did not preclude relationships between Armenians and Muslims, and interactions were frequent in mercantile, artistic, artisanal, and bureaucratic spheres, it did provide clear limitations on Armenian encounters with non-Armenians, creating a situation whereby Armenians lived alongside Muslims but apart from them. Thus the nineteenth-century Armenian novelist Raffi (1835–88) wrote in his *Parskakan Patkirner* (Persian images) that the Armenian who leaves Christianity ceases to be an Armenian.[16] The Armenian word for "foreigner" (*otar*) is used to greatest effect in situations such as these, as it etymologically refers to the act of being pushed away or becoming estranged (*otarel*).[17] This pattern continues into the present, as in many parts of the Middle East the Armenian Apostolic Church does not recognize intermarriage let alone conversion.[18] In Iran, intermarriage can lead to the community turning their back on the person in question, and even their own families are likely to reject them.[19] These divisions, and the contradictory belief in the unity of Armenians with Christianity, are the context for the following discussion about Armenians and Islam.

### *Islam through Armenian eyes*

Armenian history and Islamic history are interconnected, mainly because the narratives of each center on the same geographical area: the Middle East. However, Armenians are rarely mentioned in Islamic historical narratives, and Muslims are a peripheral element in Armenian history. In addition, Armenian histories give scant attention to the large number of Armenian converts to Islam who formed a significant component of the military class in the early modern Middle East. This is especially notable in the virtual neglect of "Armenian" janissaries in the Ottoman Empire and their equivalent in Safavid Iran, the *gholāmān*.[20] In recent years, some Armenians have brought attention to the origins of famous converts, such as the sixteenth-century Ottoman architect Sinan, but this has usually been limited to nationalistic point scoring,[21] and instead most of these Armenian Muslims are ignored. Among Iranian Armenians, there is some acknowledgment of Mirza Malkum Khan, a nineteenth-century politician and modernizer, although Armenian publications usually fail to mention that he converted to Islam.[22] This is evidential of the ways in which Armenian Muslims are either whitewashed or rejected in Armenian historiographies.

For much of their history, Christians and Muslims lived in separate settlements, including distinct quarters of major towns, and this has contributed to their alienation from the other religious groups. Seta Dadoyan has argued that until the fourteenth century, interaction between Muslims and Armenians was limited to the academic sphere, and Armenian intellectuals showed little interest in dealing with questions of Christian–Muslim relations, mainly due to the religious illiteracy of the Armenian peasantry. However, by the fourteenth century, polemical writings began to appear, which aimed to teach Armenians the nature of Christian and Islamic beliefs with the sole purpose of proving that the former was superior to the latter.[23] Polemical and apologetic works are among the strongest documentation of Christian–Muslim–Jewish interaction in the medieval period. Polemical works were designed to refute the religion of the other, and they therefore formulated an "imaginary argument" with a Christianity (or Islam or Judaism) of their own invention.[24] In sociological terms, the purpose of works like these is to define who Armenians are by defining who they are not, which in this case is Muslims. These narratives have continued over the centuries and responded to changes in Armenian identity while at the same time maintaining some consistency.

In the seventeenth and eighteenth centuries, Armenians converted to Islam infrequently, and usually to avoid discriminatory taxation. However, Armenian Christians frequently adopted Arabic, Turkish, and Persian names depending on their area of residency, meaning that they were often indistinguishable from the people among whom they lived.[25] Evidence for this is found in legal records, as well in the artistic legacies of Middle Eastern Armenian communities from this period. In Iran, for example, the glosses in the margins of the illuminated

Bibles produced by the wealthy New Julfa community during the Safavid era demonstrate that Armenians had adopted Persian or Arabic names, and even wrote in Persian, albeit using Armenian letters.[26]

Nevertheless, religion remained a gulf between Armenians and their neighbors. Islam for Armenians has traditionally been presented as the religion of the oppressor. In the seventeenth century, Arakel of Tabriz, a monk and chronicler, employed a number of stereotypes when writing about Muslims, portraying them as oppressors who were only able to convert Christians through force,[27] and often depicting them as homosexuals and immoral deviants.[28] Part of the reason why Armenians have traditionally rejected converts is the role they played in oppressing Armenian communities. For example, Mohammad Beg, who became the vizier of Shah Abbas II, actively encouraged the persecution of Christians and Jews following his appointment.[29] Similarly, another convert during the sixteenth century used his new status to pursue vendettas against his Armenian rivals, having them charged with blaspheming Islam.[30] The narrative of Muslims as oppressors, and converts as traitors, continued in later centuries. For example, the Armenian novelist Raffi stated that it was in the nature of Muslims to extort Christians and unjustly assault them.[31] Presently, this view remains pervasive, particularly under the genocide narrative where religious difference is seen as a source of prejudice, in addition to ethnic racism.

In the past century, Turks have been portrayed as the natural enemy of the Armenians and as the perpetrators of the Armenian genocide. This discourse centers on the narrative of Armenian identity, which is pervasive at the present period and has largely been portrayed as an ethnic rivalry rather than a religious one. The term "Turk" is variously applied to different actors and is used in an overwhelmingly negative fashion. Its applications include the government of Turkey—which is seen as the successor to the late Ottoman government and is consequently held responsible for the Armenian genocide—as well as all citizens of Turkey, be they "Turks," Kurds, or any other kind of non-Armenian. It is also applied to Azerbaijan and Azerbaijanis at times.[32] Since the 9/11 attacks, there has been a rise in the tendency to place the Armenian–Turkish animosity within a broader Christian–Muslim binary, especially when promoting political issues like recognition of the Armenian genocide and the independence of Nagorno-Karabakh. This has meant some Armenian groups have built alliances with right-wing politicians who support anti-Islam agendas, such as Pastor Fred Nile of Australia and Baroness Cox of the UK. However, the Christian-ness and Muslim-ness of this dichotomy is superficial and quickly evaporates into diatribes against the "Turks." For this reason, the primary focus of the case studies is about Muslims of Armenian descent in Turkey.

There are Muslims of Armenian descent throughout the world, and there are many converts, particularly in Armenia, because of marriages with Iranians; however, these do not generate the same amount of media attention, as they do not involve Turkey. Therefore, the views of Muslim Armenians from Turkey are important in understanding Armenian identity and the changes it is undergoing in the Middle East. The racialization of religion is such that in Turkey today, Armenian Muslims who wish to return to Christianity usually seek to change their names as well, since name changes have an ethnicizing effect.[33] In other words, the boundaries between ethnicities continue to be maintained in religious terms in Turkey, and this problematizes the connections between being Armenian and being Muslim, a point that is especially relevant with regard to the Hemshin people discussed below.

### *Armenian Muslims: the Hopa Hemshin*

It is estimated that there are around 50,000 Armenians remaining in Turkey, with the vast majority living in Istanbul.[34] This number is broadly similar to other Middle Eastern Armenian populations, with around 53,000 believed to live in Lebanon,[35] and 40,000 in Iran.[36] However, there is a much larger proportion of the Turkish population that has living memory of some Armenian family origin. A small number of them continue to speak Armenian, such as the Hemshin.

The Hemshin people (*Hamshen* in Armenian) are a unique sub-ethnic group who are at once Armenian and Turkish. The Hemshin are descended from Armenians living in the Hemşin region of northeastern Anatolia (presently Rize Province in Turkey) in the past millennium. The term "Hemshin" is actually applied to three groups: Armenian Christians who fled Hemşin following the Ottoman conquest, settling along the Black Sea coast in Abkhazia and Krasnodar; Muslims of Armenian origin currently living in the Hemşin district who adopted the Turkish language, albeit with a large vocabulary of Armenian words by the nineteenth century; and several Muslim communities living farther east in Artvin Province near the Georgian border who continue to speak a dialect of Armenian that they call Homshetsma.[37] The third group, often called the Hopa Hemshin after the district in which many of them live, has garnered the most attention among Armenians in Armenia and the diaspora, and are therefore the primary focus of this analysis.

The language of the Hopa Hemshin, known as Homshetsma or Hamshentsi, is a Western Armenian dialect, although it is not considered mutually intelligible with other Western Armenian dialects.[38] It is spoken by around 20,000 to 30,000 people living in villages in the Hopa and Borçka districts of Artvin Province, and is likely spoken (or at least understood) by migrant worker communities in the cities of western Turkey. Their dialect is linguistically unique in that it is unaffected by standard Armenian, especially the nineteenth-century reforms and reintroduction of classical Armenian words. It therefore retains a significant Turkish vocabulary that has otherwise been "purged" from Armenian dialects, meaning that in essence Homshetsma is one of the only "pure" dialects of Armenian.[39] In addition to speaking an Armenian dialect, the Hopa Hemshin also share a number of cultural festivals with Armenian Christians, particularly Vardavar.[40] Among Armenian Christians, Vardavar represents the Feast of the Transfiguration of Christ and is usually celebrated in July. However, the festival predates Christianity and has been celebrated in Persian-speaking territories where it is known as *tīrgān* or *āb-rīzān*.[41] The Christian connotation is removed from the Hopa Hemshin festival; however, they do participate in the tradition of throwing water onto one another, which demonstrates the continuities with their pre-Islamic, and pre-Christian, past.

In contrast to the Islamized Armenians discussed in the next section, almost all of the books published in Turkey on the topic of the Hemshin make no mention whatsoever of their Armenian descent.[42] Instead, Turkish authors tend to categorize them as a "Turkish tribe," and the Armenian linguistic connection, if it is addressed at all, is explained by their close proximity to historic Anatolian Armenian communities. Most Hemshin identify as ethnically Turkish, and this is symptomatic of the ethnicizing effect of the modern millet system. Their reluctance to acknowledge Armenian descent is understandable considering that Armenians are possibly the "most hated ethnic group in Turkey nowadays."[43] However, it also contributes to their uniqueness, since they are recognized as both Armenian and Turkish, albeit not always by the same actors.

Tessa Hofman has argued that the case of the Hemshin "questions any limitation of Armenian-ness to the religious constituent of identity. ... [And] has the 'modern' capacity to bridge the traditional gulf between Muslim and Christian identities."[44] This is especially true of the Hopa Hemshin who demonstrate several of the most crucial aspects of Armenian identity by being of Armenian descent and speaking the language, yet do not fulfill the religious criteria of being Christian. Consequently, they have been the focus of much academic and pseudo-academic speculation about Armenian identity among Armenians in Armenia, the Middle East, and elsewhere. In these instances, the primary goal has been to prove their Armenian-ness and disprove their Turkish-ness. For example, one study from Armenia used DNA analysis to argue that the Hopa Hemshin were more closely related to "Western Armenians" (of patrilineal descent from Armenians from Erzurum) than Central Asians (here, Uzbeks).[45] While the near perfect conclusion of this work makes its findings suspect, it nevertheless provides a revealing insight into how Armenians view this curious community.

Unlike the Islamized Armenians, the history of the Hemshin is not related to the Armenian genocide narrative. On the contrary, there is some suggestion that Hemshin people participated in the events as perpetrators, and there is evidence that they at least profited from the deportations by occupying Armenian villages after the First World War.[46] However, the image of Armenians forced to convert to Islam while maintaining their language and culture is highly symbolic. It is important to emphasize that in the general understanding put forward by Armenian nationalists, an Armenian would never willingly convert to Islam, except in cases of immoral individuals who convert for the sake of their own gain, usually at the expense of other Armenians. Incidences of converts becoming oppressors of Armenians, such as the example of Mohammad Beg mentioned above, are cited to support this view. Armenians manipulate these symbols to make them fit within the already existing depictions of Muslims—particularly Turks, as the oppressors of the Armenians—as well as positioning themselves as a people who have persevered and survived despite their persecution. In reality, the Hemshin more closely mirror similar communities around the Middle East, such as the Georgians of Iran, who have changed their religion but have maintained their separateness from their co-religionists in language and traditions.[47] An important development in recent years has been the emergence of Hemshin authors within Turkey who have written about these issues from the Hemshin perspective. These are not limited to the Hopa Hemshin, but include the other Turkish-speaking Hemshin communities of Anatolia. These publications cover topics such as Hemshin identity,[48] and relations between Armenians and the Hemshin before and after the First World War.[49] These writers challenge the notion that the Hemshin people are exclusively the obsession of Armenian intellectuals and have made important contributions to Armenology in their own right.

Armenian descriptions of chance meetings with the Hopa Hemshin are frequently presented as a "rediscovery" of lost cousins. Encounters like these accelerated with Turkey's rapid urbanization during the 1960s, when rural Hopa Hemshin learned of Istanbul Armenians for the first time.[50] However, the Hemshin were already known to the academic elite in Armenia, as the Armenian lexicographer and linguist Hrachia Adjarian had documented the Hemshin dialect in his research. Nevertheless, most Armenians outside of Turkey remained unaware of this group until the French philologist Georges Dumézil began to write about them in the latter half of the twentieth century.

Many Armenian academics have high hopes for the Hopa Hemshin, as many of them still speak the language. Karen Khanlari, for example, writes that as the Hemshin are not particularly religious and definitely could not be described as "Muslim fanatics," they are more likely to accept Armenian identity and show more interest in their "national consciousness."[51] Consequently, there has been a raging debate in the Armenian diaspora about whether the Hemshin could be invited to settle in Armenia, specifically in Karabakh and the Azerbaijani territories around Karabakh occupied by Armenian forces, such as Lachin.[52] These discussions involve little to no consultation with the Hemshin themselves and are purely theoretical, yet they remain highly controversial. From one perspective, Muslims will always side with other Muslims in a conflict, meaning that another war with Azerbaijan might invite Hemshin people, or Islamized Armenians for that matter, to side with them against Armenia. Furthermore, the lack of infrastructure and problems integrating Armenians expelled from Azerbaijan during the Karabakh War (1988–94) has led to the prevalence of the idea that Armenia is not ready for the Hemshin and other "Islamized" Armenians.[53] This remains at the heart of the issue and is probably one reason why the Armenian Republic may never accept them.

The "rediscovery" of the Hopa Hemshin by Armenians is an example of the complex relationship between Armenians and Muslims in Anatolia. While the Hopa Hemshin speak Armenian, they reject any suggestion that they are Armenian, describing themselves instead as Turks. On the other hand, Armenian organizations, while admiring the endurance of the Armenian language among the Hopa Hemshin, remain wary of Muslims, feeling that Islam and Armenian-ness are not mutually compatible. Nevertheless, the Hopa Hemshin, alongside the Islamized Armenians described below, are inadvertently challenging prevailing assumptions about Armenian identity.

*Islamized Armenians*

The Hemshin people, particularly the Hopa Hemshin, are relatively easy to describe since they are a specific ethno-regional group. The situation for other Turkish Muslims of Armenian descent, however, is far more complicated. This begins with the general terms in use and what they describe. In Turkey, the term "hidden" Armenians (*gizli Ermeniler*) is common, while in Armenian-language publications the name varies from "hidden" or "secret" Armenians (*t'ak'un hayer*) to crypto-Armenians (*tsptyal hayer*) to Islamized Armenians (*islamats'vats hayer*). English-language publications reflect these various uses, although "hidden" and "Islamized" Armenians are among the most common. In Kurdish-speaking regions of Turkey, Muslims of Armenian descent are known as *Misilmenî* instead of *Müslüman* in order to distinguish them from other Muslims while also implying that they are in a state of incomplete Islamization.[54] The nomenclature is further complicated regarding what the terms actually describe. For example, Khanlari placed the Hemshin and related groups (specifically Pontian Muslims of Armenian origin) under the category of "Islamized Armenians" because they consider themselves Muslim, while defining the descendants of Armenians who had been forcibly converted to Islam between 1896 and 1923, and retained memory of their origins, as the "Hidden Armenians."[55] However, the boundaries placed on these terms are inevitably contested. Perhaps the most insightful studies so far have been conducted by Ceren Özgül, who noted that the people in question reject the various terms applied to them—hidden Armenians, Muslim Armenians, crypto-Armenians, and Dönme Armenians—as inaccurate if not offensive, which is why she opted instead for "descendants of forcibly Islamized Armenians."[56]

In this chapter, I use the imperfect term "Islamized Armenians" to refer to Muslims who are descended from Armenians who converted to Islam during the period between 1915 and 1923, and who retain a memory of their origins. I have chosen this term and these boundaries as they reflect the group of people who are of most interest to Armenian scholars and commentators writing on the topic. These boundaries are deliberate in that they center on the events of the Armenian genocide, and the (presumably forcible) conversion of these Armenians is an important part of the identity discourses related to the genocide narrative. The term "crypto" is not particularly helpful here as it alludes to the descriptions by the Inquisition of the crypto-Jewish and crypto-Muslim communities of post-Reconquista Spain. It therefore tends to be applied to a person or people from a specific religious community (Armenian Christians) who are, or whose ancestors were, forcibly converted to another religion (Islam) but continue to consciously practice their previous religion, in part or in whole, while publicly professing and practicing the mainstream religion.[57] In many cases, these Muslims of Armenian descent do not consciously practice Christianity, or indeed Islam, so the term is not suitable. Furthermore, "hidden" or "secret" are not accurate adjectives because many of them openly profess their Armenian origins. Muslim Armenians would be ideal if it were not for the identity debate around religion and ethnicity as mentioned above, and such a term would encompass groups such as the Hemshin, despite their different historical origins. Therefore, I settle upon "Islamized Armenians" in this case.

Conversion to Islam was a means of escaping violence during times of persecution and reflected the ethnic nature of the millet system. Indeed, the practice of converting to Islam to escape persecution, as well as a means of changing political identities, continues to take place in the Middle East under Islamist rule.[58] Historically, many Armenian women and children also adopted Islam after being taken into Muslim homes, either as part of forced marriages in the case of women, or as slaves or adoptees in the case of children. These Armenians were converted and given Muslim names. The role of conversion in removing Armenian-ness from Anatolia was evident during the First World War, when the ruling Committee of Union and Progress Party had been considering multiple options in incentivizing Armenian conversion to Islam. Talaat Pasha authorized the forcible marriage of Armenian girls to Muslim men, and exempted Armenian converts from the deportations.[59] Some Armenians managed to escape deportation without converting but were left isolated and gradually assimilated into the local populations. The most notable example are the Yağbasan family, known as the Varto Armenians, who are believed to have never formally converted to Islam, retaining their Christian beliefs privately, but were assimilated into the Kurdish population and registered as "Turks" on their identity cards. The Armenian patriarchate of Istanbul was aware of the Varto Armenians from early on and assisted members of the family who migrated to Istanbul in finding employment.[60] This was unusual and reflected their "crypto-Christian" status, since the patriarchate, and the Armenian Apostolic Church more generally, have been extremely reluctant to baptize or even acknowledge other Muslims of Armenian descent in Anatolia, for reasons that I will outline below.

A small number of Islamized Armenians have returned to Christianity since the 1960s, although some felt pressure from their families—who had wholeheartedly embraced Islam over the generations—not to do so.[61] In many places, the difference between "official" Armenians—those specified as Armenian on their identity cards—and "hidden" Armenians had been difficult to determine because of the way the Turkish government defined Armenian-ness at the beginning of the Kemalist period. For example, in the 1960 census, Armenians who did not speak Armenian were not defined as Armenian, as few Armenians living outside of Istanbul speak Armenian. Islamized Armenians and Turkish-speaking rural Armenians who still practiced Christianity were counted as Turks.[62] In other words, the difference between an Armenian practicing Islam and one practicing Christianity in Anatolia has occasionally been considered irrelevant by the Turkish Republic. This reflects the ethnic nationalism of the Turkish Republic, which sought homogeneity in the face of diversity, sometimes bypassing long-established ethnic differentiation among religious categories to achieve this goal.

Armenian converts, specifically those kidnapped or forcibly converted, have suffered stigmatization into the next generation.[63] This has meant that many, either willingly or unwillingly, remained endogamous for much of the twentieth century. Religiosity varied, however: by the early 1980s, reports on religious freedom noted that "official" Armenians in Viranşehir, near the Syrian border, found it difficult to openly practice their religion, while Armenians in Malatya, four hours to the northwest, experienced little to no pressure to hide their faith.[64] This further blurred the "hidden-ness" and "official-ness" of their Armenian identity.

Many Armenians in the diaspora believe in the necessity for Islamized Armenians to return to their Armenian origins.[65] By this, they essentially mean rebaptism into Christianity, which demonstrates a continuation of the concept that in order to be truly Armenian, one must also be Christian. The reality is, however, that for Islamized Armenians to be able to return to or practice Christianity, or attend Armenian schools, they need to move to Istanbul.[66] This is because Istanbul provides an environment of greater religious freedom than many other places in the provinces. Additionally, the Armenian community of Istanbul was exempted from the deportations of the genocide, and therefore its institutions have remained largely intact and its members are Armenian-speaking, making it the strongest Armenian community in the republic. For this reason, while the vast majority of baptisms of Islamized Armenians have taken place in Istanbul, most of the "reconverts" (*kronadardzner*) were actually from Adıyaman, Batman, Tenceli (Dersim), Diyarbakır, Malatya, Sivas (Sebastia), and other places in Eastern Anatolia.[67]

Additionally, some have returned to Christianity following their emigration to Western countries.[68]

Neither the Turkish state nor the Armenian Apostolic Church has been particularly comfortable with these reconversions. On the one hand, while many Islamized Armenians have retained memory of their previous Armenian names, the courts often make it difficult for reconverts to officially change their names.[69] On the other hand, the Armenian Apostolic Church is reluctant to baptize Islamized Armenians, as they fear confrontation with the state as well as with religious extremists. In Turkey, the Armenian Church adopted an acquiescent approach to relations with the state, which it sees as fundamental in protecting its community. Reconversion is complicated by two factors: reversion from Islam is punishable by death under Islamic law,[70] and religion and ethnicity are intertwined. Punishments for apostasy were abolished in the Ottoman Empire in 1844, and many Armenians who were forcefully converted after this time were free to return to their original faith at a later date; however, social pressure from their Muslim neighbors and intimidation by vigilantes acted as deterrents.[71] The situation is similar in Turkey today. While the law of apostasy does not have legal recognition, it still leaves reconverts, and the churches who baptize them, vulnerable to religious extremists.[72] Outside of Turkey, the Armenian Apostolic Church is equally reluctant to baptize them. For example, in 2015, the Armenian press reported that a group of Islamized Armenians from Turkey had visited Armenia with the intention of receiving baptism, but were refused by the church. A spokesperson for the Etchmiadzin patriarchate stated that the church was suspicious of those who claimed to be Armenians, feeling that some of them were actually hostile to Armenians and were seeking to spy upon or infiltrate Armenian communities in Turkey, especially in the cities of Dersim and Diyarbakır.[73] In response to the incident, the Armenian patriarchate in Etchmiadzin indicated that it would not baptize any Turkish Muslims unless the prospective converts are able to provide a document from an imam stating that they are not recognized as Muslims in their home area.[74] As the church authorities anticipate that the likelihood of an imam being willing to provide such a document would be low, they are essentially disassociating their institution from the issue. This exemplifies the degree of controversy around the subject of Islamized Armenians.

In Turkey, awareness of Armenian ancestry is becoming less taboo and popularized. These are among the changes in Turkish identity over the past two decades allowing for more diversity and indeed a celebration, sometimes termed "neo-Ottomanism," which has been especially pervasive following the election of the Justice and Development Party in 2002. These do not necessarily involve a need to return to Christianity, although there have been a few high-profile reconverts, such as Professor Emin Alıcı, a former rector at Dokuz Eylül University in Izmir.[75] More often than not, these emerge as public acknowledgments of Armenian ancestry. An example of this is Fethiye Çetin, a well-known human rights lawyer, who published a memoir on her Armenian grandmother.[76] Her story is presented as a hidden history of Turkey, the untold secret Armenian origins of Anatolia becoming less taboo, but of course accounts such as Çetin's avoid labeling the events as genocide, since this remains a red line. Nevertheless, in the Armenian diaspora, where books like Çetin's are read or at least discussed, these memoirs are intrinsically linked to the Armenian genocide. The Hrant Dink Foundation has also worked to bring issues concerning Islamized Armenians to the forefront, running an academic conference on the topic and publishing the proceedings.[77] Publications like these have given a voice to Islamized Armenians and Hemshin people that has previously been largely absent from the discussion.

## *Conclusion*

Overall, the Armenian perception of "Armenian Muslims" as a contradiction is gradually being challenged, although the centrality of Christianity, nominal or otherwise, to Armenian identity still holds fast. In the Turkish context, the ethnic gulf that separates the Armenian Christian from the Turkish Muslim is a potent legacy of the millet system, which in the modern context has "ethnicized" religious identities. It is important to remember that it is not only the Turkish state that has created this situation; the Armenian leadership—both clerical and secular—also views this arrangement favorably and has consequently sought to promote it.

The synonymy between Armenian-ness and Christianity has developed through the leadership of the Armenian Apostolic Church, specifically the strong association of the church with the Armenian language and nation. This connection emerged over the centuries through the governing role that the church often adopted during times of occupation and dispersion, and especially under the millet system of the Ottoman Empire. For this reason, conversion to any other religion is rejected, since an Armenian who does so ceases to be Armenian. This contributes to the lack of recognition of Muslims of Armenian descent. The idea of Islam as oppositional and oppressive developed over the centuries, although this perception has also been ethicized with the principal enemy of the Armenians being presented as the Turks, instead of Muslims in general.

It is therefore interesting to see that there has been a change in attitude in the Armenian diaspora toward Muslim people of Armenian descent who are living in Turkey. Armenians hold high hopes for one such group, the Hopa Hemshin, who have continued to speak the Armenian language despite converting centuries ago. However, the issue remains controversial, and the Hopa Hemshin have until now rejected their Armenian-ness, describing themselves as Turks, and demonstrating the continuing power of the millet system in defining ethnic identity into the "secular" republican period. The second group, the Islamized Armenians, have a symbolic importance for the Armenian diaspora because of their relationship with the narrative of the Armenian genocide, particularly as Armenians forcibly converted to Islam. For this reason, most Armenian commentators see their return to Christianity as integral to their reclaiming of their Armenian-ness. However, this creates two problems, since many are reluctant to be baptized, and the Armenian Church itself, both within and outside Turkey, is cautious of baptizing them. Nevertheless, the contemplation of the potential Armenian-ness of both the Hopa Hemshin and Islamized Armenians, coupled with the enthusiastic engagement by the diaspora with these two groups, demonstrates that there is a change afoot in modern conceptions of what it is to be an Armenian.

7

# COLORBLIND OR BLINDED BY COLOR?

## RACE, ETHNICITY, AND IDENTITY IN IRAN

*Firoozeh Kashani-Sabet*

Theoretical conversations about race in Iranian studies, unlike debates about ethnicity, tribal politics, and, more recently, slavery, remain rudimentary in their investigation of identity formation, inequality, and minority cultures. Although scholars have considered the complex processes informing identity politics in Iran, including racialist discourses in nationalist mythmaking, questions about race have not evoked fervent scholarly exchanges as in other countries, especially in the United States, France, South Africa, Egypt, and Britain.[1] Some of this scholarly inertia may result from the absence of political mechanisms enabling civil dissent rooted in race—as distinct from ethnicity and religion—in Iranian society. Other forms of political opposition of an ethnic, gendered, religious, or tribal character have appeared when violence and separatism rooted in race—especially in phenotype racism—typically did not. Modern Iranian society, unlike some of the countries mentioned above, did not historically experience significant race riots or political turmoil resulting principally from racial conflicts, though ethnic divisions at times have had racial overtones. These unique political factors perhaps partly explain the inchoate nature of scholarship on race relations in Iran.

To depict Iranian society—historically or otherwise—as immune to race, however, would be a fallacy. As poignantly enacted in the movie *Bashu: The Little Stranger*, directed by Bahram Beizai in 1986, racism rooted in differences of phenotype occurs in Iranian society and has a historical precedent. Bashu, a boy who loses his family in the war-torn region of southern Iran during the Iran–Iraq War, escapes the carnage and seeks solace in the lush pastures of Gilan, where a village woman named Nai takes him in with her two young children. Nai, whose husband has left in search of employment, manages all aspects of her household. She finds Bashu and takes him in, despite the communication gap between them. Bashu speaks a different dialect from Nai, though he also knows Persian. Nai communicates principally in the Gilaki dialect, while Bashu converses in a southern dialect. When the village elders and Nai's relatives visit to see the boy, they express dismay at his manners and his dark skin. One character disdainfully compares his skin color to that of a light bulb darkened by smoke (*lamp-e dud bigifte*). In a letter, Nai herself describes Bashu to her husband as *ita siyah ray*—"a black boy." In another telling episode, Nai finds herself in an altercation with the same villagers, and in defense of Bashu promises to wash away his dark skin. As she takes him to a river to scour his dark complexion, Nai despairs that his coloring does not lighten at all.[2]

Throughout the film, the feeling of displacement frequently overwhelms Bashu, who is beset by traumatic memories of the war and especially by the loss of his mother. He recalls the distinctive melodies of southern *bandari* music and wishes to reproduce those tunes, which echo with dissonance in his new surroundings. Still, Bashu slowly integrates himself in Nai's life, despite the eruption of occasional ethnic, racial, and social clashes between him and the other villagers. Bashu does not understand Gilaki and converses either in Persian or in a southern dialect. The movie associates Bashu's darkness with his presumptive "Arab" ethnicity despite the fact that Bashu could ostensibly be Persian or South Asian—cultures that also flourished in much of southern Iran. Bashu need not necessarily be of African descent, either, and the discrimination he faces may not stem from a legacy of enslavement, but rather because he is dark-skinned. The movie thus raises interesting questions about identity and racism in Iran.

In seeking areas of commonality, one of the young boys in the village tells Bashu to speak in the language of a Persian schoolbook to bridge the communication gap between them, which Bashu eventually does. As time passes, Nai herself tries to integrate more Persian words into her speech to communicate better with Bashu. In a moving scene toward the end of the film, when Nai's husband returns home, he embraces Bashu, who realizes that the father has lost an arm and suffers from trauma himself. Although the movie ends with the family's compassionate acceptance of Bashu as an adoptive son, such attempts to reconcile differences of ethnicity, language, and race in a harmonious embrace of cultural diversity in Iran remain fraught with conflict.

Discrimination rooted in differences of skin color, culture, or ethnicity exists in certain Iranian regional communities. For example, a popular ditty commonly recited in the Gilaki dialect further encapsulates the disdainful attitude of northern, often lighter-skinned Iranians, toward dark-skinned peoples: *Bushu, bushu, man tere nakham / tu siyahi tere nakham / tu balayi tere nakham* (Go away, go away, I don't want you / You are black, I don't want you / You are devious, I don't want you). The movie, *Bashu*, which unfolds in the northern province of Gilan, portrays this initial knee-jerk racism toward the dark-skinned stranger who has intruded upon this quiet village.[3] In this rhyme, darkness becomes equated with deviousness. In the case of Bashu, this discrimination is coupled with distrust of the stranger—hence the movie's subtitle (*gharibah-i kuchak*). This limited sample of a regional cultural mindset indicates that despite the absence of rampant race riots, Iran, too, has grappled with racism.

The latest scholarship in Iranian historiography, building on previous studies of identity formation, racialist discourse, and nationalism, examines elements of ethnicity and race.[4] In particular, the burgeoning interest in the history of Afro-Iranians has spurred conversations about the legacy of slavery in Iran. However, the subject of phenotype racism has been inadequately investigated in these studies, though a general consensus has emerged that black-skinned slaves typically experienced racism in ways that white slaves did not.

Abu'l Qasim Afnan, a relative of the Babi leader Sayyid Ali Muhammad Shirazi, writes about the experiences of slaves in the household of the Bab, the leader of a spiritual movement and sociopolitical revolt during the Qajar period. Afnan contends that "[d]ark-skinned Africans and white-skinned Georgians and Caucasians might be included among the common slaves in the cities of Iran, even though the white slaves usually received preferential treatment and lived under better conditions."[5] White slaves in Iran also suffered from inequality, however, and some Georgian women became concubines of Iranian soldiers.[6]

One of the Bab's prominent disciples—Mirza Husayn Ali Nuri, known as Baha'ullah—gave rise to the religion of Bahaism, and Baha'ullah famously opposed the institution of slavery.[7] In 1911, his son Abdul Baha addressed the First Universal Races Congress at the University of London—a gathering that included a diverse host of topics related to race and ethnicity. The congress had lofty ideals, and another noteworthy participant—W. E. B. Dubois—delivered a paper there. As Canadian anthropologist Alexander Francis Chamberlain hoped, despite his questionable views on race,

> the dream of a white man's world shall fade away unregretted into the limbo of things men willingly have let die, and the real evolution of man [will] begin with the consenting co-operating and the stimulating genius of all the races of man. Toward that end the First Universal Races Congress will have done much.[8]

Although Abdul Baha did not arrive in time for the event, a letter was read on his behalf. As he explained, "The world is in a warlike condition and its races are hostile one to the other. The darkness of difference surrounds them, and the light of kindness grows dim."[9] Yet he pleaded for the unity of humankind through his divine call: "Races and nations, with their different creeds, are coming under the Word of Unity in love and in peace."[10] Abdul Baha later traveled to the United States in 1912 and promoted tolerance between blacks and whites.[11]

Despite such appeals for racial tolerance, Iran, like the other countries represented at the congress, grappled with racism, which was not limited to skin color but also extended to ethnicity. Vanessa Martin makes a distinction between social discrimination based on race and institutionalized racism as practiced in the United States and South Africa. She concludes that despite the absence of institutionalized racism of the type found in those countries, "racial awareness existed," as attested by "the sale price of slaves" given that light-skinned slaves yielded higher bids.[12] Similarly, through a fascinating analysis of literary sources, Minoo Southgate traces the etymology of various terms and expressions to show the negative connotations of the term "zangi," meaning from Zanzibar, Egypt, or Ethiopia. She shows the association of blackness (or specifically *zangi*) with "darkness, evil, sin, or a state of error" in well-known works of classical Persian literature and argues that some Persian idioms "regarded negroid features and the black skin color to be ugly."[13] As she concludes, while Iran faced invasions from the Mongols and the Ottomans in its early modern history, major works of Persian literature tended not to depict these attackers and instead focused on the ferocity of black slaves. Southgate concludes that one "is left, therefore, with color-consciousness and the perception of the blacks as 'the Other' (simply because of their physical differences) as the major source of the attack against them."[14] The literature on slavery in Iran has not addressed the issue of black slaves being feared by Iranians of the medieval era, who viewed them as members of an invading army. Classical Persian literature, as Southgate notes, regarded slave communities as distinct from indigenous Iranian communities that did not fully assimilate in the span of several centuries. One wonders what impact those conflicts may have had in hoisting barriers against their assimilation and in reinforcing Iranian discrimination against blacks in subsequent historical eras.

That such discrimination exists remains incontrovertible. Individuals of African descent typically did not hold high offices in post-emancipation Iran—a possible indicator of racist practices. Political office was not legally prohibited to Iranians based on skin color, though the lack of economic and political mobility experienced by some former slaves and peasants likely had a similar effect. We know little about the upward mobility (or what existed) of African Iranians in the post-emancipation era.[15] In fact, little information exists on the lives of former slaves, whether African or Georgian, black or white. However, the scholarship on slavery and emancipation in Iran, though related to race, has not adequately addressed racism. Perhaps ongoing research into the history of African Iranians through an analysis of photographs, visual sources, and other historical records can shed light on this subject.[16] These important distinctions differentiate Iran's experiences with race from those occurring elsewhere.

Relatedly, neither the term "Afro-Iranian" nor "Afro-Iran" was coined as a result of the current interest in recovering their history. Rather, awareness of "Afro-Iranians" as a distinct group of Iranians occurred within the burgeoning alliances forged between Afro-Asian communities during the era of decolonization.[17] Moreover, in Iran, a multiracial or multiethnic background or heritage did not typically express itself as a hyphenated identity. Official or semi-official markers of identity connoting a multicultural background (such as *irani-yeh arab* or *iraniyeh ifriqa'i* or *ifriqa'i-yeh irani*) do not formally or legally exist in Iran, though they can occur as informal descriptors. Rather, many Iranians latched on to their regional identities even as they embrace Iranian political citizenship. The idea of Iran as an ethnic amalgam, as I have argued elsewhere, though significant in the formation of modern Iranian citizenship in the post-constitutional period, did not bring about full ethnic assimilation. Iranians still maintained their regional ethnicities even as many, though not all, identified with a common homeland.

This chapter deals principally with racism rooted in ethnicity. It considers the ways in which dark skin, and not specifically black skin, became associated with various forms of "othering" and discrimination in Iran even as it demonstrates the ways in which Persians, too, faced discrimination by Arabs and the British in the Persian Gulf. It does not focus on the Afro-Iranian community per se, but it considers the origins and expression of various forms of racism, including phenotype racism, in Iran. Notably, the chapter evaluates the ways in which Arabness became associated with certain derogatory stereotypes in Iran and simultaneously considers the ways in which Arabian culture and British imperial designs and support for Arab communities have effaced the Persianiate presence there. Iran's incorporation of theories of race, its eventual intellectual move away from Aryan discourses, and the solidarity of key Iranian intellectuals with the struggles of African nations demonstrated a significant shift in the country's awareness of race and racism.

### *Theoretical conversations about race and nation*

Political dissent in the Middle East centers on differences in race, ethnicity, and religion. These tensions manifested themselves in waves of protests and separatist movements. In Iran, too, nationalism came in fits and starts, and the cultural landscape promptly became a site of contestation. A series of lopsided wars against the Great Powers brought the only two independent states of the Middle East, the Ottoman Empire and Iran, face-to-face with the imposition of imperialism and separatist movements grounded in ethnic and at times religious distinctiveness. In the Persian Gulf region, Great Britain mapped out a new and ill-conceived topography that emphasized ethno-linguistic difference, often poorly conceived, more than cultural contiguity. Under the watchful eyes of colonial powers and administrators such as Lord Curzon and Arnold Wilson, the Ottoman Empire and Iran separately adopted notions of nationhood that divided the region along ethnic and linguistic lines, which may not have corresponded to the reality on the ground.[18]

Historians and social scientists focusing on race in France, South Africa, the United States, and Latin America have written extensively on why racial politics has played a divisive and formative role in their societies.[19] In the 1980s, political theorists such as Ernest Gellner, Eric Hobsbawm, and Benedict Anderson, among others, contributed to these conversations by criticizing the primordial conceptions of nation-states. They focused attention on the tools of nation-building (journalism, censuses, maps) to "invent" a tradition of political existence.[20] Racism became embedded in discourses of nationalism as communities strove to make themselves relevant, and even superior, to regional rivals. This juxtaposition typifies the racialized discourses that have historically pitted Arabs and Persians against one another—especially in Iran, Iraq, and the Persian Gulf—and explains in part the drive for cultural hegemony currently pursued by these states.

Cultural critic Étienne Balibar argues that racism "inscribes itself in practices (forms of violence, contempt, intolerance, humiliation and exploitation), in discourses and representations ... which are articulated around stigmata of otherness (name, skin colour, religious practices)."[21] While acts of violence are to be distinguished from mindsets that convey racism—derogatory behavior, professional misconduct, or discrimination—such attitudes often breed violence rooted in racism. Middle Eastern nationalisms necessarily incorporated racist features for several reasons: first, they often derived from Western concepts of nationhood that emphasized the racial superiority of one group over another; second, they were often defensive in nature as states attempted to cohere the ethnically diverse territories they had acquired; and finally, Middle Eastern states imposed cultures of ethno-linguistic homogeneity that led to the expurgation of minority cultures and languages. Middle Eastern nationalisms deployed notions of racial hierarchy to justify authoritarian directives that imposed the superiority of one community over another.

Anthropologists have scrutinized the ways in which ethnic designations often lacked historicity. Clifford Geertz deconstructed the "primordial attachments" of various social groups.[22] As he argued, "disaffection based on race, language, or culture threatens partition, irredentism, or merger, a redrawing of the very limits of the state, a new definition of its domain."[23] In Iran, too, such attachments and primeval bonds spurred separatist movements rooted in cultural difference. One scholar has contended that religion and language are the most important determinants of ethnicity in Iran, although some communities "display certain physical characteristics."[24] These cultural ties of language and ethnicity, though forged locally, were exploited by Western colonial administrators working to advance the cause of empire, and threatened Iran's territorial integrity. Nineteenth-century European writers, with scant knowledge of local culture, created ethnographic maps to explain regional differences in dress, speech, race, and ethnicity, often based on cursory and uncorroborated observation. Designations of race and ethnicity became especially significant as Iran and its neighbors were forced to define boundary lines intended to create distinct communities along newly recognized borders.

Yet the historical process of knowledge production—that is, a careful examination of assumptions about race, language, and ethnicity in accounts of colonial administrators and Western travelers—has scarcely been explored. For at no point would it have been facile to distinguish with reasonable accuracy among large communities of itinerant Arabs, Turks, Baluchis, or Persians, in areas of long-standing and regular contact such as in the borderlands. Yet a scrupulous deconstruction of such truisms is essential to conversations about race and ethnicity in Iran and the Persian Gulf given the implications for ethnic and racial minorities in many of these communities.

My research, while building on this extensive literature, departs from some of the premises of key theorists and historians in specific ways. First, while I recognize that Iran, like other societies of the post-First World War Middle East, forged a culture of homogeneity to create unity by suppressing cultural difference, I also contend that colonial powers, most notably Britain in Iran and the Persian Gulf, emphasized and exploited racial and ethnic divides in ways that were far more complicated in reality. The manner in which some European travelers, colonial administrators, or scholars affixed ethnic or racial designations such as "Arab," "Turk," and "Persian" was at times erroneous and based on a limited understanding of local culture and languages. Such cultural labels, despite their inexactitude, often assumed the status of fact in colonial administration and nationalist mythmaking.

As anthropologist Frederik Barth contends, "Since belonging to an ethnic category implies being a certain kind of person, having that basic identity, it also implies a claim to be judged, and to judge oneself, by those standards that are relevant to that identity."[25] Barth, who was no stranger to Iran—having studied in 1958 the nomadic population of the Basseri tribe in southern Iran—composed a ground-breaking study that laid out the migrating lifestyle and cultural mores of this community. Barth observed that the Fars region "is an area of great complexity and admixture, and tribal units are best defined by political, rather than ethnic or geographical criteria."[26] He emphasized further that while members of the Basseri tribe were principally Persian-speaking, "using a dialect very close to the urban people of Shiraz town," many were also bilingual in either Arabic or Turkish. Barth emphasized the multilingualism of this community without undermining the dominant affiliation of the tribe with a particular political group. Considered the first major analysis of "Persian nomadism,"[27] Barth's research demonstrated that the metrics used to delineate identity did not remain static over time, but identity remained complex and composed of multiple cultural units. Tribal and ethnic categories in Iran and its environs, including Iraq or the Persian Gulf, drew on a multitude of cultural markers such as tribal affiliation, kinship ties, locale, language, or religion. In the absence of censuses calling for self-identification, scholars must carefully deconstruct historical assumptions about race and ethnicity in these borderlands.

Ethnic and racial designations of the inhabitants of Iran often lacked historical and scientific accuracy or genetic specificity. Politics infused the designation of ethnic and racial markers, which were manipulated at times to promote specific imperial or national objectives. Iranian debates about race and ethnicity, while broadly mimicking social patterns in other contexts, also reflected regional preoccupations. For Iran, the ethnic diversity of its population became a thorny political issue, one exploited by its neighbors, rivals, and detractors. By contrast, the Iranian presence in neighboring communities as a minority ethnic culture has received scant scholarly attention precisely because regional nationalisms have attempted to efface Persianate communities from official historical narratives outside of Iran.[28]

### *Anthropologies of race and language*

In 1771, when Sir William Jones published his monumental but flawed *Grammar of the Persian Language*, his intent was not to categorize the races of humanity.[29] Yet Jones faced questions about the origin of races and languages, and his speculations about the movements of peoples and the linguistic roots spurred discussion of race.[30] Building on the work of Jones and others, nineteenth-century observers of the Persian scene became similarly interested in "Oriental" antiquity. European travelers, many of whom were colonial officials, often hypothesized about race and strove to classify the region based on language and race, as well as religious or tribal affiliation. Philologists tried to locate the provenance of languages, while anthropologists attempted to devise ways to distinguish among races and ethnicities.

Ethnographic observations recorded by travelers and scholars—if not yet by trained anthropologists—provided the necessary fodder with which to speculate about language and race. In 1805, the term "anthropologist," with its recognizable meaning, appeared in Britain, and, by 1884, anthropology had assumed its position as a distinct discipline aligned with natural history.[31] Anthropology delved into the question of human evolution, and combined studies of culture and the natural sciences.

The rise of anthropology in the nineteenth century fueled curiosity about the divergences of race and language, and the Middle East became a locus of numerous such anthropological inquiries. The data collected by diplomats, boundary negotiators, and scholars (geographers, physicians, linguists, philologists, and ethnographers) came with theories intended to explain divergences in human experiences and cultures. More importantly, anthropologists of that generation often published their findings not only in specialist journals but also in publications for a general readership. Thus their ideas about race, language, and culture in the Middle East gained currency.[32] Anthropology provided the institutional and academic framework for the investigation of ideas related to race and language in an ethnographic context.[33]

Western writers tended to use the categories of race and ethnicity interchangeably, and a clear demarcation did not always exist between an ethnicity and a race. Thus monikers such as Arab, Turk, or Persian were described as "races" and eventually as markers of nationality, while physical characteristics and differences in phenotype also resulted in racial classification. Examples of the methods that British ethnologists and anthropologists employed to distinguish races appeared in various anthropological journals. In 1877, a leading British anthropological journal distinguished among the peoples in the Middle East through an evaluation of hair specimens. An Arab hair was described as having an "elongated irregular ellipsis." Whereas the "Aryans of Asia, the Persians, and the Hindoos, for instance, whose hair is very black, belong either to the second or third category; either their hair presents the medullary coloured thread, or nothing particular can be distinguished in the centre."[34] If differences between Middle Eastern individuals were based at times on such spurious "science" and outlandish markers of race or ethnicity, then British observations about race and ethnicity, which were used at times to justify boundary delineations in Iran and its environs, should be reconsidered.

At times, there was little consensus on the connection between the provenance of languages and races. As one observer contended, "linguistic ethnologists have spent much vain labour in attempts to prove that language is a reliable test of the Races of Man." Reviewing the many scenarios in which language and race may have been conflated in the western Persian Gulf region and Arabia, for example, this author remarked that "we cannot be sure that in remote times other races speaking other languages may not have existed in Arabia as in other parts of the world, overwhelmed or extirpated by Arabs," as in Syria and Egypt, which were "countries inhabited by races distinct from the Arabian."[35] Nonetheless, the confusion over race and language persisted in British, and more generally in European, descriptions of Middle Eastern peoples, and such accounts sometimes propagated questionable theories about the region's pedigrees of language, ethnicity, and race. The preoccupation with race reflected a desire to assert Western superiority.

Before the nineteenth century, the occasional European traveler to Iran did not always view his Iranian hosts as "white" or even as attractive. Sir John Chardin infamously wrote, "The blood of the Persian is coarse. ... They are ugly, deformed ... having a rough skin and a tainted color."[36] Chardin remarks that this physical characteristic of Persians is especially conspicuous in the borderlands of Iran and India. He differentiates, however, between Iranians of the southwest region and those in other parts of the empire. As he describes it, "the Persian blood has presently become very beautiful, due to the mixing of blood between the Georgians and Circassians, who are alluringly endowed by nature as most attractive people."[37] Without this mixing of Caucasian and Persian blood, Chardin was convinced that Persians would remain among the most unattractive peoples as their blood would have mixed with the Tatars, who inhabited the region between the Caspian Sea and China, thus giving them Asian features and their skin tone "a disagreeable tint of yellow and black."[38] Though crude and subjective, Chardin's words were nonetheless cited by several nineteenth-century writers opining on the history of race and peoples in the East.[39]

Other observers claimed that "the modern Persians are a very mixed race, formed by the commingling of Persians, Arabs, Turks, Tatars, Mongols and natives of the Caucasian isthmus."[40] James Cowles Prichard, credited with pioneering the fields of British ethnology and anthropology, offered a critique of Chardin, noting the improbability that "sufficient numbers" of Circassians had been brought to Iran "to produce any impression on the organic character of the race."[41] Prichard attributes the difference in pigmentation among Iranians of the northern and southern shores to the differences in climate. In 1865, Russian diplomat and ethnographer Nikolai Khanykov offered an interesting assessment of the Iranian peoples. As was vogue at that time, Khanykov engaged in cranial research and relied on other bodily measurements to expound on his ideas. In arguing for the similarity of the Tadjik and the Persian, Khanykov observed among them certain primitive Iranian features: "Generally, they are of a high stature; they have black eyes and black hair."[42] In addition, he perceived a distinction between the eastern and western Persian, concluding that "the Persian blood was improved by crossing during more than 2000 years with various populations, but especially with Semites and Turanians."[43] While it would be difficult to determine the quality of "Persianness" from such descriptions, it is evident that Khanykov viewed the Persian ethnicity or race as an admixture of races and cultures.

Other ethnologists offered additional explanations for the differences between such social groups. In 1867, John Crawford, writing for the Ethnological Society of London, contended that the "complexion of the European is a white of various tints; that of the Asiatic always more or less swarthy." He added that the "beauty and symmetry of person would seem to decrease as we proceed from West to East. The Persians are less handsome than the Georgians."[44] Such a view reinforced the belief that "Asiatics," including Iranians, were not considered white by some European writers.

As the debate over Aryanism raged in nineteenth-century Europe, Iran too became a locus of those conversations.[45] Many writers declared that ancient Iranian languages belonged to the Indo-European branch of languages. But what did that mean from a racial perspective? In 1874, the *American Cyclopaedia* declared that the "Iranic or Persian races form a branch of the Aryan or Indo-European family." However, it was unclear whether this characterization conferred upon Persians the label "white."[46] British philologist Hyde Clarke contended that the "Persian and Western European are diverse in every Oriental eye; and they are connected by men of science because they speak Indo-European languages and have white skins."[47] Yet some of Clarke's philological assertions did not fully convince his fellow scholars and have raised controversy.[48]

Other travelers and geographers, especially British adventurers who visited and surveyed the country in the nineteenth century, described Iran as a country of mixed races and ethnicities, thereby depicting a very heterogeneous racial and ethnic community. One might even argue that some British writers at times tended to overstate the ethno-linguistic differences among the Kurds, Baluchs, Lors, and Persians, given that it would be difficult to identify or to track a "pure" Persian race at any moment in history.[49] Yet these ethno-linguistic divisions persisted, fueling both an ardent Persian nationalist sentiment and fervent separatist movements.

### *The Arab/Persian binary*

While some European writers may have tried in vain to distinguish an Arab from a Persian in the borderlands, Islamic writers tended to have some inkling about their identity. Many indigenous medieval geographers and writers identified with specific ethnic communities.[50] As Bernard Lewis observed, in premodern Middle Eastern societies, while there was an awareness of ethnic difference, such divisions did not necessarily appear to be rooted in race: "As in the Qur'an, so also in ancient Arabian poetry, we find an awareness of difference—the sentiment of an Arab as against a Persian, Greek or other identity. We do not, however, find any clear indication that this was felt in racial terms."[51] The medieval history of Islam also provides ample evidence of the antipathy between groups, notably the Arabs and Persians. As Hamid Dabashi astutely remarks, "The constitution of 'the Persian' as the morally corrupt alterity of 'the Arab' was definitive to the medieval imperial caliphate."[52] Persian resistance to Arab imperialism became a key trope of the medieval era—and one that would assume a different character in the modern period, when much of the Middle East would be redrawn after the First World War and labeled predominantly "Arab" despite the ethnic and religious pluralism of those states.

Southern Iran and the Persian Gulf became contested terrain as Britain, the Ottoman Empire, and Iran vied for control. At the same time, various Arab tribes sought to assert their autonomy through alliances with Britain, whose officials gave prominence to Arab claims and frequently depicted the region as "Arab." Even provinces that fell within Iran's domains constantly had to assert their connection to the country. In the nineteenth century, when Mirza Ja'far Khan Mushir al-Dawlah embarked on his mission to delineate Iran's boundary with the Ottoman Empire, he provided ample evidence of Khuzistan as an integral historical portion of Iran. According to Mirza Ja'far Khan, the Ka'ab Arab tribe, which had migrated there from Najd after the rise of Islam, initially professed Sunnism, but they had abandoned the Sunni sect and embraced Shi'ism during the Safavid era.[53] Qajar writers showed sensitivity to Iran's precarious hold over the province of Khuzistan. In his travelogue, famed astronomer and geographer Abd al-Ghaffar Najm al-Mulk observed that foreign powers showed little interest in seeing Iran assert its influence there.[54]

In describing the province of Khuzistan, however, George Nathaniel Curzon, the future viceroy of India, seemed unaware of Iran's history there. He maintained that "the region is either pure Arab, or, more frequently mixed Arab and Persian." He noted that the Arab element arrived with the Islamic conquest of Iran and that "spontaneous immigration" populated the region with more Arabs. Yet the province presumably included many indigenous Persians, too, who had maintained a significant presence in Khuzistan, since rarely does the ethnic makeup of an entire region become fully subsumed under the ethnic identity of an immigrant community. As Curzon remarked, "Few of these Arab tribes have kept their blood undefiled. The majority have intermingled with Persians," to the point that "the Persian dress and even the Persian religion have been in the main adopted."[55] This inconsistency in Curzon's description of Khuzistan—as "pure Arab" on the one hand, yet dominated by the Persian element on the other—manifests his intent to emphasize the Arabness of the region despite his observations to the contrary. Like other British administrators adjudicating sovereignty over Iran's borderlands, Curzon relied on the slippery elision of race and ethnicity to marshal evidence in favor of a mixed culture that privileged the Arab component. Similarly, Colonel Thomas Holdich, who had surveyed the boundaries of Baluchistan and Afghanistan, noted in 1899 that southern Baluchistan initially had a significant Persian presence and later mixed with Arabs. Regarding the racial makeup of the region, Holdich noted that while there is a fusion of the two ethnicities, in the Indus Valley—as in Makran, "the language of all tribes alike is now that archaic form of Persian which we call Baluchi." Yet he acknowledged an "Arab extraction" in some Baluch tribes.[56]

Persianate writers of the nineteenth century, most notably Mirza Fath Ali Akhundzade and Mirza Aqa Khan Kermani, were less sanguine about the mixing of Arab and Persian communities. In his fifth sermon, Kermani contended that Caucasians were the "most superior, most authentic, and most attractive" of all human types (*jins*). He distinguished the Caucasian from other races such as the "Chinese" (*chini*) and *zangi*. Kermani embraced notions of geographic determinism, contending that the natural environment also influenced the blood type of its inhabitants. As he explained, "The blood of a *zangi* or the shape of the nose of *habashi* differs from the blood of an Englishman or the nose type of a Parisian."[57] Thus, Kermani endorsed general racial hierarchies also common in Europe to argue for the superiority of Caucasian communities. Kermani mocked regional Iranian communities as well, concluding that the "best types" (*behtarin ajnas*) of people were those who could provide for themselves and their societies without seeking outside assistance. Yet he viewed the infiltration of Arabs in Iran, which he disdainfully labeled "the Arab plague," as ill-suited to the Persian temperament.[58] These claims became explored more fully during the interwar period with the emergence of the Iranian discipline of anthropology (*mardum shinasi*).[59]

During the constitutional period of 1906–11, Persian journalists expressed grave concern over the vulnerability of Iranians in the island of Abu Musa and also about control over the port of Bandar Abbas. One writer urged the Persian community of Bandar Abbas to send a local *anjuman* (or sociopolitical organization) to Bushehr for political representation and to redouble efforts to counter any foreign control over this strategically and economically significant port.[60] The Persian word, *nezhad*, meaning race, is also used to address "the fraternity of racial Iranians" (*baradaran-i irani nezhad*).[61]

Iran struggled to maintain its territorial independence during the Great War and its aftermath. In the process, Iranians increasingly asserted their "Persianness," especially when faced with staunch British support for Arab independence movements. British efforts to eclipse Persian influence and sovereignty in contested regions of Iraq and the Persian Gulf further fueled the conflicts in those borderlands. Reza Shah suppressed the separatist aspirations of Shaykh Khazʿal in Khuzistan and also subdued the influence of other tribes throughout the country before claiming the throne. Arab nationalist historiography has attempted to assert the "Arabness" of Khuzistan, yet newspaper articles written in the early twentieth century also gave voice to a vibrant "Persian" community there that was concerned with the forfeiture of the southern Persian Gulf littoral due to British intrigues. Some Iranian writers in the south expressed grave concern over the erosion of Persian culture there.[62] In 1919, one leader, Haji Hasan Shabbut, the hereditary head of Kut in Iraq, recognized Khazʿal's mixed blood, even while claiming him an Arab. Shabbut described Khazʿal in the following way: "It is true that he is half Persian, but he has Arab ideas."[63] Even leaders indigenous to the region found it difficult to avoid the politics of race and ethnicity.

Simultaneously, the post-First World War history of the Middle East outside of Turkey and Iran became scripted largely as a history of Arab dispossession. Although Arab communities had cooperated with Allied powers during the First World War, many became victims of colonialism, and several Arab countries were unable to achieve independence until the Second World War or after. In response, Arabs also asserted their ethnic distinctiveness. As Albert Hourani explained:

> The First World War ended with the final disappearance of the Ottoman Empire. Out of the ruins of the empire a new independent state of Turkey emerged, but the Arab provinces were placed under British and French control; the whole of the Arabic-speaking world was now under European rule, except for parts of the Arabian Peninsula.[64]

By the last two decades of the nineteenth century, Hourani declared that the Ottoman Empire had become largely a "Turco-Arab" state.[65] Such a statement, however, glossed over the ethnic and racial diversity of what Hourani termed "the Arabic-speaking world," which also included peoples of Persian, Turkish, Assyrian, and Kurdish heritage, among others, and who spoke

Arabic alongside other languages. As Sukru Hanioglu has pointed out, the inhabitants of the Ottoman Empire were, in fact, quite polyglot and culturally diverse in the years leading up to the Great War. As late as 1911, when "the Union of All Ottoman Empires" publicized a call for Ottoman subjects to unite themselves, "it did so in nine languages: Ottoman Turkish, Arabic, Armenian, Bulgarian, Greek, Ladino, Serbian, Syriac (in two different scripts, Nestorian and Serta), and French."[66] Yet Hourani, himself British-trained, was not alone in ascribing too much of the modern Middle East a predominantly Arab or "Turco-Arab" character, bereft of its other long-standing ethnicities and communities.

In 1917, Gilbert Ernest Hubbard, secretary of the Ottoman–Iranian boundary commission—and presumably an official familiar with borderland populations—declared unequivocally that in "the first place all Mesopotamia is Arab country." Though Hubbard recognized the different ethnic communities living in contiguity along this vague boundary, he contended that the "neat line which provides a northern limit to Arabia on many of our maps has no basis in fact, and even the frontier between the Turkish and Persian Empires, in this particular section, marks no ethnical or linguistic boundary." Hubbard determined that "a frontier may be geographical, racial, linguistic, religious, even purely artificial."[67] By his account, delineation of the Ottoman–Iranian boundary drew on multiple modes of boundary-making, which included tribal, religious, and linguistic affiliation. As such, he contended that the frontier is "racial, in the south particularly, where it separates Iranian from Semitic, or, to be more specific, Lur from Arab."[68] Yet the process of distinguishing a Lur from an Arab was likely as fraught with ambiguity and error as the determination of the vague boundary itself.

Hubbard went so far as to assert that "the proportion of racial Turks in Irak and of racial Persians in Arabistan is almost negligible, and the spoken language is Arabic throughout."[69] Such a broad erasure of the ethnic diversity of the southern Persian Gulf littoral belied the co-existence of long-standing non-Arab (South Asian, Persian, African) communities, many of whom had arrived as itinerants, pilgrims, and merchants and had eventually made their domicile there. Hubbard's assessment of the ethnic makeup of the population of these shores is puzzling given his contention that the Arab tribes were largely "nomadic" and thus had an intermittent presence along these shores.[70] Other official British accounts similarly asserted the dominance of the "Arab race," even when an "admixture of Persian blood" occurred in the southern littoral of the Persian Gulf. In 1920, the *Persian Gulf* handbook, published by the Historical Section of the British Foreign Office, was given the mandate to prepare such documents in advance of the Paris peace conference. The handbook repeatedly emphasized the prevalence of Arab culture over the diversity of peoples represented in the region. For example, in describing the race and language of the Arabian coastal region, the handbook asserted that the population was "almost exclusively Arab, although alien elements occur."[71] The Baharina, an indigenous community, inhabiting the oases of Hasa, Qatif, and Bahrayn, was described as an "aboriginal tribe conquered or absorbed by Arabs" or as a "class formed by the conversion of certain Arab tribes to Shiism about 300 years ago," which would have also coincided with the ascendancy of the Safavid dynasty.[72]

More than a century later, British historian and Arabist Stephen Hemsley Longrigg claimed that the Baharina were "half Sunni Arab," though he grudgingly acknowledged that while "the never-relinquished Persian claim to the island need not here concern us, though the large Shi'i element is not unconnected with it."[73] However, the belief that the Arab "race" prevailed in the ethnic composition of the Baharina persisted despite the dearth of historical records supporting this position. According to the *Persian Gulf* handbook, the appellation Baharina, "as now employed on the west coast of the Persian Gulf is practically a synonym for Arab-speaking Shiah Mohammedans."[74] Presumably, Arab-speaking Shi'a Muslims could have spoken other languages, including Persian, Urdu, and Baluchi and originated from different ethnicities and cultures.[75] Yet as recently as 2014, the presumed dominance of the Arab ethnicity has continued. Historian Marc Valeri, for example, labeled the Baharina "Arab Shi'i," counting between 1,000 and 2,000 members in the Omani community.[76] Ethnic conflicts, compounded by sectarian ones, particularly between the Sunnis and the Shi'a, have only widened the chasm between the Arab, the South Asian (Baluch, Indian), and the Persian.

In Iran, Reza Shah's accession to the throne came after his execution of a fierce policy of tribal disarmament. During the interwar era, Iran molded a culture of homogeneity and secularism to forge national unity and to deflate the separatist movements rooted in ethnic difference. Caught in a web of educational reforms and sartorial shifts, the modern Iranian forcibly experimented with novel and ever-changing cultural norms. Gone were the veil and the Pahlavi hat. Instead, urban (and urbane) Iranians discovered new sports like volleyball, skiing, and swimming, and adopted the appropriate fashions to partake of these modern forms of recreation and leisure.[77] In the provinces, communities grappled more pointedly with these impositions, and local communities fought the directives levying new cultural norms for modern citizens. At the same time, Iranians of different ethnic and racial backgrounds alternately resisted or partook of the state's new ideals of citizenship, including its emphasis on Persian culture.

The interest in Persian antiquity, coupled with the European curiosity about the origins of cultures and languages, gave rise to theories and hierarchies of race, which some Iranian intellectuals embraced in order to argue for the superiority of Persians. Schoolbooks from the 1920s tended to define racial differences and categories in rather simplistic fashion. Discussions of Iranian prehistory also reinforced the notion that ancient Iranians belonged to an "Aryan race" (*aryan nizhad*). In 1927, a middle school textbook explained the origins of the Achaeminids in this way: "the founder of the Achaeminid dynasty, Hakhamanesh, was the head of one of the Aryan-race tribes in the south. He formed a government in Elam and his successors gradually controlled Fars and Elam."[78] The embrace of Aryanism continued in other ways as Iran pursued a futile project to purify the Persian language of foreign terminology.

To the west of Iran, Arab communities, including the newly created state of Iraq, began asserting their Arabness. The subject of ethnicity became a contested issue between Iraq and Iran as the neighboring states asserted their rights. In 1928, the Iranian consul at Basrah provided evidence of Persian nationality for persons affiliated with tribes inhabiting the riverain domains near the Shatt al-Arab (or Arvand Rud) waterway. Apparently, some cultivators of the riverbanks in Basrah had sent complaints "of oppression of individual Persians by Iraqi Government." However, the Iraqi government claimed "the Persian consul at Basra seduces Arab cultivators from their allegiance by issuing Persian passports to them."[79] Thus, the unresolved matter of ethnicity and sovereignty dogged this relationship.

This dispute spilled into the realm of language and culture. In 1938, an inspector from Iraq's Ministry of Education visited Iran and pursued an inquiry about opening two Arabic schools for Iraqis in Khorramshahr. According to internal memoranda, because it was perceived that the Iraqi government allowed for the operation of Persian schools in Iraq, officials in Khuzistan were advised to honor this request. The only stickler for Iran remained the mounting of a sign in Arabic outside the school. Iran had forbidden the use of non-Persian script in schools and worried about the propaganda that might accompany the opening of two Arabic-language schools in southern Iran, which it viewed as potentially "harmful."[80] Iraq had allowed Iranian schools there to hoist a sign in Farsi that also included the national emblem of the lion and the sun. At that time, Iran maintained five Persian elementary schools and one secondary school in Iraq. In order to allow for the continued operation of these schools, Iran granted the Iraqi representatives their request to open two schools. However, it forbade Iranian children from attending the Iraqi establishments. If Iranian citizens decided to send their children to such a school they would be placed under surveillance.[81] The exchange over regulation of language instruction in foreign schools also showed the insecurities and concerns of the Iranian state about attempts to undermine Persian language and culture.

During the interwar era, the debate on race and ethnicity in Iran typically focused on Aryanism and Persian exceptionalism, with less emphasis on the

Fig. 7.1: *Baba Shamal*, No. 144, 1 Bahman 1326/22 January 1948

categories of "whiteness," "blackness," mixed race, or other. This conversation took place as interwar Iran finally worked to abolish slavery in 1928. Yet this cartoon from the 1940s (fig. 7.1) shows the disparaging and offensive way in which an unspecified colored community was depicted.

The man in the picture is threatening to send the woman to Iran, where he anticipates that she will suffer a worse fate as a fully clad Muslim woman than she might in her aboriginal society. In other words, veiling was described as a primitive punishment for women. Though the cartoon pokes fun at the rigidity of Islamic dress codes, it also disparages indigenous communities as half-naked, savage, and primitive.

The desire to link Persian ethnicity with the purported virtues of Aryanism persisted in Iranian official discourse. In 1944, as Iran suffered from foreign occupation, a military textbook describing the geography of Fars reinforced the connection between the inhabitants of that province and Aryanism.[82] The text stated that the race and languages of the borderland communities of Dashtistan and Tangistan, some of whom had remained Zoroastrian, were the original Aryans, although racial intermingling had occurred after the Arab invasions of the southern Iranian shores.

### *From Aryanism to Third Worldism*

Expressions of ethnic and racial acceptance or dissent grew strident after the Second World War when Iranians engaged with global crises that brought the politics of race more heatedly to their backyard. While the theme of ethnicity remained a subject of anthropological and political interest, race and racism rose to the fore in the 1960s as intellectuals of different stripes considered their political affiliations and proclivities. Persian high culture and popular culture grappled with notions of race and color in contemporary society, and other ideologies such as Third Worldism, Islamism, and socialism also informed these intellectual and public debates.[83] In those years, Iran also expanded its network of international relations, and by 1976 it had forged ties with thirty-one African nations.[84] The conversations surrounding race, culture, and identity in the decades before the Iranian Revolution of 1979 differed sharply in content and tone from the discussions of previous eras.

Iranian writers and students considered the impact of decolonization and liberation movements globally while dealing with the postmodern challenges of their unique identity crisis. Iran's solidarity with decolonization movements was reflected in its active participation with the UN Special Committee on

Decolonization. Some of the leading intellectual figures of Iran debated the impact of colonialism and America's role in it. Embedded in these discussions remained issues of race. In the 1960s, when visiting Harvard University at the invitation of Henry Kissinger, Jalal Al-e Ahmad enjoyed meeting Ralph Ellison, the famed American writer and grandson of slaves.[85] Roy Mottahedeh said that Al-e Ahmad "thought that Ellison had a deeper view of the race question than other writers, because he saw the American black in the context of his resentments, and that Ellison's position was like the position of Camus on Algeria."[86] In his diary, Al-e Ahmad notes that the European participants in the seminar did not particularly embrace Ellison's book, *Invisible Man* which he labeled "a 'manifesto for blacks.'"[87] In defense of Ellison, Al-e Ahmad claims to have argued that other black writers, such as Richard Wright and James Baldwin, had adopted (or at least their characters had adopted) a more retaliatory posture in their works.[88]

Like his contemporaries, Al-e Ahmad grappled with the ideologies of decolonization and imperialism, and attempted to locate the place of race in that debate. Al-e Ahmad kept a diary of his travels to the United States. From his first glimpse of the Statue of Liberty, "which did have not a flame coming out of it," to his descriptions of American pop art and consumerism, Al-e Ahmad maintained a critical attitude. He and his fellow journalists authored several articles on colonization that investigated questions of identity and racial politics in international contexts. Some embraced Third Worldism through discussions of American relations with Cuba and in analyses of the related writings of Jean-Paul Sartre.[89]

In the 1960s, a close associate of Al-e Ahmad, Manuchehr Hezarkhani, had translated into Persian Aimé Césaire's "Discours sur le colonialisme," which Césaire had originally published in 1950. A Francophone writer and poet born in Martinique, Césaire had confronted many thorny issues concerning race and colonialism. Described alternately as a "declaration of war" or a "third-world manifesto," this essay scathingly attacked European barbarism in various colonial contexts.[90] As he wrote, "One can kill in Indochina, torture in Madagascar, imprison in black Africa, and clamp down in the West Indies. As of now, the colonized know that they have an advantage over the colonizer. They know that their provisional 'masters' are lying." That this polemical treatise was published at a time when Iran itself was experiencing political turmoil exposed the cracks in Iranian civil society. Students voiced their solidarity with Third World causes as demonstrated in their public rallies and demonstrations in support of Algerian revolutionaries and against Central Treaty Organization (CENTO).[91]

Ali Shariati, another towering intellectual of those years, famously published a translation of Frantz Fanon's *Wretched of the Earth* in the 1970s.[92] Shariati thus showed an affinity with the politics of decolonization and stood against the oppressive policies that accompanied imperialist regimes in Africa and elsewhere.[93] Intellectuals expressed interest in other Third World causes, including the turbulent politics of African countries and the rise of dictatorships and military coups in various countries. For example, in reference to the Nigerian Civil War, one cartoon (fig. 7.2) derided the departure of Nigerian military leader Chukwuemeka Odumegwu Ojukwu, who had established the temporary separatist state of Biafra. The caption sardonically notes that Ojukwu promised to return to Biafra whenever his Congolese counterpart, Moïse Tshombe, would return to his post in Katanga.[94] Given the growing interest in African politics, scholarly debates also began focusing on African diasporic communities in Iran and elsewhere. The terms "Afro-Iranian" or "Afro-Persian" became used in scholarly contexts in the 1960s as Arab–Persian divides were further explored in African history.[95]

It is ironic that as leading intellectuals engaged in a more sophisticated debate about race and identity, not only in Iran but the Third World, the Iranian state consumed itself with an ostentatious embrace of Aryanism, most flagrantly demonstrated in the coronation of Muhammad Reza Shah Pahlavi and his adoption of the moniker, "Arya Mehr" (Light of the Aryans), as well as the extravagant celebrations at Persepolis in 1971.

Fig. 7.2: *Tawfiq*, 2 Bahman 1348/22 January 1970

Even as Iran and its Arab neighbors supported decolonization movements and shared in the struggle to ward off imperialist politics, the divide between Arabs and Persians persisted in popular culture. The military rise of the state of Israel, however, at times complicated this relationship. Although Iran had established relations with Israel, the popular press expressed animosity toward the Jewish military leaders, especially after the 1967 war. Still, the Arab "other" was often depicted as dark-skinned and traditional. For example, when the Islamic month of Muharram—associated in Shi'a culture with the mourning of Karbala massacres—coincided with the pre-Islamic Persian New Year, the cover of *Tawfiq*, a satirical Persian periodical, depicted Shemr (fig. 7.3), the murderer of Imam Husayn, on its cover as the ultimate scoundrel for casting a pall on Iran's New Year celebrations. Like other Arabs, Shemr had dark skin

Fig. 7.3: *Tawfiq*, 1 Farvardin 1348/21 March 1969

and facial hair. In another cartoon (fig. 7.4), the famed belly dancer Jamileh is shown as performing for Amir Abbas Hoveyda, the premier at that time, who addresses her in Arabic. In this manner, Jamileh becomes associated with Arabness, and is unsurprisingly portrayed with dark skin and with visible underarm hair.[96]

After the 1967 war between Israel and its Arab neighbors, some Iranian intellectual writers identified with their Arab counterparts, complicating the facile portrait of the Arab and Persian as warring races inexorably at odds against one another. When Israel emerged unequivocally victorious against its Arab neighbors, *Tawfiq* frequently depicted Israel as the aggressor. In several issues, the journal addressed the close military ties between the United States and the Jewish state. Even as the shah pledged his support for Israel in diplomatic correspondence, the public showed far less tolerance for the new military power in the region. This cartoon (fig. 7.5), using gibberish letters in

Fig. 7.4: 11 September 1968

imitation of the Hebrew alphabet, illustrates a complacent Moshe Dayan (the Israeli Defense Minister of that period) pays no attention to the Declaration of Human Rights or to the censure of the United Nations. In another image (fig. 7.6), Prime Minister Golda Meir, frequently illustrated as a decrepit woman and referred to derisively as Metro Goldwyn Mayer, stands next to an Arab leader and shows her preference for resolving the Arab–Israeli conflict without external interference. The Arab figure remains dark-skinned, with traditional attire and facial hair.[97] Despite its frequent support for the Arab cause and its unrelenting criticism of Israel and of US–Israeli relations, *Tawfiq* reinforced entrenched negative stereotypes of Arabs, particularly the oft-ridiculed image of the Arab as a dagger-wielding desert dweller in traditional attire. Although in the enclosed image (fig. 7.7) the crab represents Israel, and Moshe Dayan more specifically, cartoon adopts derogatory stereotypes.

Fig. 7.5: Shahrivar 1348/4 September 1969

These illustrations demonstrate that Iran grappled with inclusion of its minority populations, as well as with ethnic and racial tolerance, when faced with rival nationalisms from abroad.

*Conclusion*

Racial awareness and discrimination in Iran emerged in response to political conflicts and imperialist impositions that often had ethnic–linguistic overtones. In the nineteenth century, the colonial administrators operating in Iran and its borderlands came to understand and define the cultures and communities of the region with imperfect knowledge of the terrain. The processes by which Western ethnologists produced and disseminated this information and propagated the classification of different races and ethnicities in Iran and its frontier zones betrayed the limitations of their knowledge about the Middle East. These theories—produced in a moment of cultural and linguistic flux, and at a juncture when Britain's hegemonic control of the Middle East dictated policies and cultural interpretations that favored its imperial needs over the demands of local groups—did not necessarily reflect the political aspirations of the different communities on the ground.

The imposition of monoethnic and monolingual identities in the Middle East, and especially in the borderlands of Iran, Iraq, and the Persian Gulf—as

Fig. 7.6: 28 Farvardin 1348/17 April 1969

well as the tendency to label many such communities as predominantly "Arab" or "Arabian"—has fueled the sectarian and cultural divides in these regions to this day.[98]

After the First World War, Middle Eastern communities came face-to-face with atavistic ideologies that strove to ingrain national homogeneity in defiance of the region's cultural diversity, with little ability to confront the sweeping cultural classifications that the region had inherited through colonialism. New states forced disparate populations to adopt the dominant linguistic, religious, or ethnic traits of the state. In the borderlands of Iraq, Iran, and the Persian Gulf, the mixing of races, ethnicities, languages, and religions at times made it difficult to assert the overarching presence of one culture over another. Yet these states imposed their cultures of linguistic and cultural uniformity

Fig. 7.7: *Tawfiq*, 25 Shahrivar 1348/23 August 1969

that defied the diversity of their populations and at times ignored the intermingling of races and ethnicities.

Conversations about race in Iran, rooted initially in linguistic and ethnic difference, intruded into local and international politics. While far from colorblind, the production of knowledge about race and identity moved away from colonial actors and institutions, especially non-indigenous ones, and became instead the function of state institutions, which at times reproduced the prejudices and facile social classifications introduced by colonial administrators. By the 1960s, even as the state remained stunted in its understanding of culture, ethnicity, and race, key Iranian intellectuals had moved away from discourses of Aryanism and participated instead in the struggles of peoples and nations who had long been subjected to colonial and racial discrimination. Though unable fully to remove its blinders, Iran finally began to see in color.

8

# CULTURAL CLEANSING AND ICONOCLASM UNDER THE ISLAMIC STATE

## ATTACKS ON YEZIDIS AND CHRISTIANS AND THEIR HERITAGE

*Benjamin Isakhan, José Antonio González Zarandona,*
and *Taghreed Jamal Al-Deen*

When the "Islamic State" (IS) seized large swathes of territory across Iraq and Syria, and declared a new caliphate, it unleashed a cataclysmic wave of devastating human suffering and unprecedented heritage destruction.[1] In terms of human suffering, IS executed many who questioned its nefarious ideology or those who committed petty crimes like drinking alcohol; women have been forced into marriages and raped; girls as young as nine have been used as sex slaves; boys as young as twelve have been armed and used as child soldiers; and the region's many cultural and religious groups have faced cruel and deadly persecution, including being slaughtered and dumped into mass graves. At the same time, the rapid expansion of IS also proved fatal for many of the world's most sensitive and important cultural heritage sites. It is difficult to state the extent, speed, and variety of heritage destruction that has occurred under IS rule. Targeted sites range from ancient Mesopotamian city-states through to Greek, Roman, and Byzantine sites, from classical Islamic sites to those that enshrine the history and beliefs of the region's rich diversity, as well as secular state institutions such as museums, art galleries, and libraries.

Not surprisingly, much media attention and several significant scholarly works have addressed both the human tragedy and the heritage destruction that has unfolded under IS rule. Aside from broader accounts of the roots of IS, its ideology, and its cruel fundamentalist vision,[2] others have focused on documenting the plight of various ethnoreligious minorities across the Middle East,[3] the extent to which attacks on these communities meet the varying definitions of ethnic cleansing and genocide,[4] and the problem of holding groups like IS accountable under international human rights law.[5] At the same time, a collection of scholarly articles has documented the scale of heritage destruction wrought under IS rule: its use of social media to present the destruction as dramatic spectacles to local, regional, and global audiences;[6] the extent to which its destruction draws on a tradition of religious and political iconoclasm,[7] which is used to assert and legitimize its spatio-political power;[8] the revenues IS raised from the illicit looting and trafficking of artefacts sold on the international black market for antiquities;[9] using satellite imagery to monitor the destruction;[10] and the extent to which existing international law and the responses issued by various governments and multinational bodies have been largely ineffective.[11]

While each of the factors outlined above must be considered in any nuanced account of the human suffering and heritage destruction unleashed by IS, the above studies overlook the fact that groups like IS employ violent iconoclasm to cleanse the world of a complex and cosmopolitan past, to encourage rifts and antagonism between communities, and to end blasphemy toward the creation of a holy and serene state. As a terrorist organization with a homogenizing ideological agenda, IS seeks to destroy many forms of religious and cultural pluralism, thus fracturing the rich and colorful mosaic that has long constituted the Middle East. In other words, little attention has been paid to the intersection between the human suffering and the heritage destruction undertaken by IS. Here, human and heritage destruction are intertwined: the suffering inflicted on people is projected onto their sites of ritual and worship—just as the destruction of these sites is deliberately orchestrated to inflict symbolic suffering on specific communities and to shatter the ethnic and religious diversity of the region. This chapter, therefore, explores and documents the human/heritage "cultural cleansing" undertaken by IS against two fragile minorities: the Yezidi and Christian populations of northern Iraq and Syria.[12] The chapter begins by situating this discussion within the conceptual framework of "heritage, community, violence," and concludes by discussing the consequences of such destruction for the rich cultural mosaic of the Middle East.

### *Heritage, community, violence*

Although there is no shortage of historical examples in which human suffering and heritage destruction have paralleled one another, most academic studies have not adequately demonstrated their complex interrelationship. Indeed, while investigations into contexts as diverse as the First World War and the Armenian genocide,[13] the Second World War and the Holocaust,[14] the "cultural cleansing" campaign in Cambodia,[15] the civil war in Lebanon,[16] the ethno-nationalist conflict in Northern Ireland,[17] and the Iraq war of 2003 routinely place mass human suffering alongside heritage destruction,[18] the relationship between the two is not adequately explored. The same can be said of studies that examine isolated incidents in which heritage sites have become a target of specific political actors, such as the destruction of the Babri Masjid mosque in India by Hindu radicals in 1992,[19] or the destruction of the Bamiyan Buddhas in Afghanistan by the Taliban in 2001.[20] Investigations into such phenomena achieved perhaps their greatest urgency following the devastating events that tore apart the Balkans in the 1990s. The ethnoreligious nature of the war clearly meant that the heritage of opposing factions became a direct target.[21] The "deliberate destruction of mosques, churches, museums, civil records, monuments and artefacts in the Balkans" was said to be driven by a zealous desire to suppress "evidence of a culturally diverse and hybrid past, in favour of a mythical 'golden age' of ethnic uniformity."[22] In this context, while Andras Riedlmayer has asserted a "link between the systematic persecution and expulsion of ethnic and religious communities and the destruction of the cultural and religious heritage associated with the targeted community,"[23] he does not explore the nature of this "link" and the human-heritage nexus.

Attacks on heritage sites in conjunction with genocidal pogroms or ethno-religious conflict occur precisely because heritage plays such a critical role as the tangible manifestation of community.[24] Sites of religious or historical significance, of public ritual, and of commemoration or celebration enable groups to build an "imagined community" in which individuals inculcate a sense of collective identity.[25] Heritage sites therefore "act as markers that signify the identity of the place,"[26] a physical structure that can be used (and, in many cases, abused) by various actors—from oppressive states to liberation movements, and from divisive ethnoreligious separatists to unifying civil society organizations—to rally people behind a common cause.[27] However, when differences between and within communities occur, specific groups become targets, and their heritage sites can be transformed into sites of contestation and conflict.[28] In such a situation, actors who target enemy heritage are aiming to destroy not just the site itself but the site as symbol of the given community—its history, customs, and identity.[29] However, the targeting of a community and its heritage can have divergent consequences and responses,[30] from the complete erasure of a way of life through to the re-appropriation of suffering by future generations in which communities come to commemorate their "places of pain and shame."[31] In some instances, such sites are turned into monuments where trauma is memorialized and conflict mediated.[32]

Despite such transformative potential, the targeting of heritage sites as a proxy for, or in conjunction with, attacks on human beings remains deeply problematic, and the intersection between the two phenomena remains widely understudied. For his part, Robert Bevan has argued that attacks on heritage sites and human communities during conflict ought to be thought of as indistinguishable moments of cultural cleansing "with architecture as its medium."[33] More recently, W. J. T. Mitchell has argued that "the destruction of images [iconoclasm] is directly linked to ... 'ethnic cleansing.' The removal of images, sacred sites, and persons is all one process ... to cleanse the world of these images and of the 'inhabitants' for whom they are important signs of identity and belonging to a place."[34] Further, in response to the heinous actions of IS, UNESCO's Director General, Irina Bokova, referred to the atrocities as "cultural cleansing," arguing that the destruction of heritage cannot be understood without the persecution and killing of cultural minorities. It is "intended to destroy identities, tear apart social fabrics, and fuel hatred," because "violent extremists attack anything that can sustain diversity, critical thinking and freedom of opinion—schools, teachers, journalists, cultural minorities, and monuments."[35] Drawing on this work, the remainder of this chapter seeks to document this human–heritage nexus by examining the plight of the Yezidis and Christians under IS rule, and the deliberate targeting of them as human communities and their specific heritage sites. What distinguishes the human–heritage attacks on the Yezidis and Christians from other historical iconoclastic episodes is the speed and ferocity of this deliberate symbolic campaign.[36] Another point of distinction is that while much attention has been paid to IS destruction of certain sites—particularly ancient archaeological sites with a distinct connection to biblical narratives or the origins of "Western civilization" such as Palmyra or Nimrud—little mention has been made in the Western media of the destruction of those sites that hold contemporary significance to the many ethnic and religious minorities that constitute the modern Middle East.

### *"Devil worshippers" and judgment day: Islamic State attacks on Yezidis*

Yezidis are a minority community spread across different regions of Iraq, Syria, Iran, Turkey, and Transcaucasia (Armenia, Georgia, and Azerbaijan), and there are also significant Yezidi communities in Germany, Switzerland, Sweden, and Russia.[37] Today, the biggest communities are in northern Iraq, particularly in the Lalesh Valley in the Sheikhan district west of Mosul where their holiest sites are located. It is thought that they number around 450,000 people in total.[38] Throughout their history, Yezidis have experienced repression and extermination and today face significant challenges in keeping their traditions alive in their homeland. Although their origins are somewhat opaque, scholars recognize the influence of and elements from Christianity, Islam (including Sufism), Gnosticism, and Zoroastrianism in their unique religion and system of beliefs.[39] Ethnically and linguistically, most are considered to be Kurds, although other variations exist. Thus, Yezidis are regarded as "one of the most remarkable illustrations of ethno-religious identity,"[40] because their sense of identity combines unique religious, cultural, and ethnic elements.

Yezidis have long suffered a history of persecution, which has also formed a core part of their identity.[41] In the 1970s, for example, Saddam Hussein initiated a campaign of Arabization that entailed the destruction of Yezidi villages and/or their repopulation by Sunni Arabs, as well as the relocation of hundreds of thousands of Kurds and Yezidis to the so-called "collective villages," so their independence could be suppressed by the Ba'thist regime. In the 1980s, the Ba'th regime undertook several attacks against the Kurds and Yezidis, including the brutal Anfal Campaign.[42] Needless to say, such actions forced the Yezidis to settle in urban centers, disrupting their rural way of life. Most recently, in August 2007, a series of bombs in the Sinjar region left 250 dead and 350 wounded Yezidis when four trucks exploded in three villages in northern Iraq.[43] Al-Qa'ida-linked Sunni insurgents were widely viewed as being responsible for the attacks, which a US army general described as "an act of ethnic cleansing ... almost genocide."[44]

As with many other groups, the tangible heritage sites of the Yezidis play a central role in their community and religious identity. Their main type of heritage site is the mausoleums of saints as well as temples and shrines where a mixture of Christian, Muslim, and Zoroastrian traditions converge in the rituals. Situated mainly in rural areas and on top of hills "to separate them from public spaces," these shrines, temples, and mausoleums play an important role in underscoring Yezidi identity: they are places for community and religious ritual, sacred and public gatherings, and for collective worship of the divine.[45] Yezidi temples can be easily identified by the depiction of the two revered animals of their faith on the façade: the peacock and the serpent. The first symbolizes the Peacock Angel or Melek Taus, the representative of their god, Xwade, on earth. Melek Taus is thought to have been an angel that fell to earth and transformed into the colorful bird.[46] The serpent is also revered by the Yezidis because they believe that it helped humanity to survive the Flood when the animal used its body to seal a leak in Noah's ark after it crashed into rocks.[47] The worship of a fallen angel and a serpent are controversial in the three Abrahamic faiths of Judaism, Christianity, and Islam where the fallen angel and the serpent are associated with the story of the devil. This has often led to the Yezidis being mistakenly described as "devil worshippers."

The most recent example is that of IS, which has frequently referred to the Yezidis as "devil worshippers" in its propaganda materials, as well as calling them *kafir* (non-believers) who are given the option of conversion or death. On 3 August 2014, IS staged a horrifying campaign to not only take the northwestern Iraqi city of Sinjar but to cleanse the region of its Yezidi population. In the IS propaganda magazine *Dabiq*, the jihadists explained their desire to erase the Yezidi community for fear of judgment day:

> Upon conquering the region of Sinjar in Wilayat Ninawa, the Islamic State faced a population of Yazidis, a pagan minority existent for ages in regions of Iraq and Sham. Their continual existence to this day is a matter that Muslims should question as they will be asked about it on Judgment Day, considering that Allah had revealed Ayat as-Sayf (the verse of the sword) over 1400 years ago.[48]

The consequences of its claim to be committing genocide on behalf of the divine were devastating. Up to 500 Yezidis were slaughtered in a matter of days, with tens of thousands, including up to 25,000 children,[49] fleeing their homes in fear, many ending up trapped on Mount Sinjar without food, water, or weapons.[50] According to a report commissioned by the United Nations in 2016, many Yezidi women, including girls as young as nine, were taken into slavery and raped.[51] After Sinjar was retaken in November 2015 by Iraqi and Kurdish forces, six mass graves were unearthed containing the bodies of at least 200 women aged between forty and eighty years old who were apparently deemed too old or unattractive to be used as sex slaves.[52] The physical violence committed by IS on the Yezidis and other minorities was the subject of a UN report in March 2015, which argued that IS "may have committed genocide," based on its deliberate intentions to "destroy the Yezidis as a group."[53] A similar report by the United States Holocaust Memorial Museum concluded that IS was "targeting particular groups on the basis of their identity,"[54] and that it was undoubtedly "perpetrating genocide against the Yezidi people."[55]

In addition to the violence against the Yezidi people, IS undertook an aggressive campaign to cleanse the region of the physical manifestations of their identity, including many heritage sites. Once IS had cleared the Sinjar region of Yezidis, it began to mark Yezidi houses to distinguish them from houses that belonged to Muslims. Needless to say, the Yezidi houses were "looted, and some were destroyed or severely damaged."[56] Likewise, in August 2014, IS appeared to destroy four significant Yezidi cultural sites, including the Shrine of Sheikh Mand in Jiddala, the Shrine of Sheikh Hassan in Gabara, the Shrine of Malak Fakhraddin in Sikeeniya, and the Shrine of Mahma Rasha in Solagh.[57] In 2015, IS destroyed the early thirteenth-century minaret of Qutb Al-Din Muhammad in Sinjar, filling the building with explosives before detonating it and demolishing it.[58] In Tal Afar on 25 June 2015, IS also destroyed the shrine of Khidr al-Elias (Ilyas, the Green Man), a saint revered by Christians, Muslims, and Yezidis alike.[59] Also in 2015, the second most important shrine in the Yezidi faith, the Sharaf Al-Deen shrine near Sinjar, came under several waves of attack by IS. It was successfully defended by a small group of just eighteen armed Yezidi men who stayed behind to defend the thirteenth-century shrine.[60]

Being prepared to risk their lives to defend their religious sites speaks volumes about the high value that the Yezidi community places on their heritage. The Yezidi collective identity and culture are fundamentally tied to their heritage. As one Yezidi man put it when reflecting on the IS attack on Sinjar, "It's more than our heritage ... It's our heart and soul."[61] Haider Elias, the president of Yazda, a global Yezidi organization based in Houston, also underlined the erasure of Yezidi identity via the destruction of their holy sites: "The new generation, they don't know, they don't have places of worship ... they don't know who they are. And that is terrifying for the Yezidi culture."[62] Therefore, attacks on the Yezidis, including the displacement of their population and the destruction of their shrines, are comparable to the ontological death of the community.[63] As human rights activist Nadia Murad, a Yezidi who was kidnapped and sold into sex slavery by IS, said: "[it is a] genocide against our identity." She added that IS "came with the sole aim of destroying the Yezidi identity through force, rape, recruitment of children and destruction of all our temples."[64] This highlights the interconnection between the violent genocide perpetrated by IS against the Yezidis and the parallel destruction of their heritage sites, and points to the terrifying relationship between human/heritage suffering.

### *"N" for "Nasarene:" Islamic State attacks on Christians*

Christians have long played a significant role in the Middle East's rich sociocultural life, contributing to the region's diversity, an influence that has been dramatically reduced in the twentieth and twenty-first centuries. The geopolitics of the Middle East has deeply shaped the history of Christianity as well as its survival in the region of its birth.[65] As one anthropologist asserts, Christianity in the Middle East needs to be "understood as a cultural and political system in addition to being a religion."[66] Christians in the Middle East belong to a broad spectrum of different sects, including Chalcedonians or Eastern Orthodox (Greek Orthodox, Russian Orthodox); Chalcedonian Monothelites (Maronites); non-Chalcedonians or Oriental Orthodox (Syrian or Syriac Orthodox, Coptic, Armenian, and Ethiopian Orthodox); non-Ephesians (Nestorians or Assyrians); and Eastern Catholics (Uniate). Like the Yezidis, Christians in the Middle East are scattered across different regions: Copts mostly live in Egypt; Armenians mainly live in Syria, Lebanon, Armenia, Turkey, and Iran; Maronites and Catholics are predominantly in Lebanon; Greek and Syriac Orthodox branches live in Syria; and Nestorians, Syrian Orthodox, and Chalcedonians live in Iraq.[67] Beyond their doctrinal differences, the Christians of the Middle East are not monolithic, differing along divergent cultural, political, and ethnic identities. No matter where they are, the communal identity of Middle Eastern Christians—as with Christians elsewhere—is embodied in various forms of material culture, particularly churches that are identified by the prominence of a sacred cross. Worship occurs in these sacred spaces, where people also gather for ritual ceremonies like christenings, weddings, and funerals, and to mark important religious events, like Easter and Christmas.

As with many religious and ethnic minorities, Christian communities have also endured centuries of persecution and oppression in the Middle East at the hands of different forces. To some extent, this has been shaped by actual and perceived political connections between the Christians of the Middle East and the West, a legacy that dates back to the Crusades, but it also influenced attitudes towards Christians during the colonial period and more recent military interventions.[68] Historically, many governments of the region have undertaken degrees of discrimination and persecution against the Christians. These range from restricting religious education or banning their ancient languages (Aramaic, for example) through to direct persecution, such as the Armenian genocide at the end of the First World War or the Simele massacre undertaken by the Iraqi state in 1933.[69] In fact, the persecution and oppression have played an important part in the construction of identity discourses related to the genocide narrative, particularly in the case of the Christian Armenian community.[70] Under strict interpretations of Islamic law, while the Yezidis are considered *kafir* and devil worshippers, the Christians are considered *Ahl Al-Kitab* (people of the book) and are granted protection as long as they pay the *jizya* tax. With the rise of various fundamentalist groups such as IS, Christians have once again faced persecution, with many choosing to flee the region. Experts have demonstrated that the Christian population of the Middle East has plummeted dramatically over the last century: in 1910, Christians represented 13.6 percent of the Middle East's population, but in 2010 they comprised just 4.2 percent, with that number likely to decline further given the post-Arab-uprisings environment, and the rise of groups like IS.[71]

Indeed, when IS swept across Syria and Iraq, the region's many Christians were given a stark ultimatum: either convert to Islam, pay the *jizya* tax, leave their ancient homelands, or be executed.[72] In Syria alone, 600,000 Christians have fled the country since the start of the civil war in 2011, driven out by extremist groups like Nusra Front and IS.[73] The abuse of human rights that they are subjected to is devastating. As an example, many Christians have been crucified by IS and left to die in public spaces over the course of several days.[74] Similarly, since the Iraq war of 2003, nearly a million Christians have fled Iraq and only about 300,000 remain in the country.[75] In Mosul, IS marked all Christian properties across the city with a red Arabic letter "N" for "Nasarene," a derogatory name for Christians taken from the city of Nazareth where Jesus is said to have spent his youth. Many of the marked buildings were later looted by IS and demolished. In terms of Christian heritage sites, IS has destroyed

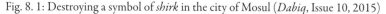

Fig. 8. 1: Destroying a symbol of *shirk* in the city of Mosul (*Dabiq*, Issue 10, 2015)

hundreds of statues, defaced murals, desecrated Christian cemeteries, taken sledgehammers to church façades, blown up ancient monasteries, and removed crosses from churches and replaced them with the black flag of IS before converting them to mosques or for other purposes. Nuri Kino, founder and president of a group called "A Demand for Action" campaigning for the rights of ethnoreligious minorities such as Christians and Yazidis in the Middle East, notes: "If they changed a church to a mosque it is further proof of their cleansing, something that many call a genocide. They destroy our artefacts, our churches and try to erase us in any way they can."[76] This has been confirmed by priests in Mosul, with one explaining: "Some of these churches date back to ancient historical periods." By destroying the churches, "IS and the extremists in Mosul want to fully erase the history of the Christians."[77]

For example, in Mosul, IS destroyed the Tomb of the Prophet Jonah (Nebi Yunus) in July 2014, with reports of a statue of the Virgin Mary also being destroyed.[78] Furthermore, the 1,400-year-old monastery of St. Elijah (Deir

Mar Elian) was completely leveled during August or September 2014.[79] This monastery was the oldest in Iraq, having been established by one of the first Christian communities in the world. Other religious sites attacked in Iraq include the September 2014 destruction of the seventh-century Assyrian St. Ahoadamah Church (or Green church) in Tikrit;[80] the February 2015 destruction of the seventh-century Al-Tahera church in Mosul;[81] the March 2015 destruction of the tenth-century Chalcedonian Catholic church of St. Markourkas in Mosul;[82] the early March destruction of the Christian cemetery of Tel Kaif in Mosul; and the 19 March 2015 demolition of the tombs associated with the Syriac Catholic monastery dedicated to the martyrs Mar Behnam and Mart Sarah, originally erected in the fourth century in Qaraqosh, southeast of Mosul, Iraq.[83]

Additionally, in July 2015, IS destroyed a Chalcedonian church, known as the Mother of Aid Church in Mosul, which is thought to be more than 1,000 years old.[84] Although not destroyed, the church of Saint Ephraim—the seat of the Syriac Orthodox archdiocese in Mosul—was occupied over the course of a year, while IS emptied the church of anything it could sell and then converted the premises into the location of its state council. In June 2015, IS had devised plans to convert the church into what would be called "the mosque of the mujahideen."[85] The attack on Mosul's Christian heritage is particularly strategic because, as a historian has pointed out, "Mosul was a key center of spirituality for the Church of the East."[86] The second largest city in Iraq was not only an important city in terms of the Islamic State's desire to dominate significant cities, but it was also important because of the cosmopolitan heritage of the city with its many cultural and ethnic peoples.

Similar attacks on Christian heritage sites occurred in Syria. In August 2015, the Christian monastery of Deir Mar Elian in Al-Qaryatain, thought to date from the sixth century, was bulldozed by members of IS, leaving the site in ruins.[87] Osama Edward, director of the Assyrian Human Rights Network, described the destruction: "The monastery has been completely removed ... these actions send a message to Christians in the area that we don't have a place anymore."[88] Likewise, after conquering the northern city of Raqqa in late 2013—the de facto capital city of IS—the group shuttered all three of the major churches in the city and removed the crosses and hung black flags over the buildings. The largest church, the Armenian Catholic Martyrs Church, was turned into a recruitment center where gruesome videos are shown of IS operations and conquests.[89] A similar case occurred with the Church of St. Simeon—famous for having spent his life atop a column. A sublime example of a Byzantine-era church (AD 490), located 35 kilometers east of Aleppo, was used by Islamist forces as a military base in 2013.[90] Perhaps the most well-known example is the complete destruction of the Armenian Holy Martyrs Church in the al-Roshdeyah neighborhood in Deir ez-Zour, Syria, by IS—or its once affiliate, Jabhat al-Nusra, in September 2014.[91] This church, built from the mid-1980s and consecrated in 1991,[92] is known as the Armenian Genocide Memorial Church or Holy Martyrs Armenian Church and housed one of the world's largest and most significant archives on the 1915 Armenian genocide, as well as a crypt with the remains of hundreds of victims.[93] Each year, thousands of Armenians gather at the church on 25 April, the date they commemorate the start of the genocide dedicated to the one and a half million Armenians slaughtered in 1915. Most of the church archives, dating back to 1841 and containing thousands of documents on the Armenian genocide, were burned to ashes, while the bones of hundreds of victims, packed into the church's crypt in memory of the mass killings a century ago, were thrown into the street beside the ruins.[94]

Also very symbolic is the attack against Christians in the Khabur River in the Jazirah region of Syria, where an Assyrian community settled in 1933—in thirty-five villages stretching between Al-Hasaka and Ras al-Ain—after having left Iraq because of the Simele massacre at the hands of the Iraqi state. In February 2015, at around the same time that IS seized global media attention with its destruction of the Mosul Museum, the group had also captured the villages along the Khabur River, displacing thousands of Christians,[95] and kidnapping between 220 and 250 Assyrian civilians.[96] The group burned down a church in the village of Tal Hurmoz—one of the oldest churches in the region—and destroyed three more churches in the town of Tal Tamer.[97] Other reports claim that IS had also set fire to churches in the villages of Tel Shamiran, Qabr Shamly, and Tel Baloua.[98] On Easter Sunday 2015, in the village of Tal Nasri, IS blew up the Assyrian Church of the Virgin Mary, an eighty-year-old structure, and turned it to rubble. As they went on to do at many churches along the Khabur River, IS then set booby traps at the church, including landmines, in the hope of killing more Christians as they returned to their villages and holy sites.[99] In total, nineteen churches, all built after 1933, were destroyed, damaged, or vandalized along the Khabur River.[100]

Needless to say, this is an unprecedented act of heritage destruction that not only emphasizes the sectarian violence against Assyrians in Syria but that also seeks to erase the community's history and collective identity. Demonstrating the significance of the human–heritage nexus in the actions of

IS against Christian communities, these attacks highlight the emphasis that groups such as IS place on both the targeting of humans and their sacred sites. As one Syrian Christian refugee put it, when asked whether he would return to his village in Hasaka, "Go back to what? I watched ISIS blow up our church."[101] This speaks volumes about the intent and effectiveness of the IS campaign to not only erase the Christian people but to also remove the sites most sacred to them.

*Conclusion*

Despite the fact that the days of IS controlling significant territory across Iraq and Syria appear to be drawing to a close,[102] the organization has left behind a horrific legacy. Key to interpreting and analyzing this legacy will be an appreciation of the devastating brutality and heritage destruction carried out by IS, which has included deliberate attacks against two of the most vulnerable minorities in Iraq and Syria: Yezidis and Christians. This has been a two-pronged campaign: it included violent genocidal pogroms that ended in enslavement, gang rape, torture, and mass graves, on the one hand, and a very deliberate parallel effort to destroy the key heritage sites and symbols that enshrine the respective collective identity of these communities, on the other. Such attacks on the human/heritage dimension of a given community ultimately rupture their identity, dismembering their connections to each other and to their collective past.

Beyond this, however, lies an even darker dimension to the human/heritage destruction wrought by the IS. Many of the organization's attacks on the Yezidis and Christians are deliberately orchestrated to connect with earlier waves of genocide endured by these groups. For example, many of the IS attacks against the Yezidis have included the destruction of their villages and their forced migration to urban centers, reminiscent of the Arabization programs undertaken by the Ba'th in the 1970s and 1980s. More to the point, attacks by IS on Christian sites such as the Armenian church in Deir ez-Zour and the villages along the Khabur River appear to have been deliberately designed to conjure sharp memories of the Armenian genocide and the Simele massacre. Reenacting earlier waves of genocide allows IS to connect its contemporary brutality—ideologically, temporally, and physically—to those moments in Yezidi and Christian history that are most sensitive and painful. This deliberate layering of genocide means that moments of direct persecution extend beyond the human/heritage suffering of the present to invoke the traumas of the past. The message could not be clearer: where the Armenian genocide or the Anfal campaign failed, the holy mandate of IS will succeed. It intends to erase any vestige of a cosmopolitan and diverse Middle East toward the creation of a monolithic and oppressive caliphate governed by the most perverse interpretations of Islamic law.

However, it is in the IS rejection and suppression of difference that we find the seeds of the group's undoing. The rich and colorful mosaic of the Middle East has always been central to its unique history and way of life. Beyond political and military efforts to defeat IS lies the even more urgent need to defeat the organization ideologically. What the Middle East—and Iraq and Syria more specifically—needs is a robust and sensitive process in which the traumas of the past are openly and honestly engaged with. This would serve as but one antidote to the ongoing chaos and as a critical first step toward mending inter-ethnic and religious relations, creating a cohesive region and a modern, peaceful, and multicultural Middle East where all citizens are free to live in peace regardless of their ethnicity, religion, or political leanings.

# NOTES

## INTRODUCTION: COMMUNITIES IN THE PLAYING FIELD OF PLURALISM

1. William E. Connolly, *Pluralism*, Durham: Duke University Press, 2005, p. 5.
2. Nicolas Pelham, *Holy Lands: Reviving Pluralism in the Middle East*, New York: Columbia Global Reports, 2016, p. 17. Also see Shadi Hamid, "The End of Pluralism," *The Atlantic*, 23 July 2014.
3. For instance, Marwan Muasher, *The Second Arab Awakening: And the Battle for Pluralism*, New Haven: Yale University Press, 2014.
4. Orit Bashkin, *The Other Iraq: Pluralism and Culture in Hashemite Iraq*, Stanford: Stanford University Press, 2008, p. 17.
5. Diana Eck, "What Is Pluralism?," the Pluralism Project at Harvard University; http://pluralism.org/pages/pluralism/what_is_pluralism (accessed 25 June 2018).
6. Courtney Bender and Pamela Klassen, "Habits of Pluralism," in Courtney Bender and Pamela Klassen (eds), *After Pluralism: Reimagining Religious Engagement*, New York: Columbia University Press, 2010, p. 6.
7. Maria Baghramian and Attracta Ingram, "Introduction," in Maria Baghramian and Attracta Ingram (eds), *Pluralism: The Philosophy and Politics of Diversity*, London: Routledge, 2013, p. 3.
8. I rely on the taxonomy proposed by John Rex, "The Concept of a Multicultural Society," in John Rex and Montserrat Guibernau (eds), *The Ethnicity Reader: Nationalism, Multiculturalism and Migration*, 2nd edn, Cambridge: Polity Press, 2010, pp. 217–29.
9. Ali R. Abootalebi, "Nationalism, Power Politics, and Pluralism in Divided Societies," in Fonkem Achankeng (ed.), *Nationalism and Intra-State Conflicts in the Postcolonial World*, Lanham: Lexington Books, 2015, p. 113.
10. Kabir Tambar, *The Reckoning of Pluralism: Political Belonging and the Demands of History in Turkey*, Stanford: Stanford University Press, 2014, p. 5.

11. Ibid.
12. Anthony P. Cohen, *Symbolic Construction of Community*, London: Routledge, 2001, p. 12.
13. Gerard Delanty, *Community*, London: Routledge, 2003, p. 12.
14. James C. Scott, *Domination and the Arts of Resistance: Hidden Transcripts*, New Haven: Yale University Press, 1990.
15. For a specific case study on Palestine, see Julia Droeber, *The Dynamics of Coexistence in the Middle East: Negotiating Boundaries between Christians, Muslims, Jews and Samaritans in Palestine*, London: I. B. Tauris, 2014.
16. Representative scholarship that expands on the pluralism theory of pioneering figures such as William James, Isaiah Berlin, Stuart Hampshire, and John Rawls includes Connolly, *Pluralism*; Robert Talisse, *Pluralism and Liberal Politics*, New York: Routledge, 2012; Richard E. Flathman, *Pluralism and Liberal Democracy*, Baltimore: Johns Hopkins University Press, 2005; Peter Lassman, *Pluralism*, Cambridge: Polity Press, 2013; Thomas E. Hill, *Respect, Pluralism, and Justice: Kantian Perspectives*, Oxford: Oxford University Press, 2010; David B. Wong, *Natural Moralities: A Defense of Pluralistic Relativism*, Oxford: Oxford University Press, 2009.
17. On traditional legal pluralism, see Ido Shahar, *Legal Pluralism in the Holy City: Competing Courts, Forum Shopping, and Institutional Dynamics in Jerusalem*, London: Routledge, 2016; Anver M. Emon, *Religious Pluralism in Islamic Law: Dhimmīs and Others in the Empire of Law*, Oxford: Oxford University Press, 2012; Karen Barkey, "Aspects of Legal Pluralism in the Ottoman Empire," in Lauren A. Benton and Richard Jeffrey Ross (eds), *Legal Pluralism and Empires, 1500–1850*, New York: New York University Press, 2013, pp. 83–108; Timur Kuran, "The Economic Ascent of the Middle East's Religious Minorities: The Role of Islamic Legal Pluralism," *The Journal of Legal Studies*, 33, 2 (2004), pp. 475–515; Shlomo Deshen and Walter P. Zenner (eds), *Jews among Muslims: Communities in the Precolonial Middle East*, London: Macmillan, 1996.
18. Tambar, *The Reckoning of Pluralism*, p. 5.
19. Ibid., p. 14.
20. Ibid., p. 14.
21. Monique Deveaux, *Cultural Pluralism and Dilemmas of Justice*, Ithaca: Cornell University Press, 2000, p. 6.
22. For some of the more recent work that engages with this new set of challenges, see Stefano Moroni and David Weberman (eds), *Space and Pluralism: Can Contemporary Cities Be Places of Tolerance?*, Budapest: Central European University Press, 2016; Will Kymlicka, *Multicultural Odysseys: Navigating the New International Politics of Diversity*, Oxford: Oxford University Press, 2009; Thomas F. Banchoff, *Democracy and the New Religious Pluralism*, Oxford: Oxford University Press, 2007.
23. For a reflective essay on this shift, see Zygmunt Bauman, *Community: Seeking Safety in an Insecure World*, Cambridge: Polity Press, 2013.

24. James Tully, "Middle East Legal and Governmental Pluralism: A View of the Field from the Demos," *Middle East Law and Governance*, 4, 2–3 (2012), pp. 225–63.
25. For a study that examines the case of Syrian refugees in Turkey through solid ethnographic fieldwork and that goes beyond the official discourse of "state generosities" granted to displaced persons, see Ibrahim Sirkeci, Kadir Onur Unutulmaz, and Deniz Eroglu Utku (eds), *Turkey's Syrians: Today and Tomorrow*, London: Transnational Press, 2017. Also see Robert G. Rabil, *The Syrian Refugee Crisis in Lebanon: The Double Tragedy of Refugees and Impacted Host Communities*, Lanham: Lexington Books, 2016.
26. It is no coincidence that the urgency of the consequences and implications of migration in the aftermath of Arab Spring is reflected in a plethora of scholarship, including Martina Tazzioli, *Spaces of Governmentality: Autonomous Migration and the Arab Uprisings*, London: Rowman & Littlefield, 2015; Natalia Ribas-Mateos (ed.), *Migration, Mobilities and the Arab Spring: Spaces of Refugee Flight in the Eastern Mediterranean*, Cheltenham: Edward Elgar Publishing, 2016; Leïla Vignal (ed.), *The Transnational Middle East: People, Places, Borders*, New York: Routledge, 2016; Marion Boulby and Kenneth Christie (eds), *Migration, Refugees and Human Security in the Mediterranean and MENA*, New York: Palgrave Macmillan, 2018; Peter Seeberg and Zaid Eyadat (eds), *Migration, Security, and Citizenship in the Middle East: New Perspectives*, New York: Palgrave Macmillan, 2013.
27. Sami Zubaida, "The Question of Sectarianism in Middle East Politics," in Steven Vertovec (ed.), *Routledge International Handbook of Diversity Studies*, London: Routledge, 2015, p. 197. Dawn Chatty, *Displacement and Dispossession in the Modern Middle East*, New York: Cambridge University Press, 2010, p. 279.
28. Imad Salamey, *The Decline of Nation-States after the Arab Spring: The Rise of Communitocracy*, New York: Routledge, 2017, p. 17.
29. Bender and Klassen, "Habits of Pluralism," p. 15; emphasis added.
30. For the latest scholarship on minority rights in the Middle East, see Will Kymlicka and Eva Pföstl (eds), *Multiculturalism and Minority Rights in the Arab World*, Oxford: Oxford University Press, 2014; Ibrahim Zabad, *Middle Eastern Minorities: The Impact of the Arab Spring*, London: Routledge, 2017; Joshua Castellino and Kathleen A. Cavanaugh, *Minority Rights in the Middle East*, Oxford: Oxford University Press, 2013; Ofra Bengio and Gabriel Ben-Dor (eds), *Minorities and the State in the Arab World*, London: Lynne Rienner, 1999; Bas Ter Haar Romeny (ed), *Religious Origins of Nations? The Christian Communities of the Middle East*, Leiden: Brill, 2010.
31. See, e.g., Zulfikar Hirji (ed), *Diversity and Pluralism in Islam: Historical and Contemporary Discourses amongst Muslims*, London: I. B. Tauris, 2010; Yaser Ellethy, *Islam, Context, Pluralism and Democracy: Classical and Modern Interpretations*, New York: Routledge, 2015; Robert W. Hefner, ed. *Remaking Muslim Politics: Pluralism, Contestation, Democratization*, Princeton: Princeton

University Press, 2005; Abdou Filali-Ansary and Sikeena Karmali Ahmed (eds), *The Challenge of Pluralism: Paradigms from Muslim Contexts*, Edinburgh: Edinburgh University Press, 2009.

32. For an earlier chapter on this tension between religious and secular legal frames, see Saïd Amir Arjomand, "Religious Human Rights and the Principle of Legal Pluralism in the Middle East," in John Witte and Johan D. Van Der Vyver (eds), *Religious Human Rights in Global Perspective*, The Hague: Kluver Law International, 1996, pp. 331–47. See also Alessandro Ferrari and James Toronto, *Religions and Constitutional Transitions in the Muslim Mediterranean: The Pluralistic Moment*, New York: Routledge, 2017; Enayat Hadi, *Islam and Secularism in Post-Colonial Thought*, Cham: Palgrave Macmillan, 2017.
33. For a series of scholarly essays that probe into the relationship between Islamic law and international law, see Anver M. Emon, Mark Ellis and Benjamin Glahn (eds), *Islamic Law and International Human Rights Law: Searching for Common Ground?*, Oxford: Oxford University Press, 2012.
34. Shelly Culbertson and Louay Constant, *Education of Syrian Refugee Children: Managing the Crisis in Turkey, Lebanon, and Jordan*, Santa Monica, CA: Rand Corporation, 2015.
35. For a new study on Turkey, see Murat Ergin, *"Is the Turk a White Man?" Race and Modernity in the Making of Turkish Identity*, Leiden: Brill, 2017.
36. Paul Rowe, John Dyck, and Jens Zimmermann (eds), *Christians and the Middle East Conflict*, London: Routledge, 2014.
37. Benjamin Isakhan, José Antonio González Zarandona, and Taghreed Jamal Al-Deen, "Cultural Cleansing and Iconoclasm under the Islamic State: Attacks on Yezidi and Christian Humans/Heritage," Chapter 8 in this volume.

## 1. BETWEEN FAITH AND STATE: CONTEMPORARY CONFLICTS OVER DIVERSITY

1. See Saba Mahmood's study in which she argues that it was not the failure of secularism to take root in the Middle East that caused religious tensions and inequalities in the region, but rather the presence of modern secular governance. Saba Mahmood, *Religious Difference in a Secular Age: A Minority Report*, Princeton: Princeton University Press, 2015.
2. David Kennedy, "The International Human Rights Movement: Part of the Problem?," *15 Harvard Human Rights Journal*, 15 (2002), pp. 101–25, here 115.
3. Ibid., pp. 101–25, 101.
4. Refah Partisi (Welfare Party) and Others v. Turkey (ECHR GC) 14 B.H.R.C. 1, (2003) 37 E.H.R.R. 1.
5. Ibid., para. 123.
6. While this view is not exclusive to the Muslim world, as similar narratives running through more textualist readings of Judaism, Hinduism, and Christianity can also

be found, for the purposes of this chapter I will focus on the engagement of the human rights project in the MENA region where Islam is the dominant religion.

7. This term, applied to religion, was first used in a blog by Slavoj Žižek, "Passion in the Era of Decaffeinated Belief," www.lacan.com/passion.htm
8. One critique that hangs heavy over the human rights project is that it has been unable to render itself free from, as Kennedy notes, its "tainted origin" as a "product of a specific cultural and historical origin (Post-enlightenment, rationalist, secular, Western, modern, capitalist)." See Kennedy, "Part of the Problem?," p. 114.
9. José Casanova, "Immigration and the New Religious Pluralism: A EU/US Comparison" (Paper presented at the "The New Religious Pluralism and Democracy" conference, Washington, DC: Georgetown University, 21–2 April 2005), see pp. 6–7 (on file with author).
10. Kennedy, "Part of the Problem?," p. 114.
11. Henry Maine, *Early Law and Custom*, New York: Henry Holt, 1883, p. 5.
12. A. S. Diamond, *Primitive Law Past and Present*, London: Routledge, 1971, p. 47.
13. In Javier Martínez Torrón and W. C. Durham Jr, "Religion and the Secular State/La religion et l'état laïque," Interim National Reports Issued for the Occasion of the XVIIIth International Congress of Comparative Law, Provo: International Center for Law and Religion Studies, 2010, p. 2.
14. Ibid.
15. Ibid.
16. José Casanova, "Religion, European Secular Identities, and European Integration," in Timothy A. Byrnes and Peter J. Katzenstein (eds), *Religion in an Expanding Europe*, Cambridge: Cambridge University Press, 2006, p. 79.
17. Torrón and Durham, "Religion and the Secular State," p. 3.
18. www.bundesverfassungsgericht.de/SharedDocs/Entscheidungen/EN/2003/09/rs20030924_2bvr143602en.html
19. Ibid., para. 3.
20. Ibid., para. 64–71.
21. Anayasa Mahkemesi [Constitutional Court], 5 June 2008, Esas no. 2008/16 [Basis Number], Karar No. 2008/116 [Decision Number] (TC Resmi Gazete [Official Gazette of Republic of Turkey], 2008, No. 27032) (Turk.).
22. Sahin v. Turkey, App. no. 44774/98 (Eur. Ct. H.R. 10 November 2005) (Grand Chamber), *referral of* Sahin v. Turkey App. no. 44774/98 (Eur. Ct. H.R. 29 June 2004) at para. 12. The judgments and other decisions of the European Court of Human Rights are available online at http://www.echr.coe.int
23. Note that this "ban" was lifted in Turkey in 2008.
24. Sahin v. Turkey, App. no. 44774/98 (Eur. Ct. H.R. 10 November 2005) (Grand Chamber), *referral of* Sahin v. Turkey App. No. 44774/98 (Eur. Ct. H.R. 29 June 2004).
25. Ibid.

26. In this case, ECHR explicitly quoted the French National Assembly's bill of February 2004, which banned "visible" religious symbols in state primary and secondary schools.
27. Daniel Bodansky (ed.), INTERNATIONAL DECISION: Sahin v. Turkey; "Teacher Headscarf" Case (Cindy Skach): ECHR and German Constitutional Court decisions on wearing of Islamic head-scarves, 100 A.J.I.L. 186, p. 7.
28. Ibid., p. 5.
29. In English, the Justice and Development Party.
30. Casanova, "Immigration and the New Religious Pluralism," pp. 6–7.
31. Handyside v. United Kingdom (1979) 1 E.H.R.R. 737.
32. Talal Asad, *Formations of the Secular: Christianity, Islam, Modernity*, Stanford: Stanford University Press, 2003, pp. 6–7.
33. Ibid., p. 8.
34. Kathleen Cavanaugh, "Narrating Law," in Anver Emon, Mark Ellis, and Benjamin Glahn (eds), *Islamic Law and International Human Rights Law: Searching for Common Ground?*, London: Oxford University Press, 2012, p. 26.
35. Azzam Tamimi and John L Esposito (eds), *Islam and Secularism in the Middle East*, New York: NYU Press, 2000, p. 9.
36. Martti Koskenniemi, "International Law and Hegemony: A Reconfiguration," *Cambridge Review of International Affairs*, 17, 2 (2004), p. 199.
37. Samuel Moyn, *The Last Utopia: Human Rights in History*, Cambridge: Harvard University Press, 2010, p. 7.
38. Koskenniemi, "International Law and Hegemony," p. 198.
39. Also referred to as scholastic traditionalists. For more on this typology, see Moussa Abou Ramadan, "Notes on the *Shari'a*: Human Rights, Democracy and the European Court of Human Rights," *Israel Law Review*, 40, 1 (2007). For contemporary writers adopting this approach, see the works of Fazlur Rahman, Mohammed Arkoun, Mohammad Shahrour, and Khaled Abou El Fadl.
40. Tariq Ramadan, *Western Muslims and the Future of Islam*, London: Oxford University Press, 2004, p. 9.
41. Ibid., p. 9.
42. There are six main schools of thought in Islamic law. Four of these are Sunni schools: the Hanbali School, named after Ahmad Ibn Hanbal (d. 855); the Hanafi School, named after Abu Hanifa (d. 767); the Shafi'I, named after al-Shafi'I (d. 819); the Maliki is named after Anas bin Malik (d. 795). Two are Shi'a schools: the Zaydi School, named after Zayd Ibn Ali (d. 740); and the Ja'fari School, named after Ja'far al-Sadiq (d. 765). However, the multiplicity of readings provides for many more detours and points of departures, some of which are specific to a region or state.
43. Anver Emon, Mark Ellis, and Benjamin Glahn, "From Common Ground to Clearing Ground: A Model for Engagement in the 21st Century," in Emon, Ellis, and Glahn, *Islamic Law and International Human Rights Law*, p. 7.

44. Ibid., p. 6.
45. Ann Mayer, *Islam and Human Rights*, Boulder, CO: Westview, 2007, p. xiii.
46. Ibid., p. xi.
47. Mashood Baderin, *International Human Rights and Islamic Law*, Oxford: Oxford University Press, 2003, p. 13.
48. The division between formal source and legal reasoning and method is not consistently applied. Some scholars adjoin the sources of shari'a and *fiqh* while others indicate that these are in fact separate with one being a source and the other a method. I have opted for the latter definition as it more accurately reflects the function and form of each.
49. *Ijtihad* (independent legal reasoning) is sometimes (but not consistently) included, among scholars of Islamic law, as a fifth source of shari'a.
50. What Abdullahi Ahmed An-Na'im calls minor or subsidiary techniques and Tariq Ramadan refers to as "tools." See Abdullahi Ahmed An-Na'im, *Toward an Islamic Reformation: Civil Liberties, Human Rights and International Law*, Syracuse: Syracuse University Press, 1990, p. 25, and Tariq Ramadan, *Western Muslims and the Future of Islam*, Oxford: Oxford University Press, 2003, p. 37, respectively. Also, An-Na'im, *Toward an Islamic Reformation*, pp. 25–6.
51. Only a small number of Qur'anic verses have a legal element. Most of the verses relate to worship rituals, leaving only about eighty verses that, in strict terms, deal with legal subject matter. *Hudud* are fixed punishments generally prescribed for six offenses—for theft: amputation of a hand (*sariaqah*); for armed robbery or rebellion (*hirabah*): amputation of the hand and foot, banishment, crucifixion, or death; for adultery: stoning to death; for fornication (*zina*): 100 lashes; for apostasy (*riddah*): death; for intoxication (*sharb al-khamr*): forty or eighty lashes. *Qisas* are offenses for which the punishment is discretionary and rests with the victim of the offense (or his/her heirs) and the judge (or state).
52. Noel Coulson, *A History of Islamic Law*, Edinburgh: Edinburgh University Press, 1994, p. 12.
53. Ramadan, *Western Muslims and the Future of Islam*, p. 145
54. Baderin, *International Human Rights and Islamic Law*, p. 37
55. Ibid., p. 87
56. *Mujtahid* (singular). Scholars note that there are two types of Islamic legists, one who extracts legal rulings from scriptural sources without reference to a particular juridical school (*mujahid al-mutlaq*); and one for whom the extractions are tied to a particular juridical school (*mujtahid al-muqayyad*).
57. The Prophet was to have said: "My people shall never be unanimous in error."
58. Baderin was writing this with regard to the practice of slavery and arguing that by understanding *ijma* as consensus among Muslim states, one can conclude that "the doctrine of the overall objective of shari'a strongly supports the consensus on the total abolition of slavery under Islamic law." See Baderin, *International Human Rights and Islamic Law*, p. 88.

59. An-Na'im, *Toward an Islamic Reformation*, p. 25.
60. This goes some way to explaining the necessity to clarify, define, omit, and constantly restate the unsettled part of Islamic law so often seen in texts on the subject matter.
61. An-Na'im, *Toward an Islamic Reformation*, p. 104.
62. Ibid., p. 105.
63. Ann Mayer, "Reviewed Work: *The Islamic Criminal Justice System*, by Cherif Bassiouni," *The American Journal of Comparative Law*, 31 (Spring 1983), p. 363.
64. Sadiq Reza, "Due Process in Islamic Criminal Law," *George Washington International Law Review*, 1 (2013), p. 3.
65. Ibid., p. 2
66. Mayer, "A Critique of An-Na'im's Assessment of Islamic Criminal Justice," p. 47.
67. While this is not a position that is universally adopted, a number of writers share his view that there are differences among scholars (and indeed schools) regarding the offenses of apostasy and intoxication.
68. The six crimes for which *hadd* punishments are fixed; these are: theft (amputation of the hand), illicit sexual relations (death by stoning or 100 lashes), making unproven accusations of illicit sex (eighty lashes), drinking intoxicants (eighty lashes), apostasy (death or banishment), and highway robbery (death).
69. An-Na'im, *Toward an Islamic Reformation*, p. 112
70. Although this private–public divide is more anchored in Western thought, and a right to privacy is a notion that does not have conceptual autonomy, Islamic law does emphasize the private sphere of the family and the Qur'an notes that certain realms within family life, including unlawful intrusion in the private life, home, correspondence with others, are prohibited. Qur'an (24:27) states: "Do not enter houses other than your own unless you have asked permission and greeted the inhabitants!" There is also a general injunction not to pry and spy on people (Qur'an 49:12). Reza, "Due Process in Islamic Criminal Law," p. 12.
71. Baderin, *International Human Rights and Islamic Law*, p. 84, 85.
72. Reza, "Due Process in Islamic Criminal Law," p. 19.
73. Ibid., p. 20.
74. Ibid., p. 18.
75. Mayer, *Islam and Human Rights*, p. 10.
76. See Derek Gregory, *The Colonial Present*, Malden: Blackwell, 2008, p. 18. See also M. E. Sörli, N. P. Gledisch and H. Strand, "Why Is There So Much Conflict in the Middle East?," *Journal of Conflict Resolution*, 49, 1 (2005), p. 141
77. Elizabeth Shakman Hurd, "Politics of Sectarianism: Rethinking Religion and Politics in the Middle East," *Middle East Law and Governance*, 7 (2015), pp. 61–75, 61.
78. Ibid., p. 61.
79. See, e.g., John R. Bradley, *After the Arab Spring: How the Islamists Hijacked the Middle East Revolts*, London: Palgrave Macmillan, 2012.

80. Although the Muslim Brotherhood's political wing did not emerge until 2011, it had already established a number of charitable organisations, as well as a network of mosques, both of which provided services to the poor. For additional information on the Muslim Brotherhood, see Samer Shehata and Joshua Stacher, "The Brotherhood Goes to Parliament," *Middle East Report*, 240 (Fall 2006), pp. 30–9.
81. A piece published by *The Economist* immediately after the first round of elections in Egypt captured such a framing. [Leader], "From Arab Spring to Islamists Winter," *The Economist*, 10 December 2011.
82. The narrative that was uncritically accepted was that the removal of FJP was necessary to protect vulnerable communities (minorities and women).
83. On Iran and religious minorities in particular, see Eliz Sanasarian, *Religious Minorities in Iran*, Cambridge: Cambridge University Press, 2000; and on gender in Iran and in Muslim states, Ziba Mir-Hosseini, *Islam and Gender: The Religious Debate in Contemporary Iran*, Princeton: Princeton University Press, 1999; Mir-Hosseini (with Richard Tapper), *Islam and Democracy in Iran: Eshkevari and the Quest for Reform*, London: I.B. Tauris, 2006; and Mir-Hosseini (with Vanja Hamzic), *Control and Sexuality: The Revival of Zina Laws in Muslim Contexts* (Women Living under Muslim Laws, 2010). For a more nuanced analysis on Saudi Arabia, see Madawi al-Rasheed, *Contesting the Saudi State: Islamic Voices from a New Generation*, Cambridge: Cambridge Middle East Studies, 2006.
84. Eric Davis "Rebuilding a Non Sectarian Iraq," *Strategic Insights*, 6 (2007), p. 6.
85. For more on the concept of legal pluralism (including critique), see Franz von Benda-Beckmann, "Who's Afraid of Legal Pluralism?," *Journal of Legal Pluralism & Unofficial Law*, 47 (2002), p. 37; David M. Engel, "Legal Pluralism in an American Community: Perspectives on a Civil Trial Court," *American Bar Foundation Research Journal*, 5, 3 (1980), p. 425; Marc Galanter, "Justice in Many Rooms: Courts, Private Ordering, and Indigenous Law," *Journal of Legal Pluralism & Unofficial Law*, 13, 19 (1981), pp. 1, 28–34; John Griffiths, "What Is Legal Pluralism?," *Journal of Legal Pluralism & Unofficial Law*, 24, 1 (1986); Sally Engle Merry, "International Law and Sociolegal Scholarship: Toward a Spatial Global Legal Pluralism," *Studies in Law Politics and Society*, 41 (2007); Engle Merry, "Legal Pluralism," *Law & Society Review*, 22 (1988), pp. 869, 870; Sally Falk Moore, "Law and Social Change: The Semi-Autonomous Social Field as an Appropriate Subject of Study," *Law & Society Review*, 7 (1973), p. 719; Balakrishnan Rajagopal, "The Role of Law in Counter-hegemonic Globalization and Global Legal Pluralism: Lessons from the Narmada Valley Struggle in India," *Leiden Journal of International Law*, 18 (2005), p. 345; Brian Z. Tamanaha, "A Non-Essentialist Version of Legal Pluralism," *Journal of Law & Society*, 27 (2000), p. 296.
86. See Marie Rose Zalzal, "Secularism and Personal Status Codes in Lebanon: Interview with Marie Rose Zalzal," *Middle East Report*, 203, Lebanon and Syria: The Geopolitics of Change (Spring 1997), pp. 37–9.
87. One example of this is the practice of Female Genital Mutilation, which, while

practiced in Muslim states, is not mentioned in the Qur'an. That said, proponents of FGM have ascribed certain verses of the Qur'an, most notably 16:123, to give the practice an Islamic basis.

88. Kathleen Cavanaugh and Joshua Castellino, *Minority Rights in the Middle East*, Oxford: Oxford University Press, 2012, p. 32.
89. Kathleen Cavanaugh and Edel Hughes, "Rethinking What Is Necessary in a Democratic Society: Militant Democracy and the Turkish State," *Human Rights Quarterly*, 38 (2016), p. 654.
90. Joan E. Scott, "Deconstructing Equality-Versus-Difference: Or, the Uses of Poststructuralist Theory for Feminism," *Feminist Studies*, 14 (1988), p. 43.
91. Ibid.
92. Kennedy, "The International Human Rights Movement," p. 114.
93. Andrew March, "Rethinking Religious Reasons in Public Justification," *American Political Science Review*, 107, 3 (2013), p. 535.

## 2. FORMAL EDUCATION SYSTEMS AS ARENAS OF INCLUSION AND EXCLUSION: COMPARATIVE CASE STUDIES FROM LEBANON AND SYRIA

1. Annika Rabo, "Tapping a Potential For the Good Of All," paper delivered at TEND 2000: Proceedings of the Technological Education and National Development Conference, "Crossroads of the New Millennium" (2nd, April 8-10, 2000, Abu Dhabi, United Arab Emirates), https://files.eric.ed.gov/fulltext/ED446265.pdf.
2. See, e.g., United Nations Development Programme and Arab Fund for Economic and Social Development, *The Arab Human Development Report 2003: Building a Knowledge Society*, New York: United Nations Publications, 2003.
3. I will use material collected in the project *Perceptions of Development in the Middle East*, financed by the Swedish Research Council in the Humanities and Social Sciences between 1988 and 1990, where I did fieldwork in Jordan and Syria; and from the project *Future Citizens in Pedagogic Texts and Educational Policies: Examples from Lebanon, Sweden and Turkey*, financed by the Education Committee of the Swedish Research Council between 2011 and 2013. Originally, Syria was part of the project but was taken out in 2012 and substituted with Lebanon. I have, however, tried to follow the educational developments inside Syria, and among exiled Syrians as much as possible since then. I want to thank Marie Carlson, Sabine Gruber, and Tuba Kanci for their efforts in this project, and in particular Rima Bahous and Mona Nabhani, for the collaboration in collecting and analyzing the Lebanese material, some of which is used here. In these projects, the textbook focus has been on grades eight and nine.
4. Rabo, "Tapping a Potential For the Good Of All."
5. For more details on curriculum theory, see, e.g., Ulf P. Lundgren, "Educational Research and the Language of Education," in Stephen J. Ball and Staffan Larsson

(eds), *The Struggle for Democratic Education: Equality and Participation*, New York: Falmer Press, 1989, pp. 191–210; Göran Linde, *On Curriculum Transformation: Explaining Selection of Content in Teaching*, Stockholm: HLS, 1993.

6. Ernest Gellner, *Nations and Nationalism*, Oxford: Blackwell, 1989, p. 34.
7. John Boli, *New Citizens for a New Society: The Institutional Origins of Mass Schooling in Sweden*, Oxford: Pergamon Press, 1989, p. 108.
8. Ibid., p. 109.
9. Ibid., p. 41. For a highly original and thought-provoking analysis of modern education, see Peter McLaren, *Schooling as a Ritual Performance*, 3rd rev. edn, London: Routledge & Kegan Paul, 1999 [1986].
10. Boli, *New Citizens for a New Society*, p. 41.
11. In *Education, Globalization and the Nation State*, Houndmills Basingstoke: Macmillan Press, 1997, p. 142, Andy Green notes that since the 1980s education has been tightly linked to national economic competitiveness rather than to nation-building and national cohesion.
12. For a useful early overview of this field, see Ingemar Fägerlind and Lawrence J. Saha, *Education and National Development: A Comparative Perspective*, Oxford: Pergamon Press, 1983.
13. Joseph S. Szyliowicz, *Education and Modernization in the Middle East*, Ithaca: Cornell University Press, 1973.
14. If a reader sees—reads—beyond the book's outdated theoretical framework, it actually includes a great deal of highly interesting and valuable data on the educational developments in the Middle East generally, and on Turkey, Iran, and Egypt specifically, in the nineteenth and twentieth centuries.
15. See, e.g., *Towards Knowledge Societies: UNESCO World Report*, Paris: UNESCO Publications, 2005.
16. United Nations Development Programme and Arab Fund for Economic and Social Development, *Arab Human Development Report 2002: Creating Opportunities for Future Generations*, New York: United Nations Publications, 2002. This report has been followed by reports in 2003, 2004, 2005, and 2009; Osama Abi-Mershed (ed.), *Trajectories of Education in the Arab World: Legacies and Challenges*, London: Routledge, 2010, is one highly interesting example of the reactions to the report.
17. *Arab Human Development Report 2002*, p. 55.
18. See, e.g., Muhammad Faour and Marwan Muasher, "Education for Citizenship in the Arab World," in *The Carnegie Papers*, New York: Carnegie Middle East Center, 2011; and Rima Karami Akkary, "Facing the Challenge of Educational Reform in the Arab World," *Journal of Educational Change*, 15 (2014), pp. 179–202.
19. André Elias Mazawi, "Naming the Imaginary: 'Building an Arab Knowledge Society' and the Contested Terrain of Educational Reforms for Development," in Abi-Mershed, *Trajectories of Education in the Arab World*, pp. 215–16.

20. For the Arab world, see, e.g., Muna Amr, "Teacher Education for Inclusive Education in the Arab World: The Case of Jordan," *Prospects*, 41 (2011), pp. 399–413.
21. Annika Rabo, "Talet om mångfald i svensk utbildning," in Anders Gustavsson et al. (eds), *Främlingskap och Tolkning: En Vänbok till Charles Westin*, Stockholm: Stockholms Universitets Förlag, 2008, p. 133.
22. Palestinians in pre-2011 Syria could attend Syrian public schools or schools run by UNRWA. The latter catered to about 45,000 pupils in Syria and about 40,000 in Lebanon before 2011. The issue of education for Palestinians in Lebanon and Syria is highly relevant and important when discussing inclusion and exclusion, but it is too vast to be included in this particular text.
23. Considering the low quality of education in many schools in Lebanon and the low public spending on education, it is perhaps surprising that the literacy rate is high: 94 percent of the population above age fifteen were literate in 2015 according to UNESCO statistics.
24. For critical analysis of changes in multicultural policies in Swedish education, see Sabine Gruber and Annika Rabo, "Multiculturalism Swedish Style: Shifts and Sediments in Educational Policies and Textbooks," *Policy Futures in Education*, 12 (2014), pp. 56–66. See also Rabo, "Talet om mångfald i svensk utbildning," pp. 132–51.
25. For a very interesting comparison between the practice of French and Swedish teachers, see Jannete Hentati, "Skolan utom sig," PhD diss., Stockholm University, 2017. For a wider and innovative comparison, see Werner Schiffauer et al. (eds), *Civil Enculturation: Nation-State, School and Ethnic Difference in the Netherlands, Britain, Germany and France*, New York: Berghahn Books, 2004.
26. Rima Bahous, Mona Nabhani, and Annika Rabo, "Parochial Education in a Global World? Teaching History and Civics in Lebanon," *Nordidactica: Journal of Humanities and Social Science Education*, 1 (2013), p. 145.
27. See also Zeena Zakharia, "Language-in-Education Policies in Contemporary Lebanon: Youth Perspectives," in Abi-Mershed, *Trajectories of Education in the Arab World*.
28. Tabitha Petran, *Syria*, London: Ernest Benn, 1972, p. 69.
29. This was changed to nine years in the 1980s, and in the early twenty-first century there was a plan to increase it to ten years.
30. This was according to official statistics, which did not always take drop-outs into account. The high percentage of pupils underlines, of course, that Syria had a very young population.
31. The Syrian state obtained less rent from abroad and started far-reaching reforms. See, e.g., Eberhard Kienle (ed.), *Contemporary Syria: Liberalization between Cold War and Cold Peace*, London: I. B. Tauris, 1994.
32. From Rima Nehme, "The Standardized History Textbook for Lebanon: Impact of Politics on Education," MA diss., Beirut: Lebanese American University, 2006, pp. 47–8.

33. Munir Bashshour, "The Deepening Cleavage in the Educational Systems," in T. Hanf and N. Salam (eds), *Lebanon in Limbo: Postwar Society and State in an Uncertain Regional Environment*, Baden-Baden: Nomos Verlagsgesellschaft, 2003, p. 163.
34. Ibid., pp. 164–5.
35. Bahous, Nabhani, and Rabo, "Parochial Education," p. 67.
36. Werner Schiffauer and Thijl Sunier, "Representing the Nation in History Textbooks," in Schiffauer et al., *Civil Enculturation*, p. 33.
37. In 2012, I bought used civics textbook for grades seven, eight, and nine. In one of them, a former pupil had written "how BORING" on the first page. From what I understand, pupils are not very enthusiastic about this school subject.
38. Teachers and student teachers I talked to said that eighth-grade books were rarely read to the end. Instead, they start on ninth grade books to prepare for exams the year ahead. This way of teaching and learning is not unique to Lebanon, of course. See Bahous, Nabhani, and Rabo, "Parochial Education," p. 68.
39. Saladin, for example, is depicted not as a Muslim, but rather as an Arab hero. Among Kurds in Syria, however, he is appropriated as a Kurdish hero.
40. I have not systematically scrutinized textbooks used in the twenty-first century, but my impression is that there has not been much change.
41. For a very detailed and important contribution to textbook analysis in history, see Ulrike Freitag, *Geschichtsschreibung in Syrien 1920–1990: Zwischen Wissenschaft und Ideologie*, Hamburg: Deutsches Orient-Institut, 1991.
42. Unlike Jordanian textbooks where religion was greatly emphasized.
43. Monika Bolliger, "Writing Syrian History while Propagating Arab Nationalism: Textbooks about Modern Arab History under Hafiz and Bashar al-Asad," *Journal of Educational Media, Memory, and Society*, 3 (2011), pp. 96–112, notes that a new textbook from 2004 for the twelfth grade had a chapter on globalization.
44. Religious education was compulsory, but the grade was not included in the overall points in examination.
45. For highly diverging views on religious education in Syria, compare Joshua Landis, "Syria, Secularism, Arabism, and Sunni Orthodoxy," in E. A. Doumato and G. Starrett (eds), *Teaching Islam: Textbooks and Religion in the Middle East*, Boulder, CO: Lynne Rienner, 2007, pp. 177–96, and Monique C. Cardinal, "Religious Education in Syria: Unity and Difference," *British Journal of Religious Education*, 31 (2009), pp. 91–101. Landis claims that the curricula is intolerant and ignores religious minorities, Cardinal claims it is tolerant. For in-depth analysis of Hafiz al-Asad regime's complicated relationship with religion, see Annabelle Böttcher, *Syrische Religionspolitik unter Asad*, Freiburg: Arnold-Bergstraesser-Institut, 1998.
46. The *national* in the Syrian subject (*qawmiyya*) has a very different connotation in the Mashreq compared with the *national* in the Lebanese subject (*wataniyya*).

*Qaum* is clearly associated with the ethnos—the people—and a central concept in Ba'th ideology. In Syria, there is furthermore no *civil* (*madani*) in the title of the subject.

47. Perhaps this stress should be linked to the situation in Syria after the so-called events in the early 1980s when militant Muslim Brothers (and leftists) revolted and were crushed.
48. The subject is still taught in regime-controlled areas and for those pupils in Lebanon or Turkey who sit the "national" Syrian examination.
49. The members of the second largest Christian community in Lebanon, the Greek Orthodox in Lebanon, have generally associated themselves as Arabs.
50. I use the present tense in this section because although much of the Syrian school system is in ruins at the time of writing, in regime-controlled areas there has been no change of curricula and no effort made to rethink the Ba'th variety of Arab nationalism or to stop lauding the al-Asad family.
51. The president, however, should be Muslim according to the constitution.
52. With Syriacs, I mean those Syrian Orthodox or Syrian Catholics who do not have Arabic as their mother tongue or who regard themselves as non-Arab. The history of Armenian and Assyrian/Syriac education from the Ottoman period and onward is varied and complex. See, e.g., Nicola Migliorino, "'Kullna suriyyin'? The Armenian Community and the State in Contemporary Syria," *Revue du mondes musulmans et de la méditerranée*, 115–16 (2006), pp. 97–115, special issue entitled *La Syrie au quotidien: Cultures et pratiques du changement.*
53. These non-Arab "guests" have a very long history in what became Syria, but many also arrived to the north and northeast of Syria in the turbulent years around the First World War.
54. The situation for Kurds in pre-2011 Syria is quite complex and outside the scope of this text, but the presence of Kurds was not denied by the regime or non-Kurdish people at large. Many who lived in the center of the country were Arabized for centuries but still retained a Kurdish identity and were regarded as such.
55. *Arab Human Development Report 2002*, executive summary, p. 2.
56. I have not made or seen any systematic research on the visibility or invisibility of migration in Arab curricula as a whole, but I suspect that the situation is similar to that of Lebanon and Syria.
57. For discussion on the complex issue of "majority/minority" debates and sensitivities in pre-2011 Syria, see, e.g., Annika Rabo, "Conviviality and Conflict in Contemporary Aleppo," in Anh Nga Longva and Anne Sofie Roald (eds), *Religious Minorities in the Middle East: Domination, Self-Empowerment, Accommodation*, Leiden: Brill, 2011, pp. 123–47.
58. Zeina Bali, "Domination, Privilege and Fear: Uncovering a Hidden Curriculum of Oppression in the Syrians' Narratives on School," MA diss., Lund University, 2015. The dissertation is highly critical of the regime, and the author has inter-

viewed former pupils who have experienced oppression and who sided with the uprising in 2011.

59. Most of the information about education for Syrians after 2011 is taken from the research report (supervised by Dawn Chatty), Hashem Ahmadzadeh et al., "Ensuring Quality Education for Young Refugees from Syria (12–25 Years): A Mapping Exercise," Refugee Studies Centre, University of Oxford, September 2014. This publication can be downloaded from the center's website.
60. Syrians who have fled to the neighboring countries are mainly self-settled and not all are registered with the UNHCR.

## 3. THE RULING FAMILY'S HEGEMONY: INCLUSION AND EXCLUSION IN QATARI SOCIETY

1. Mohammed Arkoun defines the "social imaginaire" as the "Dynamic, imaginative mould by which a society orders her experiences and structures her relations both inward and outward. This mould is imaginative because it is primarily a matter of collective representation and not one of rationally formulated concepts. Such concepts, however, do find their origin in the social imaginaire and can themselves become part of it in the process of historical change." Rein Fernhout, Henry Jansen, and Lucy Jansen-Hofland, *Canonical Texts: Bearers of Absolute Authority. Bible, Koran, Veda, Tipitaka; A Phenomenological Study*, Amsterdam: Rodopi, 1994, p. 234. For further discussion on the concept of the *imaginaire*, refer to Mohammed Arkoun, *The Unthought in Contemporary Islamic Thought*, London: Saqi Books, 2002.
2. Abd means slave. It is a term used in the Arab states of the Persian Gulf to refer to citizens of slave background. Hawalah are Arab tribes that migrated to Persia during times of drought and famine in Arabia, and then migrated back to the Arabian peninsula when conditions improved. The purity of these tribes' Arab blood is contested due to the possibility of their having mixed with Persians through intermarriages.
3. Social inclusion and exclusion is a dynamic process of social estrangement based on categorical perceptions that affect individuals' membership of their society, hence resulting in an adversarial relationship between the excluding and excluded that threatens social cohesion.
4. Adham Saouli, *The Arab State: Dilemmas of Late Formation*, New York: Routledge, 2012, pp. 16–19.
5. Zakariya Al Shalaq et al., *Al Tarikh Al Syassy Ledewal Al Khaleej Al Arabiyya: Al Hadith Wal Moaaser*, 7th edn, Doha: Renoda Modern Printing, 2015, p. 82.
6. Jill Crystal, *Oil and Politics in the Gulf: Rulers and Merchants in Kuwait and Qatar*, Cambridge: Cambridge University Press, 1990, p. 133.
7. Ibid.
8. Zahlan, *The Creation of Qatar*, p. 99.

9. Great Britain, Admiral Naval Staff, Naval Intelligence Division, and Geographical Section, *A Handbook of Arabia*, vol. 1, Oxford: Oxford University Press, 1920, p. 328.
10. John Gordon Lorimer, *Gazetteer of the Persian Gulf*, Westmead: Gregg International Publishers, 1970, pp. 1530–1.
11. Ibid., p. 2288.
12. Crystal, *Oil and Politics in the Gulf*, p. 119.
13. Max Weber, *From Max Weber: Essays in Sociology*, Oxford: Oxford University Press, 1946, p. 181; Robert C. Tucker (ed.), *The Marx–Engels Reader*, 2nd edn, New York: W. W. Norton, 1978, p. 441.
14. Islam Hassan, "Social Stratification in Qatari Society: Family, Marriage, and Khaleeji Culture," in "Family in the Arabian Peninsula," ed. Lauren-Elizabeth Wanucha and Zahra Babar, CIRS Special Issue of *HAWWA* (forthcoming).
15. Zahlan, *The Creation of Qatar*, p. 99.
16. Crystal, *Oil and Politics in the Gulf*, p. 146.
17. Ibid., pp. 146–7.
18. Saouli, *The Arab State*, pp. 8–9.
19. Ibid., pp. 16–17.
20. Ibid., p. 19.
21. Ibid., p. 16.
22. Ibid., pp. 18–19.
23. Ibid., p. 20.
24. Ibid., pp. 19–21.
25. Antonio Gramsci, *Selections from the Prison Notebooks of Antonio Gramsci*, ed. and trans. Quentin Hoare and Geoffrey Nowell-Smith, London: Lawrence & Wishart, 1971, p. 244.
26. Ibid., p. 12.
27. Ibid.
28. Ibid.
29. James Harold Farney, *Social Conservatives and Party Politics in Canada and the United States*, Toronto: University of Toronto Press, 2012, pp. 21–23.
30. Lyle A. Scruggs and James P. Allan, "Social Stratification and Welfare Regimes for the 21st Century: Revisiting the 'Three Worlds of Welfare Capitalism,'" paper delivered at the Fifteenth International Conference of Europeanists, Chicago, 2006, p. 3; http://councilforeuropeanstudies.org/files/Papers/ScruggsAllan.pdf
31. Ibid., p. 4.
32. Ibid., p. 6.
33. Thomas R. Bates, "Gramsci and the Theory of Hegemony," *Journal of the History of Ideas*, 36, 2 (April–June 1975), p. 355.
34. Mehran Kamrava, "State–Business Relations and Clientelism in Qatar," *Journal of Arabian Studies*, 7, 1 (2017), p. 7.

35. For further discussion on this topic, refer to Karen Exell, *Modernity and the Museum in the Arabian Peninsula*, New York: Routledge, 2016; E. Davis, "Theorizing Statecraft and Social Change in Arab Oil-Producing Countries," in E. Davis and N. Gavrielides (eds), *Statecraft in the Middle East: Oil, Historical Memory and Popular Culture*, Miami: Florida International University, 1991, pp. 1–35; and Crystal, *Oil and Politics in the Gulf.*
36. Anthony D. Smith, *National Identity*, Reno: University of Nevada Press, 1991, p. 14.
37. Steven Wright, "Qatar," in Christopher M. Davidson (ed.), *Power and Politics in the Persian Gulf Monarchies*, New York: Columbia University Press, 2011, p. 121.
38. Smith, *National Identity*, 14.
39. Kamrava, "State–Business Relations and Clientelism in Qatar," p. 2.
40. Exell, *Modernity and the Museum in the Arabian Peninsula*, p. 136.
41. Nazih Ayubi, *Over-Stating the Arab State: Politics and Society in the Middle East*, London: I. B. Tauris, 2009, p. 224.
42. Ali Al Shawi, "Political Influences of Tribes in the State of Qatar: Impact of Tribal Loyalty on Political Participation," PhD diss., Mississippi State University, 2002, p. 22.
43. Rebecca L. Torstrick and Elizabeth Faier, *Culture and Customs of the Arab Gulf States*, Westport: Greenwood Press, 2009, p. 111.
44. For further discussion on tribes as political parties of Yemen, see Mohammad M. Al-Dhahiri, *The Tribe's Political Role in Yemen*, Cairo: Madboly, 1996.
45. Al Shawi, "Political Influences of Tribes in the State of Qatar," p. 23.
46. Ibid.
47. Constitution of the State of Qatar, Article 1.
48. *Qatar: Year Book 2009*, Doha: State of Qatar Ministry of Foreign Affairs, 2009, p. 2.
49. For further discussion, refer to Exell, *Modernity and the Museum in the Arabian Peninsula*, p. 42; Christopher Davidson, *The United Arab Emirates: A Study in Survival*, Boulder, CO: Lynne Rienner, 2005, pp. 77–80;
50. Exell, *Modernity and the Museum in the Arabian Peninsula*, p. 34; and M. MacLean, "Museums in Context: Built Environment, National Identity, and Emirati History," paper presented at the Fifth Annual Gulf Research Meeting, University of Cambridge, Cambridge.
51. Mohammed Alsudairi and Rogaia Mustafa Abusharaf, "Migration in Pre-oil Qatar: A Sketch," *Studies in Ethnicity and Nationalism*, 15, 3 (2015), pp. 511–21, here p. 518.
52. Constitution of the State of Qatar, Article 1.
53. *Acquisition of Qatari Nationality*, Law no. 38 of Year 2005, Article 2.
54. Wall text for Bin Jelmood House, 2016, Msheireb Museums, Doha.
55. Ibid.

56. Kishwar Rizvi, *The Transnational Mosque: Architecture and Historical Memory in the Contemporary Middle East*, North Carolina: University of North Carolina Press, 2015, p. 155.
57. Mehran Kamrava, *Qatar: Small State, Big Politics*, Ithaca: Cornell University Press, 2013, p. 134.
58. Allen James Fromherz, *Qatar: A Modern History*, London: I. B. Tauris, 2012, p. 93.
59. Kamrava, *Qatar*, p. 123.
60. Ibid., p. 61.
61. Ibid., p. 123.
62. Interview by Islam Hassan. Personal interview. Doha, Qatar, 14 November 2016.
63. Wall text for Bin Jelmood House, 2016, Msheireb Museums, Doha.
64. Ramadan is a holy month in the Islamic year during which Muslims are required to fast from sunrise to sunset. Eid is an important Islamic festival. Eid al-Fitr marks the end of Ramadan, and Eid al-Udha marks the end of the Haj, or pilgrimage to Mecca, season.
65. Smith, *National Identity*, p. 14.
66. *Qatar: Year Book 2009*, p. 3.
67. Qatari Government. "The National Day," Hukoomi website; http://portal.www.gov.qa/wps/portal/about-qatar/nationalday (accessed 13 November 2015).
68. *Qatar: Year Book 2009*, p. 3.
69. Sheila B. Kamerman and Alfred J. Kahn, *Family Change and Family Policies in Great Britain, Canada, New Zealand, and the United States*, New York: Clarendon Press, 1997, p. 7.
70. Ibid.
71. Ibid.
72. Ibid.
73. Chiara Saraceno, "Family Policies. Concepts, Goals and Instruments," Turin, Italy, 2011, pp. 3–4; www.carloalberto.org/assets/working-papers/no. 230.pdf
74. Ibid., p. 4.
75. Wright, "Qatar," p. 120.
76. Constitution of the State of Qatar, Article 67.
77. Ibid., Article 21.
78. Ibid., Article 24.
79. "The Family Law," Law no. 22 of Year 2006.
80. *Al-Qanuwwn Raqm (1) Lsnat 2000 Biaṣḍar Qanuwwn Ṭnẓiyym bʿḍ A'wḍaʿ w I'gra'at al-taqaḍi fiyy Masa'il al-Aḥwal al-Shakhṣiyya.*
81. Ibid., Article 26.
82. Ibid., Article 27.
83. Ibid., Article 29.
84. Ibid., Article 31.
85. *Al-Kafa'ah Fyy Al-Nasab ... Ro'yyah Sharʿyyah*. Islamweb, 9 May 2007; http://

fatwa.islamweb.net/fatwa/index.php?page=showfatwa (accessed 20 November 2016).

86. Bernard Lewis, *Race and Slavery in the Middle East: An Historical Enquiry*, New York: Oxford University Press, 1990, p. 85.
87. *Al-Kafa'ah Fyy Al-Nasab ... Ro'yyah Shar'yyah.*
88. "Qatari Nationality Law (Repealed)," Law no. 2 of Year 1961, Article 12.
89. Wright, "Qatar," p. 121.
90. "Acquisition of Qatari Nationality," Law no. 38 of Year 2005, Article 2.
91. Ghada Al-Subaey, "Women's Citizenship Laws in the Gulf: Understanding Citizenship Laws in Qatar and UAE," Certificate of Arab and Regional Studies Thesis, Georgetown University, 2013, p. 19.
92. Ibid.
93. Ibid.
94. "Acquisition of Qatari Nationality," Law no. 38 of Year 2005, Article 2.
95. "Marriage to Foreigners," Law no. 21 of Year 1989, amended by Law no. 11 of Year 1994, and Law no. 8 of Year 2005.
96. Ibid., Article 1.
97. Ibid., Article 3.

## 4. THE SHI'I STATE AND THE SOCIOECONOMIC CHALLENGES OF THE SUNNI COMMUNITIES IN IRAN: HISTORICAL AND CONTEMPORARY PERSPECTIVES

1. Constitution of the Islamic Republic of Iran, Articles 12 and 13.
2. It is also important to note that the constitution acknowledges ethnic pluralism in the country, but it does not give any ethnic group an automatic minority status.
3. Lois Beck, "Iran's Ethnic, Religious, and Tribal Minorities," in Lawrence G. Potter (ed.), *Sectarian Politics in the Persian Gulf*, London: Hurst, 2014, pp. 245–6.
4. Ibid.
5. Stéphane A. Dudoignon, "Sunnis and Shiites in Iran since 1979: Confrontations, Exchanges, Convergences," in Brigitte Maréchal and Sami Zenmi (eds), *The Dynamics of Sunni–Shia Relationships: Doctrine, Transnationalism, Intellectuals and the Media*, London: Hurst, 2013, pp. 143–4.
6. Sekandar Amanolahi, "A Note on Ethnicity and Ethnic Groups in Iran," *Iran & the Caucasus*, 9, 1 (2005), pp. 39–40.
7. Amin Moghadam, "The Other Shore, Iranians in the United Arab Emirates: Between Visibility and Invisibility," in Annabelle Sreberny and Massoumeh Torfeh (eds), *Cultural Revolution in Iran, Contemporary Popular Culture in the Islamic Republic*, London: I. B. Tauris, 2013, p. 248.
8. Sabri Ateş, *Ottoman–Iranian Borderlands: Making a Boundary, 1843–1914*, Cambridge: Cambridge University Press, 2013, pp. 50–1; and Firuz Kazemzadeh,

*Russia and Britain in Persia: Imperial Ambitions in Qajar Iran*, London: I. B. Tauris, 2013.

9. Akbar Zavari-Rezayi, "Et'telā' āt-i Darbārey-i Kūresonnī-hāy-i Azarbāyjān" [Some information regarding the Küresünlī of Azerbaijan], personal Weblog of Akbar Zavari-Rezayi, 13 May 2011; http://azrurmia.blogfa.com/post-2557.aspx
10. Fariba Adelkhah and Zuzanna Olszewska, "The Iranian Afghans," *Iranian Studies*, 40, 2 (April 2007), p. 141.
11. Tarāneh Banī'yaghūb, "Mādarān-i Sargardān, Farzandān-i Bi'shenās'nāmeh: Zendeh'gī-i Zanān-i Irānī bā Hamsarān-i Afghān" [Distressed mothers and children without identity papers: Life of Iranian women with Afghan spouses], *Iran* newspaper, 3 Mordād-i 1395/26 July 2016, p. 9.
12. Adelkhah and Olszewska, "The Iranian Afghans," p. 143.
13. Moojan Momen, *An Introduction to Shi'i Islam: The History and Doctrines of Twelver Shi'ism*, New Haven: Yale University Press, 1985, pp. 103–4.
14. Colin Turner, *Islam without Allah? The Rise of Religious Externalism in Safavid Iran*, Richmond: Curzon Press, 2000, pp. 48–50; Rasūl Ja'fariyān, *Ṭārīkh-I ṭashay'yo dar Irān: az āghāz tā tolou-i dawlat-I Safavi* [A history of Shi'ism in Iran, from the beginning to the rise of Safavid state], Tehran: Nāshr-i Elm, 2007 [1386], pp. 774–6 and 809–20.
15. Turner, *Islam without Allah?*, p. 209.
16. Andrew J. Newman, *Safavid Iran, Rebirth of a Persian Empire*, London: I. B. Tauris, 2006, pp. 55–60; Turner, *Islam without Allah?*, pp. 79–90; Aghājarī, *Moghadame'ī bar monāsebāṭ-i dīn va dawlat dar Irān-i asr-i safavī* [A prelude to faith and state relations in the Safavid era], pp. 129–40, 258–74, 513.
17. Ervand Abrahamian, *Iran between Two Revolutions*, Princeton: Princeton University Press, 1982, pp. 45–7.
18. Homa Katouzian, "Arbitrary Rule: A Comparative Theory of State, Politics and Society in Iran," *British Journal of Middle Eastern Studies*, 24, 1 (May 1997), p. 59.
19. Kazemzadeh, *Russia and Britain in Persia*.
20. Ibid., pp. 52–4; Steven R. Ward, *Immortal: A Military History of Iran and Its Armed Forces*, Washington, DC: Georgetown University Press, 2008, pp. 74–5, 78–81.
21. Robert G. Watson, *A History of Persia: From the Beginning of the Nineteenth Century to the Year 1858*, London: Smith, Elder & Co., 1866, pp. 262–5; Carina Jahani, "The Baloch as an Ethnic Group," in Lawrence G. Potter (ed.), *The Persian Gulf in Modern Times: People, Ports and History*, New York: Palgrave Macmillan, 2014, pp. 276–7.
22. Ibid.
23. Abrahamian, *Iran between Two Revolutions*, 30.
24. Asghar Asqarī-Khānghāh and Mohammad-Sharīf Kamālī, *Irāniyān-i Torkaman, Pajūhesh-i dar Mardom-shenāsī va Jam'eiyat-shenāsī* [Iranian Turkmens, an anthro-

pologic and demographic research], Tehran, Asātir, 1995 [1374], 29–31; and Adrienne Lynn Edgar, *Tribal Nation: The Making of Soviet Turkmenistan*, Princeton: Princeton University Press, 2006, pp. 18, 24–5.

25. William Irons, "Variation in Political Stratification among the Yomut Turkmen," *Anthropological Quarterly*, 44, 3, Comparative Studies of Nomadism and Pastoralism (Special Issue) (July 1971), pp. 150–2.
26. Amin'ollah Golī, *Tārīkh-i Siyāsī va Ejtemāee-i Torkaman'hāy-i Irān* [The political and cultural history of Iran's Turkmens], Tehran: Elm, Winter 1366/1988, p. 170.
27. Fereydoun Ādamiyat, *Amīr Kabīr va Irān* [A biography of Mirzā Taqī Khan Amir Kabir], 6th edn, Tehran: Khārazmī, 1362/1983, copyright 1348/1969, pp. 249–52; Philip Carl Salzman, "Politics and Change among the Baluch in Iran," *Middle East Strategy at Harvard Middle East Papers*, 2 (20 June 2008), pp. 2–3.
28. Kasravi, *Tārīkh-i Hijdah Sāleh-yi Azarbāyjān* Vol. 2 [A history of the later Constitutional period, 1909–21], vol. 2, 9th edn, Tehran: Amir-Kabir, 2537/1979, copyright 1319/1940, pp. 725–30.
29. David McDowall, *A Modern History of the Kurds*, London: I. B. Tauris, 2007, p. 103.
30. Akbar Aghajanian, "Ethnic Inequality in Iran: An Overview," *International Journal of Middle East Studies*, 15, 2 (May 1983), p. 212.
31. Philip C. Salzman, *Black Tents of Baluchistan*, Washington, DC: Smithsonian Institution Press, 2000, pp. 134–6.
32. Bī'bī Rābe'a Lughashwa, *Turkmen'hāy-i Irān* [Iranian Turkmens], trans. Sirūs Izadī and Hossein Tahvilī, Tehran: Shabāhang, 1359/1980, pp. 47–8.
33. Moghadam, "The Other Shore, Iranians in the United Arab Emirates," pp. 247–55.
34. Abrahamian, *Iran between Two Revolutions*, p. 150.
35. Ibid.
36. Moghadam, "The Other Shore, Iranians in the United Arab Emirates," p. 250.
37. Aghajanian, "Ethnic Inequality in Iran," p. 213.
38. Lugashwa, *Turkmen'hāy-i Irān*, pp. 47–8.
39. Hamid Zargari, *Mikhāstim Shāh rā Sāghet Konim* [Memoires of Hamid Zargari (b. 1926), junior army officer and member of the Tudeh Party], Prague: 2011, pp. 8–9.
40. Ibid.
41. Mahmoud Zand-Moghadam, *Hekāyat-i Baloch*, vol. 2, Tehran: Tirājeh, 1371/1992, pp. 155–6.
42. Ibid.
43. Abrahamian, *Iran between Two Revolutions*, p. 141.
44. McDowall, *A Modern History of the Kurds*, pp. 225–6.
45. Ibid.
46. Ibid.

47. Philip Carl Salzman, "Continuity and Change in Baluchi Tribal Leadership," *International Journal of Middle East Studies*, 4, 4 (October 1973), pp. 428–30; Ahmad Reza Taheri, *The Baloch in Post Islamic Revolution Iran: A Political Study (1979–2008)*, n.p.: 2010, pp. 35–8.
48. Ibid.
49. Ibid.
50. Taken from Salzman's PhD thesis in Selig S. Harrison, *In Afghanistan's Shadow: Baluch Nationalism and Soviet Temptations*, Washington, DC: Carnegie Endowment for International Peace, 1981, p. 95.
51. Ibid.
52. William Irons, "The Yomut Turkmen: A Study of Social Organization among a Central Asian Turkic-Speaking Population," Anthropological Papers Museum of Anthropology, University of Michigan no. 58, 1975, p. 74.
53. Lugashwa, *Turkmen'hāy-i Irān*, pp. 146–9.
54. Golī, *Tārīkh-i Siyāsī Ejtemā'ee Turkmen'hā*, pp. 192–3.
55. Hamid Ahmadi, *Ghomiyat va Ghomiat'garārāyī dar Irān, Afsāneh va Vāghe'iyat* [Ethnicity and ethno-nationalism, myth and realty], Tehran: Nashr-i Ney, 1378/1999, pp. 222–4.
56. Abrahamian, *Iran between Two Revolutions*, pp. 217–18, 398–401; McDowall, *A Modern History of the Kurds*, pp. 239–44.
57. Lughashwa, *Turkmen'hāy-i Irān*, p. 148; McDowall, *A Modern History of the Kurds*, pp. 225–6.
58. Aghajanian, "Ethnic Inequality in Iran," p. 213.
59. Amuzegar, *Iran's Economy under the Islamic Republic*, p. 5.
60. Ibid., p. 5.
61. Aghajanian, "Ethnic Inequality in Iran," p. 214.
62. Amir-Assadollah Alam, *Yaād'dāshthā-yi Alam, Matn-i Kāmel* [Alam diaries, complete text], vol. 4: Year 1353/1974, ed. Ali-Naqi Ālī'khānī, Tehran: Maziār & Mo'een, 1391/2012, 2000, pp. 67–8.
63. Aghajanian, "Ethnic Inequality in Iran," pp. 215–17.
64. Taheri, *The Baloch in Post Islamic Revolution Iran*, pp. 60–1.
65. Habib'ollah Tābānī, *Bar'resī-i Ozā'ee Tabi'ee Eghtesādī va Ostānī Kordestān dar Nemūneh-yi Kordestān-i Mokrī* [Reviewing Kurdistan's natural, economical, and provincial situation with Mokrī Kurdestan as an example], Mahabad: Seyedān, 1358/1979, pp. 47, 58, 62, 72, 120.
66. Alam, *Yaād'dāshthā-yi Alam*, vol. 6: Years 1355/1976 and 1356/1977, p. 173.
67. Ibid., vol. 2: Years 1349/1970 and 1351/1972, p. 244.
68. Mohammad Borgha'ie, *Nazarī be Balochestān, Safarnāmeh*, [Balochistan at a glance, a travel journal], Tehran: Sepid 1352/1972, pp. 65, 81–3, 97–9, 125–7.
69. Aghajanian, "Ethnic Inequality in Iran," p. 213.
70. Ibid., p. 222.

71. Katouzian, *The Political Economy of Modern Iran*, p. 128.
72. Amuzegar, *Iran's Economy under the Islamic Republic*, p. 4.
73. Abrahamian, *Iran between Two Revolutions*, pp. 152–4.
74. Parviz Sabeti, *Dar dāmgah-ihādes'i, bar'resi-i elatha va avāmel-i forūpāshi-i hokūmat-i Shāhanshāhi, goft'o'gūyī bā Parvīz Sābetī* [The memoir of Parviz Sabeti, high-ranking member of imperial Iran's main security agency, Savak], ed. Erfān Qane'eī'fard, Los Angeles: Ketab Corps, 2012, p. 541.
75. Interview with Mowlavi Abdul-Hamid Esmā'īl'zehī, "Tārīkh-i Dār al-olūm-i Zādedān va Masjed-i Jeme'i Mak'kī" [History of Zahedan's religious school and Makki mosque], *Nedaye Eslam*, 55, 56 (Summer 1392/2013), pp. 24–5.
76. Djavad Salehi-Isfahani, "Revolution and Redistribution in Iran: How the Poor Have Fared 25 Years Later" (May 2006), p. 35, http://siteresources.worldbank.org/INTDECINEQ/Resources/1149208-1147789289867/IIIWB_Conference_Revolution&Redistribution_Iran.pdf
77. Persian Deutsche Welle, "Cherā Bikārī dar Miyān-i Aghaliyat'hāy-i Ghomi'i Iran Bishtar Ast?" [Why is unemployment higher among Iran's ethnic minorities?], 23 April 2011; www.dw.com/fa-ir/a-6505594
78. Sho'ār-i Sāl, "Aghvām-I Sāken dar Ostān-i Golestan" [The ethnicities of Golestan province], 20 September 2016; http://shoaresal.ir/fa/news/29716/ (1 August 2017).
79. Rahim Bardī Anā-Morād'nejād, "Tahvolāt-t Ejtemā'ee Panjāh Sāl-i Akhīr dar Ashāyer-i Torkaman (Motā'le'ey-i Moredī: Bandar Torkaman)" [Social developments among Turkmen tribes in the past fifty years (research example: Bandar Turkmen)], *Majaleh-yi Elmī-Takhasosī Barnāmeh'rīzī Fazāyī*, year 1, no. 1 (Summer 1390/2011), p. 55.
80. Ibid., p. 55.
81. Persian Deutsche Welle, "Negāhi beh Eshteghāl dar Kordestān" [A glance at employment in Iran's Kurdistan], 23 April 2011; http://www.dw.com/fa-ir/a-15025855
82. Reza Namak-Shenas (economic deputy of Sistan and Balochistan's financial and economic organization), "Sherkat'hāyi San'atī-i Ostān-i Sistām va Balūchestān, Chālesh'hā va Āyandeh" [A report on Sistan-Baluchistan's industrial mini-cities;: Challenges and future, *Majaleh-yi Eghtesādī*, year 5, nos. 49–50, Azar va Dey 1384/January 2005, pp. 98, 113–14.
83. Kamāl al-Dīn Ghorāb, *Balūchistān, Yādgār-i Matrūd-i Ghorūn* [Baluchistan, the rejected reminiscence of time: A mixture of history, social analysis, and travel journal of an Iranian revolutionary to Baluchistan, pp. 138–9 and "Kār'khāneh-yi Bāft-i Balūchi Irān'shahr Niāzmand-i Ehyā Ast" [A report on the state of the Bāft factory and its need for restoration], 12 May 2013, the official website of Sistan-Baluchistan province; www.sbportal.ir/fa/news/4436; "Damidan-i Jān-i Dobāreh beh Kār'khāneh-yi Bāft-i Balūchi Irān'shahr" [A report on the re-opening of Bāft

factory under government control by the direct intervention of Supreme Leader Khameni], 2 January 2016; www.isna.ir/news/94101206191

84. Mohammad-Karīm Ra'isī, "Elal va Piāmad-i Mohājerat Az Navāhi Jonūbī Balūchestān (Mokrān) beh Keshvarhāy-i Arab-i Hawzeh-yi Khalīj-i Fārs" [Causes and consequences of immigration from southern Baluchistan to the Gulf Arab countries], *Political & Economic Ettela'at*, 21, 233–4 (February–March 2007), pp. 172–9.
85. Persian Deutsche Welle, "Cherā Nerkh-i Bīkārī dar Miyīn-i Aghaliyat'hāyi Qomī dar Irān Bishtar Ast?"
86. Persian Deutsche Welle, "Eterārz-i Balūch-hā beh Tab'īz dar Vāgozāri-i Mas'uliyat'hā-yi Ostānī" [Baluch object to discrimination in allocation of provincial responsibilities], 12 April 2013; www.dw.com/fa-ir/a-16741173
87. Muʿizz al-Dīn Mahdavī, *Ākharīn Maʾmūrīyat, Owʾzāʿ-i Kermān va Balūchistān va Banāder* [Last assignment: The situation of Kerman, Baluchistan, and southern ports. By a mid-ranking educational officer], Tehran: Chāpkhānah-i Bahman, 1342/1963, p. 88.
88. Iranian Labor News Agency (ILNA), "Ra' īs-i Shorāy-i Shahr-i Chābahār: Hashtād Darsad Az Mashāghel-i Amūzesh-i Chābahār dar Ekhtiyār-i Gheir-i B ūmi'hāst" [Chairman of Chabahar's city council: 80 percent of Chabahar's educational jobs are occupied by non-natives], 22 Shahrivar 1393/13 September 2014; http://ilna.ir/news/news.cfm?id=203910
89. Tabnak, "Sahm-i Nāchīz-i Balūch'ha dar Post'hāy-i Kalāni Ostān" [The Baluchi's insignificant share in province's senior posts], 9 April 2013; www.tabnak.ir/fa/news/312482
90. Interview with Mohammad Hassan Hossein'bor, Alarabiya website, Persian section, 3 December 2012; www.alarabiya.net/articles/2012/12/03/253118.html
91. Carina Jahani, "The Baloch as an Ethnic Group," in Potter, *The Persian Gulf in Modern Times*, pp. 285–6.
92. Ibid., p. 285.
93. Radio Zamaneh, "Ra' īs-i Polic-i Mobā'rezeh bā Ghāchāq-i Kālā va Arz: Beh Kūl'barān Shelīk Mīkonim" [Chief of anti-smuggling police: We will shoot Kūl'barān], 23 Shahrivar 1393/14 September 2014; www.radiozamaneh.com/175541
94. Radio Zamaneh, "Jān dar Gero'ee Nān; Gozāresh-i Az Koshtār-i Sistemātic Kūl'barān va Kāseb'kārān-i Kurd" [A report on the systematic slaughter of Kurdish Kūl'bars and dealers], 22 Mehr 1394/14 October 2015; www.radiozamaneh.com/241070
95. Fazel Hawramy, "Iran Struggles to Address Smuggling in Kurdish Areas," Al-Monitor, 19 July 2017; www.al-monitor.com/pulse/originals/2017/07/iran-kolbar-kurdistan-smuggling-social-security-coverage.html
96. Najmeh Bozorgmehr, "Bordertown in Iranian Kurdistan Booms through Trade

with Iraq," *Financial Times*, 18 December 2014; www.ft.com/content/5da8864 67a4511e4895800144feabdc0

97. Reza Kalhor, Colonel Nozar Amir-Sāremī, and Colonel Hāmed Niyāvarāni, "Ta'sīr-i Eghdāmāt-i Badūkiha dar Sīstān va Balūchestān bar Amniyāt-i Marz'hay-i Iran va Pakestān" [The effects of Badūki activities in Sistan-Baluchistan on Iran–Pakistan's border security], 168–80, *Motāli'āt-i Modiriyāt-i Entezāmi*, no. 2, Summer 1387/2008, p. 174.
98. Ibid.
99. Akbar Hashemi-Rafsanjani, *Ronagh-i Sāzandegī, Karnāmeh va Khāterāt-i Hāshemī-Rafsanjānī Sāl-i 1371* [Diaries of Hashemi Rafsanjani, year 1371 (March 1992–March 1993)], ed. Hasan Lahūtī and Qāder Bāstānī, Tehran: Nashr-i Ma'āref-i Eslāmī 1394/2015, copyright 2014, p. 507.
100. Persian Deutsche Welle, "Ghāchāq-i Sūkht bā Chāhārpāyān-i Davāzdah Miliyūn Tomānī dar Balūchestān" [Smuggling fuel with fourteen million Tooman donkeys in Baluchistan], 14 July 2014, www.dw.com/fa-ir/a-17820718
101. "Panjāh va Do Khārejī Heyn-i Ghāchāq-i Sūkht dar Iran Koshteh Shodo'and" [Fifty-two foreign nationals have been killed in Iran while smuggling fuel], BBC Persian, 28 July 2011; www.bbc.com/persian/rolling_news/2011/07/110728_l03_rln_fuel_smuggling
102. "Tajamo'ee Mardom-i Sīrīk dar E'terāz beh Koshteh Shodan-i Do Malavān-i Baloch" [Demonstration in Sīrīk in protest at the killing of two Balochi sailors], BBC Persian, 3 November 2013; www.bbc.com/persian/iran/2013/11/131103_nm_balooch_sirik_protest
103. Persian Deutsche Welle, "Nā'ārām ī dar Irān'shahr Control Shod" [Unrest in Iran'shahr resolved], 5 November 2015; http://www.dw.com/fa-ir/a-18443333
104. Marziyeh Esfandiyārī, "Bāzārcheh'hāy-i Marzī-i Sistān va Balūchestān," *Majaleh-yi Eghtesādī*, nos. 37–8 (Azar and Dey 1383/November and December 2004), pp. 18–22.
105. Persian Deutsche Welle, "Estefādeh Az Marz'neshīnān-i Irān Barāyeh Afzāyesh-i Sāderāt-i Naftī" [Using Iran's borderlanders to increase oil exports], 31 May 2013; www.dw.com/fa-ir/a-16851524
106. Radio Zamaneh, "Sālī Bīst Miliyārd Dolār Kālā dar Irān Ghachāgh Mīshavad" [Each year $20 billion worth of goods are smuggled in Iran], 1 July 2016; www.radiozamaneh.com/286137
107. Jafar Hagh'panāh, "Ghachāgh Mavād-i Mokhader va Tā'sir on bar Amnī'yat-i Melī Jomhūri eslāmi" [Drug trafficking and its effect on the Islamic Republic's national security], pp. 143–70; *Faslnāmeh-i motāli'āt-i rāhbordi*, Tehran: Pajūhesh'kade-i motāli'āt-i rāhbordi, no. 2 (Summer 1377/1998), pp. 149–50.
108. United Nations Office on Drugs and Crime, "Drug Trafficking and Border Control Situation Analysis," www.unodc.org/islamicrepublicofiran/drug-trafficking-and-border-control.html
109. Jafar Hagh'panāh, "Ghachāgh Mavād-i Mokhader," p. 152.
110. Ibid.

111. Interview with Mohammad Hassan Hossein'bor, Al-arabiya Persian section, 3 December 2012; www.alarabiya.net/articles/2012/12/03/253118.html
112. Umar Farooq, "The Secret War between Iran and Pakistan," Daily Beast, 29 December 2014; www.thedailybeast.com/articles/2014/12/29/the-dangerous-drug-funded-secret-war-between-iran-and-pakistan.html
113. Seymour M. Hersh, "Preparing the Battlefield," *New Yorker*, 7 July 2008, www.newyorker.com/magazine/2008/07/07/preparing-the-battlefield
114. Syed Saleem Shahzad, "Where Pakistan's Militants Go to Ground," Asia Times Online, 23 October 2009; www.atimes.com/atimes/South_Asia/KJ23Df03.html
115. "Rūz'shomār-i Nafashā-yi Yek Terrorist, Az Dastforūshī tā Sar Boridan va Amaliyāt-i Entehārī" [Life of a terrorist, from peddler to cutting throats and suicide missions], 4 Esfand 1393/23 February 2015; www.asrehamoon.ir/fa/doc/news/65605
116. Esmā'īl Ahmadī-Moghadam, "Rāhbord'hāy-i Entezāmī dar Joghrāfi'yāy-i Sistān va Balūchestān" [Policing strategies in Sistan-Baluchistan], *Pajūhesh'Nāmeh-ti Nazm va Amniyat-i Entezāmī*, no. 29 (Winter 2010), pp. 1–32.
117. Colum Lynch, "Iran Wins World Record for Most Executions Per Capita," Foreign Policy, 27 October 2015; http://foreignpolicy.com/2015/10/27/rouhani-zarif-state-department-human-rightsiran-wins-world-record-for-most-executions-per-capita
118. "Molaverdi Summoned to Court for 'Telling Lies,'" International Iran Times, 15 April 2016; http://iran-times.com/molaverdi-summoned-to-court-for-telling-lies
119. Renad Mansho, "Edām-i seh kūr-i sonnī dar orūmiyeh" [Execution of three Küresünlī in Urmia], 7 October 2011; www.radiofarda.com/content/f3_execution_in_iran/24366803.html

## 5. INCLUSION AND EXCLUSION IN THE ARAB CITY: DISCOURSES ON IDENTITY AND URBANISM IN THE MIDDLE EAST

1. See Anthony D. King (ed.), *Culture, Globalization, and the World-System*, Basingstoke: Macmillan in association with the Department of Art and Art History, SUNY Binghamton, 1991.
2. Roland Robertson, "Social Theory, Cultural Relativity, and the Problems of Globality," in King, *Culture, Globalization, and the World-System*.
3. Many conceptions of globalization have been developed in the social sciences or are rooted in economic theories. This chapter mainly draws from the field of cultural studies.
4. Jane T. Wolff, "The Global and the Specific: Reconsidering Conflicting Theories of Culture," in King, *Culture, Globalization, and the World-System*.
5. See Stuart Hall, "Old and New Identities, Old and New Ethnicities," in King, *Culture, Globalization, and the World-System*; Nezar AlSayyad, "Neither

Homogeneity Nor Heterogeneity: Modernism's Struggles in the Muslim World," in *Homogenisation of Representations*, ed. Modjtaba Sadria, Geneva: Aga Khan Award for Architecture, p. 87.

6. I elaborate on this point specifically in Nezar AlSayyad, "From Modernism to Globalization: The Middle East in Context," in Sandy Isenstadt and Kishwar Rizvi (eds), *Modernism and the Middle East: Architecture and Politics in the Twentieth Century*, Seattle: University of Washington Press, 2014, pp. 255–66; AlSayyad, "Neither Homogeneity Nor Heterogeneity," p. 88.
7. Nezar AlSayyad, "From Vernacularism to Globalism: The Temporal Reality of Traditional Settlements," *Traditional Dwellings and Settlements Review*, 7, 1 (1995), pp. 13–24; AlSayyad, "Neither Homogeneity Nor Heterogeneity," pp. 89–90.
8. Nezar AlSayyad, "Urbanism and the Dominance Equation," in Nezar AlSayyad (ed.), *Forms of Dominance: On the Architecture and Urbanism of the Colonial Enterprise*, London: Avebury, 1992.
9. AlSayyad, "Neither Homogeneity Nor Heterogeneity," p. 92.
10. Nezar AlSayyad and Manuel Castells (eds), *Muslim Europe or Euro-Islam*, Lanham, MD: Lexington Books, 2002; AlSayyad, "Neither Homogeneity Nor Heterogeneity," pp. 92–93.
11. Nezar AlSayyad, "Urbanism and the Dominance Equation."
12. See Benjamin Barber, *Jihad vs. McWorld*, New York: Ballantine Books, 1995.
13. Timothy Mitchell, "McJihad: Islam in the U.S. Global Order," *Social Text*, 20, 4 (Winter 2002), pp. 1–15; AlSayyad, "Neither Homogeneity Nor Heterogeneity," p. 93.
14. I elaborate on this point in Nezar AlSayyad, "Identity, Culture, and Urbanism: Remarks from Colonialism to Globalization," in Soumyen Bandyopadhyay and Guillermo Garma Montiel (eds), *The Territories of Identity: Architecture in the Age of Evolving Globalization*, London: Routledge, 2013, pp. 135–44.
15. Nezar AlSayyad, "Culture, Identity, and Urbanism in a Changing World," in Michael A. Cohen et al. (eds), *Preparing for the Urban Future*, Washington, DC: Woodrow Wilson Center Press, 1996; AlSayyad, "Neither Homogeneity Nor Heterogeneity," p. 94.
16. Nezar AlSayyad, "Whose Cairo?," in Diane Singerman and Paul Amar (eds), *Cairo Cosmopolitan*, Cairo: American University in Cairo Press, 2006, pp. 539ff.
17. Ananya Roy and Nezar AlSayyad, "Medieval Modernity: Citizenship in Contemporary Urbanism," *Applied Anthropologist*, 25, 2 (2005), pp. 147–65.
18. "Include, v.," Oxford English Dictionary Online, 2nd edn, 1989; http://dictionary.oed.com (23 October 2006).
19. "Exclude, v.," Oxford English Dictionary Online, 2nd edn, 1989; http://dictionary.oed.com (23 October 2006).
20. "Identity, n.," Oxford English Dictionary Online, 2nd edn, 1989; http://dictionary.oed.com (23 October 2006).

21. "Difference, n.," Oxford English Dictionary Online, 2nd edn, 1989; http://dictionary.oed.com (23 October 2006).
22. Nezar AlSayyad, "Urbanism and the Dominance Equation," p. 19.
23. Nezar AlSayyad, "Prologue: Hybrid Culture/Hybrid Urbanism; Pandora's Box of the 'Third Place,'" in Nezar AlSayyad (ed.), *Hybrid Urbanism*, Westport: Praeger, 2001, p. 4.
24. Vanessa Watson, "Deep Difference: Diversity, Planning and Ethics," *Planning Theory*, 5, 1 (2006), p. 32.
25. Vanessa Watson, "Conflicting Rationalities: Implication for Planning Theory and Ethics," *Planning Theory & Practice*, 4, 4 (2003), p. 402.
26. Ira M. Lapidus, *Muslim Cities in the Later Middle Ages*, Cambridge: Cambridge University Press, 1984, p. xi.
27. Ibid., p. 87.
28. Ibid., p. 92.
29. Ibid., p. 95.
30. AlSayyad, "Notes on the Islamic City," p. 15.
31. Ibid., p. 16.
32. Emily Gottreich, *The Mellah of Marrakesh: Jewish and Muslim Space in Morocco's Red City*, Bloomington: Indiana University Press, 2006.
33. Ibid.
34. Ibid.
35. Roy and AlSayyad, "Medieval Modernity," p. 158.
36. Manuel Castells, "The World Has Changed: Can Planning Change?," *Landscape and Urban Planning*, 22, 1 (1992), pp. 73–8; AlSayyad, "Neither Homogeneity Nor Heterogeneity," pp. 94–95.
37. AlSayyad, *Hybrid Urbanism*; AlSayyad, "Neither Homogeneity Nor Heterogeneity," p. 95.

## 6. MILLET ETHNICITY: ISLAMIZED ARMENIANS AND ARMENIAN IDENTITY

1. Feroz Ahmad, *Turkey: The Quest for Identity*, Oxford: Oneworld Publications, 2003, p. 89.
2. Sener Akturk, "Persistence of the Islamic Millet as an Ottoman Legacy: Mono-Religious and Anti-Ethnic Definition of Turkish Nationhood," *Middle Eastern Studies*, 45, 6 (2009), p. 893.
3. Ceren Belge and Ekrem Karakoç, "Minorities in the Middle East: Ethnicity, Religion, and Support for Authoritarianism," *Political Research Quarterly*, 68, 2 (2015), p. 283.
4. Akturk, "Islamic Millet as an Ottoman Legacy," p. 904.
5. Razmik Panossian, *The Armenians: From Kings and Priests to Merchants and Commissars*, New York: Columbia University Press, 2006, p. 88.

6. Ibid., p. 94.
7. George Bournoutian, *A History of the Armenian People, Volume One: Pre-History to 1500 AD*, Costa Mesa: Mazda Publishers, 1993.
8. John Binns, *An Introduction to the Christian Orthodox Churches*, Cambridge: Cambridge University Press, 2002, p. 68.
9. Theo Maarten van Lint, "The Formation of Armenian Identity in the First Millennium," *Church History and Religious Culture*, 89, 2 (2009), pp. 251–78, here pp. 269–70.
10. Bournoutian, *Armenian People, Volume One*, p. 20.
11. Kevin Blackburn, "Mapping Aboriginal Nations: the 'Nation' Concept of Late Nineteenth-Century Anthropologists in Australia," *Aboriginal History*, 26 (2002), pp. 131–58, here p. 137.
12. John Hutchinson and Anthony Smith, "Introduction," in John Hutchinson and Anthony Smith (eds), *Ethnicity*, Oxford: Oxford University Press, 1996, pp. 3–16, here pp. 6–7, 10.
13. Anthony Smith, "The Origins of Nations," *Ethnic and Racial Studies*, 12, 3 (1989), pp. 340–67, here p. 347.
14. In the late seventeenth century, for example, the economically powerful archbishop of New Julfa (Iran) managed to force the abdication of a catholicos in Etchmiadzin due to his disapproval of, among other things, the Western Armenian practices introduced by the Edessa-born catholicos. Vazken Ghougassian, *The Emergence of the Diocese of New Julfa in the Seventeenth Century*, Atlanta: University of Pennsylvania Press, 1998, p. 116.
15. Henry Astarjian, "Our Muslim Brothers," *The Armenian Weekly*, 24 June 2011; http://www.armenianweekly.com/2011/06/24/our-muslim-brothers/ (accessed 25 June 2011).
16. Quoted in Houri Berberian, *Armenians and the Iranian Constitutional Revolution 1905–1911: "The Love of Freedom has no Fatherland"*, Boulder, Westview Press, 2001, p. 42.
17. Jenny Phillips, *Symbol, Myth and Rhetoric: The Politics of Culture in an Armenian American Population*, New York: AMS Press, 1989, p. 111.
18. Ali Granmayer, "Minorities and Press in Post-Revolution Iran," in T. Parfitt and Y. Egorova (eds), *Jews, Muslims and Mass Media: Mediating the "Other"*, London: Routledge Curzon, 2004, pp. 55–67, here p. 60.
19. See, e.g., Aileen Esma'ili, "Zan (armanī): Ezdevājam rā az chahār sāl az khānevādeham penhān kardam" [(Armenian) woman: I hid my marriage from my family for four years], Hooys, 31 August 2013; http://farsi.hooys.com/?p=1353 (accessed 24 March 2016); Aileen Esma'ili, "Mard (armanī): Dar goẕashteh barāyam mohem būd kasī nafahmad hamsaram gheyr-e armanī ast" [(Armenian) man: In the past, it was important to me that people did not know my wife is not Armenian], Hooys, 20 August 2013; http://farsi.hooys.com/?p=1269 (accessed 24 March 2016).

20. James Barry, "Merchants, Mercenaries and Monarchs: Christians in Safavid Iran," in A. A. di Castro and D. Templeman (eds), *Asian Horizons: Giuseppe Tucci's Buddhist, Indian, Himalayan and Central Asian Studies*, Melbourne: Monash University Publishing, 2015, pp. 184–96, here p. 184.
21. See, e.g., Tigran Petrossyants and Garegin Ghazaryan, *1000 Hayazgi Generalner yev Tsovakalner* [1,000 Armenian generals and admirals], Yerevan: Heghinakayin Hratarakutiwn, 2009, p. 45.
22. See, e.g., Zhanet Lazarian, *Dāneshnāmeh-ye īrānīān-e armanī* [Encyclopaedia of Armenian Iranians], Tehran: Hirmand Publications, 2003, pp. 98–101
23. Seta Dadoyan, *The Armenians in the Medieval Islamic World: Paradigms of Interaction, Volume Three, Medieval Cosmopolitanism and Images of Islam (Thirteenth to Fourteenth Centuries)*, New Brunswick: Transaction Publishers, 2013, p. 25.
24. Jacob Neusner, *Telling Tales: Making Sense of Christian and Judaic Nonsense, the Urgency and Basis for Judeo-Christian Dialogue*, Eugene: Wipf and Stock, 1993, p. 6.
25. Elyse Semerdjian, "Armenian Women, Legal Bargaining and the Gendered Politics of Conversion in Seventeenth- and Eighteenth-Century Aleppo," *Journal of Middle East Women's Studies*, 12, 1 (2016), pp. 10–11.
26. Alice Taylor, *Book Arts of Isfahan: Diversity and Identity in Seventeenth-Century Persia*, Malibu: J. Paul Getty Museum, 1995, pp. 67–8.
27. Arakel of Tabriz, *Book of History* (Patmowt'iwn Aṙak'el Vardapeti Dawriżec'woy), trans. and ed. George Bournoutian, Cosa Mesa: Mazda Publishers, 2010, pp. 412–13.
28. Ibid., p. 408.
29. Aptin Khanbaghi, *The Fire, the Star and the Cross: Minority Religions in Medieval and Early Modern Iran*, London: I. B. Tauris, 2006, p. 121.
30. Ghougassian, *The Diocese of New Julfa*, p. 112.
31. Raffi [Hakob Melik Hakobian], *Yerkeri Zhoghovatsu: Hator Innerord* [Collected works: Volume 9], Yerevan: Soviet Writers Publishing, 1987, p. 6.
32. Stephan Astourian, "State, Homeland and Diaspora: The Armenian and Azerbaijani Cases," in T. Atabaki and S. Mehendale (eds), *Central Asia and the Caucasus: Transnationalism and Diaspora*, London: Routledge, 2005, pp. 80–112, here p. 86.
33. Ceren Özgül, "Legally Armenian: Tolerance, Conversion and Name Change in Turkish Courts," *Comparative Studies in Society and History*, 56, 3 (2014), pp. 622–49, here p. 627.
34. Ulf Björklund, "Armenians of Athens and Istanbul: The Armenian Diaspora and the 'Transnational' Nation," *Global Networks*, 3, 3 (2003), pp. 337–54, here p. 344.
35. Nicola Migliorino, *(Re-) Constructing Armenia in Lebanon and Syria*, New York: Berghahn Books, 2008, p. 128.

36. James Barry, "'This Is Not Our Country': Declining Diversity in the Islamic Republic of Iran,'" *The Muslim World*, 105, 3 (2015), pp. 281–98, here p. 285.
37. Hovann H. Simonian, "History and Identity among the Hemshin," *Central Asian Survey*, 25, 1 (2006), pp. 157–78, here p. 160.
38. Bert Vaux, "Homshetsma: The Language of the Armenians of Hamshen," in Hovhann H. Simonian (ed.), *The Hemshin: History, Society and Identity in the Highlands of Northeast Turkey*, New York: Routledge, 2007, pp. 257–78, here pp. 257, 259.
39. Ibid., p. 257.
40. Simonian, "History and Identity among the Hemshin," p. 162.
41. Lina Melkonian, *Gozīdehī az taʿāmolāt va tashābohāt farhangī beyn-e īrān va armenestān az dīrbāz tā konūn* [A selection of cultural interactions and similarities between Iran and Armenia from ancient times to the present], Tehran: Nairi, 2010, p. 87.
42. Simonian, "History and Identity among the Hemshin," p. 165.
43. Ibid., p. 166.
44. Tessa Hofman, *One Nation; Three Sub-Ethnic Groups: The Case of Armenia and Her Diaspora*, Yerevan: Narek Publishers, 2011, p. 29.
45. Ashot Margaryan et al., "Paternal Lineage Analysis Supports an Armenian rather Than a Central Asian Genetic Origin of the Hamshenis," *Human Biology*, 84, 4 (2012), pp. 405–22, here p. 418.
46. Hofman, *One Nation*, pp. 28–9.
47. See, e.g., Babak Rezvani, "The Fereydani Georgian Representation of Identity and Narration of History: A Case of Emic Coherence," *Anthropology of the Middle East*, 4, 2 (2009), pp. 52–74.
48. Mahir Özkan, "Hemşinli Kimliği: Kültür, Dil ve Din" [Hemshin identity: Culture, language, and religion], in Altuğ Yılmaz (ed.), *Müslümanlaş(tırıl)mış Ermeniler: Konferans Tebliğleri Kasım 2013* [Islamized Armenians: Conference proceedings, November 2013], Istanbul: Hrant Dink Foundation, 2015, pp. 99–106.
49. Halil Erhan, *1915'ten 1980'e Karadeniz: Ermeniler, Eşkıyalar, İnsanlar, Yaşamlar* [From 1915 to 1980 in the Black Sea: Armenians, bandits, people, lives], Istanbul: İletişim Yayınları, 2015.
50. Simonian, "History and Identity among the Hemshin," p. 157.
51. Karen Khanlari, "Hay Ēt'nokronakan Tarrě Arewmtyan Hayastanum, 1991–2005t't'" [Armenian ethno-religious elements in Western Armenia, 1991–2005], *21st Century*, 3, 9 (2005), pp. 123–37, here pp. 127–8.
52. Asbarez Correspondents, "Hamshen Armenians to Resettle in Karabakh," Asbarez, 11 May 2011; http://asbarez.com/95834/hamshen-armenians-to-resettle-in-karabakh (accessed 26 July 2016).
53. Julia Hakobyan, "A Different Tradition: Hamshen Armenians Struggle for Identity and Recognition," Armenia Now, 2 February 2007; https://www.armenianow.

com/features/7103/a_different_tradition_hamshen_arme (accessed 26 July 2016).

54. Ramazan Aras, "'Misilmenî': Exploring Perceptions about Christian and 'Muslim Armenians' in the Kurdish Community in Turkey," *Milel ve Nihal*, 11, 1 (2014), pp. 91–117, here p. 110.
55. Karen Khanlari, "'Pashtonakan' Hayerě T'urk'iayi Hanrapetut'iwnum, 1923–2005t't'" ["Official" Armenians in the Turkish Republic, 1923–2005], *Teghekagir*, 22 (2008), pp. 45–97, here p. 46.
56. Özgül, "Legally Armenian," p. 626.
57. Maurus Reinkowski, "Hidden Believers, Hidden Apostates: The Phenomenon of Crypto-Jews and Crypto-Christians in the Middle East," in Dennis Washburn and A. Kevin Reinhart (eds), *Converting Cultures: Religion, Ideology and Transformations of Modernity*, Leiden: Brill, 2007, pp. 409–33, here p. 413.
58. See, e.g., Benjamin Isakhan, Antonio Gonzalez, and Taghreed Al-Deen, "Cultural Cleansing and Iconoclasm under the 'Islamic State': Attacks on Yezidi and Christian Humans/Heritage," in this volume.
59. Uğur Ümit Üngör, "Orphans, Converts, and Prostitutes: Social Consequences of War and Persecution in the Ottoman Empire, 1914–1923," *War in History*, 19, 2 (2012), pp. 173–92, here pp. 181–2.
60. Ruben Melkonian, *Islamats'vats Hayeri Khndirneri Shurj: T'urkiayi Islamats'vats Hayut'yan Khndri Usumnasirut'iwn* [Regarding the question of the Islamized Armenians: A survey of the question of Turkey's Islamized Armenian community], Yerevan: Noravank, 2009, pp. 46–7.
61. Üngör, "Orphans, Converts, and Prostitutes," p. 185.
62. Khanlari, "'Pashtonakan' Hayerě T'urk'iayi Hanrapetut'iwnum," p. 73.
63. Aras, "'Misilmenî,'" p. 108.
64. Khanlari, "'Pashtonakan' Hayerě T'urk'iayi Hanrapetut'iwnum," p. 83.
65. Melkonian, *Islamats'vats Hayeri Khndirneri Shurj*, p. 81.
66. Khanlari, "'Pashtonakan' Hayerě T'urk'iayi Hanrapetut'iwnum," p. 94.
67. Melkonian, *Islamats'vats Hayeri Khndirneri Shurj*, p. 29.
68. Üngör, "Orphans, Converts, and Prostitutes," p. 186.
69. Özgül, "Legally Armenian," pp. 622–3.
70. James Barry, "Pragmatic Dogma: Understanding the Ideological Continuities in Iran's Response to the Charlie Hebdo Attacks," *Islam and Christian–Muslim Relations*, 27, 1 (2016), pp. 77–93, here p. 83.
71. Selim Deringil, "'The Armenian Question Is Finally Closed': Mass Conversions of Armenians in Anatolia during the Hamidian Massacres of 1895–1897," *Comparative Studies of History and Society*, 51, 2 (2009), pp. 344–71, here p. 347.
72. Melkonian, *Islamats'vats Hayeri Khndirneri Shurj*, p. 35.
73. Alik Correspondents, "Aknark: Inchu Hay Aṛak'elakan yekeghetsi'in hrazharwets' mkrtel Dersimi hayerin" [Sketch: Why the Armenian Apostolic Church refused

to baptize the Armenians of Dersim], *Alik*, 30 October 2015; http://alikonline.ir/hy/news/social/item/26859- (accessed 21 June 2016).

74. Ibid.
75. Melkonian, *Islamats'vats Hayeri Khndirneri Shurj*, p. 34.
76. Fethiye Çetin, *My Grandmother: A Memoir*, trans. Maureen Freely, Melbourne: Spinifex Press, 2007.
77. Yilmaz, *Müslümanlaş(tırıl)mış Ermeniler*.

## 7. COLORBLIND OR BLINDED BY COLOR? RACE, ETHNICITY, AND IDENTITY IN IRAN

1. Mostafa Vaziri, *Iran as Imagined Nation: The Construction of National Identity*, New York: Paragon, 1993; Mohamad Tavakoli-Targhi, *Refashioning Iran: Orientalism, Occidentalism and Historiography*, Basingstoke: Palgrave, 2001; Afshin Marashi, *Nationalizing Iran: Culture; Power and State, 1870–1940*, Seattle: University of Washington Press, 2008; Ali Ansari, *The Politics of Nationalism in Modern Iran*, Cambridge: Cambridge University Press, 2012; David Motadel, "Iran and the Aryan Myth," in Ali Ansari (ed.), *Perceptions of Iran: History, Myth and Nationalism from Medieval Persia to the Islamic Republic*, London: I. B. Tauris, 2013, pp. 119–45; Motadel, *Islam and Nazi Germany's War*, Cambridge, MA: Belknap Press of Harvard University Pres, 2014; Reza Zia-Ebrahimi, *The Emergence of Iranian Nationalism: Race and the Politics of Dislocation*, New York: Columbia University Press, 2016; F. Kashani-Sabet, *Frontier Fiction: Shaping the Iranian Nation, 1804–1946*, Princeton: Princeton University Press, 1999.
2. For a parallel reading of this scene, see Hamid Naficy, *A Social History of Iranian Cinema: Volume 4; The Globalizing Era, 1984–2010*, Durham: Duke University Press, 2012, pp. 35–7. Also, Hamid Dabashi, *Close Up: Iranian Cinema, Past, Present, and Future*, London: Verso, 2001, p. 102. My public lectures at the University of Pennsylvania, especially in the fall of 2014, discussed the racial, ethnic, and cultural overtones of this film in the context of the Iran–Iraq War and Iranian modernity. I provided more precise translations and interpretations of the Gilaki dialect used in the movie as I analyzed the film in class. For a subsequent online essay that discusses the notion of "blackness" in *Bashu*, see Beeta Baghoolizadeh, "Blackness on the Iranian Periphery: Ethnicity, Language, and Nation in Bashu, the Little Stranger"; https://ajammc.com/2015/09/23/blackness-on-the-iranian-periphery/. In addition, Nasrin Rahimieh's flawless translation of the Gilaki emphasizes this racial tension: Nasrin Rahimieh, "Marking Gender and Difference the Myth of the Nation: A Post-Revolutionary Iranian Film," in Richard Tapper (ed.), *The New Iranian Cinema: Politics, Representation and Identity*, London: I. B. Tauris, 2002, p. 244. However, I make a distinction here between dark-skinned and black-skinned (and the conflation of such descriptions) in deconstructing notions of racial identity in Iran.

3. My novel, *Martyrdom Street*, also grapples with race and acceptance. One of the characters, Yasaman, reflects on her racial identity: "The bloom of Jasmine. The luster of pearl. The jingle of ivory. The flow of coconut milk. The fall of snowflakes. The innocence of clouds. What is white?" Further, she notes, "Imagine white granulated sugar melting in a pot. That's me. A deep caramel brown. My grandmother told me that when I was born, my mother was convinced I did not belong to her. I couldn't. I was too dark. When the hospital refused to take me back, my father came after me. He knew I came from him. He was not white." Kashani-Sabet, *Martyrdom Street*, Syracuse: Syracuse University Press, 2010, p. 28.
4. For historical studies on slavery in Iran, see Thomas M. Ricks, "Slaves and Slave Traders in the Persian Gulf, 18th and 19th Centuries: An Assessment," *Slavery and Abolition*, 9, 3, (1988), pp. 60–70; Ricks, "Slaves and Slave-Trading in Shi'i Iran, 1500–1900," *Journal of Asian and African Studies*, 36, 4 (1988), pp. 407–18; Ricks, "Persian Gulf Seafaring and East Africa: Ṇinth-Twelfth Centuries," *African Historical Studies*, 3, 2 (1970), pp. 339–57. Abu'l-Qasim Afnan, *Black Pearls: Servants in the Household of the Báb and Bahá'u'lláh*, Kalimat Press, 1988/99. Vanessa Martin, "Slavery and Black Slaves in Iran in the Nineteenth Century," in *The Qajar Pact: Bargaining, Protest and the State in Nineteenth-Century Persia*, London: I. B. Tauris, 2005; Willem Floor, "The Trade in and Position of Slaves in Southern Iran, 1825–1925," *Studia Iranica*, 41, 2 (2012), pp. 255–94. In her book, *A History of Slavery and Emancipation in Iran, 1800–1929*, Austin: University of Texas Press, 2017, Behnaz Mirzai erroneously claims to have "developed the term Afro Iranian" (see p. 287, n. 174). As shown below, the term was coined well before the author's assertion to have developed it in 1998. Despite the author's important and detailed analysis of the slave trade, the book scarcely deals with race. Moreover, Mirzai has omitted some of the available scholarship on slavery in Iran (including studies by Vanessa Martin and Willem Floor). Absent also from her bibliography is the collected volume on slavery in Iran compiled by Narges Alipour, *Asnad-i Barda furushi va man'i an dar 'asr Qajar* (2012). Moreover, she does not engage with works on Iranian nationalism that have delved into the intellectual background of racial theories such as Ali Ansari, *The Politics of Nationalism in Modern Iran*, Cambridge: Cambridge University Press, 2012, and Reza Zia-Ebrahimi, *Emergence of Nationalism*, New York: Columbia University Press, 2016. In addition, Mirzai's liberal adoption of Iranian nationalist and "frontier" paradigms omits key books in Iranian historiography that have theorized on these concepts and that provide the framework for her discussion of the slave trade along Iran's frontiers. Her incorporation of such ideas without full and transparent citation to the source of information occurs starkly on p. 15, where she notes that the idea of Iranzamin is not an "innovation," citing two authors who do not trace the origin of Iran's nomenclature and who do not use the word "innovation" to discuss Iran and its land in those pieces and in that context. Compare this with F. Kashani-Sabet, "Fragile Frontiers:

The Diminishing Domains of Qajar Iran," *International Journal of Middle East Studies* (May 1997), which expressly argues that "Iran and its corresponding territory then were not nineteenth-century innovations," and offers an extensive bibliography and a theoretical paradigm on frontiers to frame Iran's diplomatic and territorial experiences in the nineteenth century. Finally, Mirzai's narrative of enslavement at times inappropriately elides the experiences of "ray'at" (peasant; subject) with that of enslaved people (see pp. 86–7). Relatedly, her documentary, *Afro-Iranian Lives*, which joins a small number of films and photographic collections on the Afro-Iranian community, provides interesting footage of southern Iran and its local communities. Regrettably, the film suffers from the author's voyeuristic attempt to document Afro-Iranian culture. Her inquisitorial stance and almost juvenile fascination with Iranians of African heritage when "introducing" audiences to Afro-Iranians further alienates, rather than integrates, this community. For a film review, including a critique of the above work, see Pedram Khosronejad, "A Review," *Canadian Journal of History*, 52, 2 (Autumn 2017), pp. 323–5. For a related discussion on Afro-Iranians, see Beeta Baghoolizadeh in conversation: http://kgou.org/post/historian-beeta-baghoolizadeh-sheds-light-iran-s-unique-forgotten-history-slavery. For background on the slave trade, see John Barrett Kelly, *Britain and the Persian Gulf, 1795–1880*, Oxford: Clarendon Press, 1968; and Ann Lambton, *Continuity and Change in Medieval Persia*, London: Tauris, 1988; and Peter Avery, Gavin Hambly, and Charles Melville (eds), *Cambridge History of Iran*, vol. 7, Cambridge: Cambridge University Press, 1991.

5. Abu'l Qasim Afnan, *Black Pearls*, Los Angeles: Kalimát Press, 1999, preface, p. 29. Also, Anthony Lee, *The Baha'i Faith in Africa: Establishing a New Religious Movement, 1952–1962*, Leiden: Brill, 2011.
6. Muriel Atkin, *Russia and Iran, 1780–1828*, Minneapolis: University of Minnesota Press, 1980, p. 110.
7. Juan Ricardo Cole, *Modernity and the Millennium: The Genesis of the Baha'i Faith in the Nineteenth-Century Middle East*, New York: Columbia University Press, 1998, chapter 2.
8. Alexander F Chamberlain. "Review: Papers on Inter-Racial Problems Communicated to the Universal Races Congress, Held at the University of London, July 26–29, 1911 by G. Spiller," *The Journal of Race Development*, 2, 4 (1912), pp. 494–7.
9. Gustav Spiller, *Papers on Inter-Racial Problems: Communicated to the First Universal Races Congress, Held at the University of London, July 26–29, 1911*, vol. 1, London: P. S. King and Son, 1911, p. 156.
10. Ibid., p. 156.
11. Moojan Momen, *The Bahai Faith: A Short Introduction*, Oxford: Oneworld, 1999. Also, Hussein Ahdieh and Hilary Chapman, *'Abdu'l-Bahá in New York*, Hong Kong: Juxta, 2015.

12. Vanessa Martin, *The Qajar Pact*, offers interesting commentary on the slave trade and the lives of slaves (*kaniz*) in Iran, especially chapter 8. Martin briefly touches on racism and slavery as well, largely endorsing Bernard Lewis's views on the subject. See Bernard Lewis, *Race and Slavery in the Middle East: An Historical Enquiry*, New York: Oxford University Press, 1992. Also, Willem Floor, "Barda," *Encyclopedia Iranica* (1988), which offers a detailed history survey of slavery in Iran, but not an analysis of racism. Accessed online.
13. Minoo Southgate, "The Negative Images of Blacks in Some Medieval Iranian Writings," *Iranian Studies*, 17, 1 (Winter 1984), pp. 3–36.
14. Ibid., p. 26.
15. Such historical realities effectively disprove Behnaz Mirzai's assertion that Afro-Iranians' "equal membership in the host society provided them opportunity for social assimilation." Behnaz Mirzai, "African Presence in Iran: Identity and Its Reconstruction," *Outre-mers*, 89, 336 (2002), p. 235. This piece is also bereft of references to works on Iranian historiography that discuss the politics of ethnicity in Iran's southern provinces. It would be difficult to argue for the political or social equality or assimilation of Afro-Iranians historically. Moreover, the community of Afro-Iranians remains small, making their political involvement and advocacy at best marginal, if nonetheless vital and significant. Mirzai does not reference Southgate, whose novel analysis of literary and historical sources informs this subject.
16. Mahdi Ehsaei, *Afro-Iran: The Unknown Minority*, Heidelberg: Kehrer Verlag, 2016. Pedram Khosronejad, as cited in "The Face of African Slavery in Qajar Iran: in Pictures," *The Guardian*, 14 January 2016.
17. In 1964, the *Area Handbook for Iran* described the country as "a part of the Islamic, as well as the Afro-Asian world." *Area Handbook for Iran*, Washington, DC: American University Press, 1964, p. 368. For uses of the terms "Afro-Iran" and "Afro-Iranian," see the following publications: Gopikāmohana Bhaṭṭācārya, *All-India Oriental Conference*, Twenty-Seventh Session (1974): Summaries of Papers, p. 50. For an instance of the term, "Afro-Iran," see *Industrial Bulletin*, 11 (1970), p. 40. Also, Joseph E. Harris, *The African Presence in Asia: Consequences of the East African Slave Trade*, Evanston: Northwestern University Press, 1971, for related discussions.
18. Kashani-Sabet, "Fragile Frontiers."
19. Books that have informed my thinking in this chapter include: Matthew F. Jacobson, *Whiteness of a Different Color: European Immigrants and the Alchemy of Race*, Cambridge, MA: Harvard University Press, 1999; Vivek Bald, *Bengali Harlem and the Lost Histories of South Asian America*, Cambridge, MA: Harvard University Press, 2013; N. Zakharov, *Race and Racism in Russia*, Basingstoke: Palgrave, 2015; Rotem Kowner and Walter Demel, *Race and Racism in Modern East Asia: Western and Eastern Constructions*, Leiden: Brill, 2012; Kimberlé

Crenshaw et al., *Critical Race Theory: The Key Writings that Formed the Movement*, New York: New Press, 1995; Howard Winant, *The New Politics of Race: Globalism, Difference, Justice*, Minneapolis: University of Minnesota Press, 2004; John Solomos (ed.), *Theories of Race and Racism: A Reader*, New York: Routledge, 2000; Henry Louis Gates Jr. (ed.) "Race," *Writing, and Difference* (1985); Stephen Jay Gould, *The Mismeasure of Man*, New York: Norton, 1996 [1981]; Richard J. Herrnstein and Charles Murray, *Bell Curve: Intelligence and Class Structure in American Life*, New York: Free Press, 1994; Nicholas Wade, "Scientists Measure the Accuracy of a Racism Claim," *New York Times*, 14 June 2011; www.nytimes.com/2011/06/14/science/14skull.html?_r=0; Didier Fassin, "Racialization: How To Do Races with Bodies," in Frances E Mascia-Lees (ed.), *A Companion to the Anthropology of the Body and Embodiment*, Malden, MA: Wiley-Blackwell, 2011; Didier Fassin and Eric Fassin, De la question sociale à la question raciale (2006); Abdoulaye Gueye, Aux Nègres de France: La Patrie Non Reconnaissante (2010). For another relevant study, see Jonathan Glassman, *War of Words, War of Stones: Racial Thought and Violence in Colonial Zanzibar*, Bloomington: Indiana University Press, 2011. I owe a special debt of gratitude to Didier Fassin and to all the participants of the "Borders" seminar convened in the 2015–16 academic year at the Institute for Advanced Study, Princeton, NJ, for the enriching readings and debates on borders, race, ethnicity, and culture.

20. Benedict Anderson, *Imagined Communities: Reflections on the Origin and Spread of Nationalism*, London: Verso, 1991; Ernest Gellner, *Nations and Nationalism*, Oxford: Blackwell, 1983; Eric Hobsbawm and Terence Ranger, eds., *The Invention of Tradition*, Cambridge: Cambridge University Press, 1992.
21. Etienne Balibar, "Is There a 'Neo-Racism'?," in Etienne Balibar and Immanuel Wallerstein (eds), *Race, Nation, Class: Ambiguous Identities*, London: Verso, 2011, pp. 17–18.
22. Clifford Geertz, *The Interpretation of Cultures: Selected Essays*, New York: Basic Books, 1973, p. 259.
23. Ibid., p. 261. Also, more generally, pp. 259–69.
24. Sekandar Amanolahi, "A Note on Ethnicity and Ethnic Groups in Iran," *Iran & the Caucasus*, 9, 1 (2005), pp. 37–41.
25. Fredrik Barth, "Introduction," *Ethnic Groups and Boundaries*, London: George Allen and Unwin, 1969, p. 14.
26. Fredrik Barth, *Nomads of South Persia: The Basseri Tribe of Khamseh Confederacy*, n.p.: Spaight Press, 1961, p. 1. For an informative review of foreign anthropologists in Iran, see Ali Bulookbashi, "Foreign Anthropologists' Contributions to Iranology," in Shahnaz Najmabadi (ed.), *Conceptualizing Iranian Anthropology: Past and Present Perspectives*, 2009, pp. 19–29. The entire volume provides useful perspectives on the development and practice of anthropology in Iran.
27. Carleton S. Coon, "Review of Frederik Barth, Nomads of South Persia: The Basseri Tribe of Khamseh Confederacy," *American Anthropologist*, 64 (1962).

28. For an essay addressing this issue, see my article, "Persian Captivity and Migration in Central Asia: The 'Daughters of Quchan' Revisited," forthcoming in print. Originally proposed for, and accepted by the Iranian Studies Conference, 2014. Also, my essay, "Passages through the Persian Gulf: Histories of Commerce and Consumption," presented at Princeton University, October 2015, and my paper, "Crossing Empires: Shia Pilgrims of the Sultan and the Shah," Princeton, Institute for Advanced Study, January 2016.
29. William Jones, *A Grammar of the Persian Language*, London, 1771. Also, Garland Cannon, "Sir William Jones, Persian, Sanskrit and the Asiatic Society," *Histoire épistémologie langage*, 6, 2 (1984), pp. 83–94.
30. Kenneth A. R. Kennedy, "The Legacy of Sir William Jones: Natural History, Anthropology, Archaeology," *Bulletin of the Deccan College Research Institute*, 54, 55 (1994), pp. 23–33; Garland H. Cannon, "Sir William Jones's Persian Linguistics," *Journal of the American Oriental Society*, 78, 4 (October–December 1958), pp. 262–73; Sasan Samiei, *Ancient Persia in Western History: Hellenism and the Representation of the Achaemenid Empire*, London: I. B. Tauris, 2014, pp. 15–18. However, Samiei's discussions on historical Iran lack important bibliographic references to works on Iranian nationalism that have thoroughly investigated such subjects. See also M. Tavakoli-Targhi for a discussion of Jones and the impact of indigenous writings on Jones's scholarship: M. Tavakoli-Tarhi, "Orientalism's Genesis Amnesia," *Comparative Studies of South Asia, Africa and the Middle East*, 16, 1 (Spring 1996), pp. 1–14. However, Tavakoli-Targhi does not discuss the discipline of anthropology or the theories of race and language within the origins of anthropology and in an ethnological context.
31. Henrika Kuklick, *The Savage Within: The Social History of British Anthropology, 1885–1945*, Cambridge: Cambridge University Press, 1991, pp. 2–3.
32. Ibid., p. 8.
33. Samiei, *Ancient Persia in Western History*, p. 15. In his analysis of British anthropology, Samiei contends that the British preoccupation with race and empire fueled the rise of the discipline, especially at a time when Britain pushed for the abolition of slavery and grappled with various ideologies, from social Darwinism to Marxism.
34. Pruner-Bey, "On Human Hair as a Race Character: Examined by Aid of a Microscope," *The Journal of the Anthropological Institute of Great Britain and Ireland*, Vol. 6 (1877), p. 77.
35. *The Ethnological Journal: A Monthly Record of Ethnological Research and Criticism* (1865), p. 119.
36. Jean Chardin, Voyages Du Chevalier Chardin, En Perse, Et Autres Lieux De L'Orient: Enrichi de Figures en Taille-douce, qui représentant les Antiquités & les choses remarquables du Païs. Contenant une Description générale de l'Empire de Perse; & les Descriptions particulieres des Sciences & des Arts, qui y sont en usage; du Gouvernement Politique, Militaire, & Civil, Volume 3 (1735): 45.

37. Ibid.
38. Ibid.
39. Louis François Jéhan, *Nouvelle encyclopedie theologique, ou deuxieme serie de dictionnaire sur toutes les parties de la science religeuse ... publie par M. l'abbe Migne: Dictionnaire d'anthropologie, ou Histoire naturelle de l'homme et des races humaines anatomie, physiologie, psychologie, ethnologie*, vol. 42 (1853), p. 268. Jéhan states that many of the tribes in Iran were not of the Persian race and that there had been intermingling with other "races," by which he meant to include Turks, Mongols, and Afghans.
40. Richard S. Fisher, *The Book of the World: Being an Account of All Republics, Empires, Kingdoms, and Nations* (1852), p. 435.
41. James Cowles Prichard, *Researches Into the Physical History of Mankind: Researches into the History of the Asiatic Nations* (1844), p. 64. For a study of Prichard, see Hannah Franziska Augstein, *James Cowles Prichard's Anthropology: Remaking the Science of Man in Early Nineteenth-Century Britain*, Amsterdam: Rodopi, 1999. Augstein states that Prichard "introduced" ethnology as a mode of establishing the "Identity and Diversity of Species" (see p. xi).
42. Nikolai Khanykov, "Natural History of the Iranians," *Transactions of the Ethnological Society of London* (1866), p. 56.
43. Ibid., pp. 39–58; Nikolai Vladimirovich Khanykov, *Mémoires sur l'ethnographie de la Perse* (1866).
44. John Crawford, "European and Asiatic Races," *Transactions of the Ethnological Society of London* (1867), p. 60.
45. Charles Morris, *The Aryan Race: Its Origins and Its Achievements*, Chicago: S. C. Griggs, 1888; T. Ballantyne, *Orientalism and Race: Aryanism in the British Empire*, Basingstoke: Palgrave, 2016; Thomas R. Trautmann, *Aryans and British India*, Berkeley: University of California Press, 2006; Léon Poliakov, *A History of Racist and Nationalist Ideas in Europe*, New York: Barnes & Noble, 1977; and Fereydun Junaydi, *Zindigi va muhajirat-i nezhad-i arya* (1979).
46. *American Cyclopaedia* (1874), p. 346.
47. Hyde Clarke, "On the Prehistoric and Protohistoric Relations of the Populations of Asia and Europe," *The Journal of the Anthropological Institute of Great Britain and Ireland* (1872), p. 55.
48. Hilary Henson argues that while anthropologists early on "accepted the linguists' claim that their subject was a historical one," some anthropologists did question application of the philology to the origins of race and "that the equation of language and race was false." See Hilary Henson, "Early British Anthropologists and Language," in Edwin Ardener (ed.), *Social Anthropology and Language*, London: Taylor and Francis, 2013, p. 4.
49. F. Kashani-Sabet, "Baluchistan: Nature, Ethnicity, and Empire in Iran's Borderlands," *The Journal of the Middle East and Africa*, 4 (2013), pp. 187–204.

50. Kashani-Sabet, "Fragile Frontiers"; Hamid Dabashi, *The World of Persian Literary Humanism*, Cambridge, MA: Harvard University Press, 2012; Ibn Khaldun, *The Muqaddimah*, trans. by Franz Rosenthal (1981).
51. Lewis, *Race and Slavery in the Middle East*, p. 22.
52. Dabashi, *Persian Literary Humanism*, p. 83. For an excellent historical assessment of Arab-Persian relations, see Ahmed al-Dailami, "'Purity and Confusion': The Hawala between Persians and Arabs in the Contemporary Gulf," in Lawrence Potter (ed.), *The Persian Gulf in Modern Times*, Basingstoke: Palgrave, 2014, pp. 299–326. Also, Joseph Massad, *Desiring Arabs*, Chicago: University of Chicago Press, 2007, discusses many literary sources that pitted Arabs against Persians in Orientalist and Arab writings.
53. Mirza Sayyid Ja'far Khan Mushir al-Dawlah, *Risalah-i Tahqiqat-i Sarhaddiyah* (1969), p. 59. The date of publication is also significant as Iran tried to hold on to its territorial claims in the Persian Gulf shortly after Britain's decision to relinquish control over there.
54. Kashani-Sabet, "Fragile Frontiers," pp. 222–3, and Kashani-Sabet, "Cultures of Iranianness," in Nikki R. Keddie and Rudi Matthee (eds), *Iran and the Surrounding World*,
55. George Nathaniel Curzon, *Persian and the Persian Question*, vol. 2, London: Longmans, Green & Co, 1892, p. 321.
56. Thomas Holdich, "The Arab Tribes of our Indian Frontier," *The Journal of the Anthropological Institute of Great Britain and Ireland*, 29 (1899), pp. 10–18.
57. Mirza Aqa Khan Kermani, *Sad Khatabah*, edited by Muhammad Jafar Mahbub (online version), no. 5, pp. 14–15.
58. Ibid., p. 16,
59. Nematollah Fazeli, *The Politics of Culture in Iran*, New York: Routledge, 2006. Also, Soheila Shahshahani, "History of Anthropology in Iran," *Iranian Studies*, 19, 1 (1986), pp. 65–86. For his important involvement in this debate, see Henry Field, *Contributions to the Anthropology of Iran*, 1939.
60. *Nida-yih Vatan*, 144 and 145, 6 January 1908, pp. 5–8. Also, *Nida-yih Vatan*, no. 149, pp. 2–3; nos. 157/8, pp. 4–7. For the island of Abu Musa, see *Nida-yih Vatan*, no. 142, 4 January 1908, p. 2.
61. *Nida-yih Vatan*, no. 151, 12 January 1908, p. 4.
62. *Junub*, no. 2 (Dhulhijja 1328/1910/1911?—date unclear), p. 5.
63. *Iraq Administration Reports*, vol. 3, 1919, p. 11. Interestingly, a British analysis of Mesopotamia had described the Shaykh of Muhammerah as "a Persian." Iraq Administration Reports, (1914–1918), vol. 1, p. 24.
64. Albert Hourani, *A History of the Arab Peoples*, Cambridge, MA: Belknap Press of Harvard University Press, 1991, p. 164.
65. Ibid.
66. Sukru Hanioglu, *A Brief History of the Late Ottoman Empire*, Princeton: Princeton

University Press, 2010, p. 33. The discussion continues in interesting ways in the succeeding pages.

67. Gilbert Hubbard, *From the Gulf to Ararat: An Expedition through Mesopotamia and Kurdistan*, New York: Dutton, 1917, pp. 19–20.
68. Ibid.
69. Ibid., p. 33.
70. Ibid.
71. *Persian Gulf*, Handbooks Prepared Under the Direction of the Historical Section of the Foreign Office, no. 76, London: H. M. Stationery Office, 1920, p. 29.
72. Ibid.
73. Stephen Longrigg, *The Geography of the Middle East*, New York: Routledge, 2009, p. 169.
74. *Persian Gulf*, p. 29.
75. Ibid.
76. Marc Valeri, "Identity Politics and Nation-Building under Sultan Qaboos," in Lawrence Potter (ed.) *Sectarian Politics in the Persian Gulf*, London: Hurst, 2013, p. 184. This is a very interesting chapter on the ways in which the Omani state has grappled with the issue of minority culture and ethnic diversity within its borders. According to the 1920 *Persian Gulf* Handbook, the Baharina numbered around 100,000.
77. Houchang E. Chehabi, "The Juggernaut of Globalization: Sport and Modernization in Iran," *The International Journal of the History of Sport*, 19, 2–3 (2002), pp. 275–94.
78. *Tarikh-i Mukhtasar-i Iran, zamimah-i tarikh-I 'alam-i iqbal, jahhat sal-i panjum va shishum-i madaris-i ibtida'I* (1927), pp. 11–12.
79. FO 416/83, 4 August 1928, Parr to Sir Austen Chamberlain.
80. Vizarat-i Dakhilah, Iran, 10/11/1316–30 January 1938. Also, Vizarat-i Mu'arif va Awqaf, 17/11/1316–6 February 1938.
81. Vizarat-I Dakhilah, Iran, 16/11/1316–5 February 1938.
82. For an analysis of Iran during the Second World War, see my forthcoming article, "From Culture Wars to a World War: The Allied Occupation of Iran and Its Aftermath." For a compilation of sources on the subject, see Mohammad Gholi Majd, *Iran under Allied Occupation in World War II: The Bridge to Victory & a Land of Famine*, Washington, DC: University Press of America, 2016.
83. Nikki Keddie, *Iran and the Muslim World: Resistance and Revolution*, Basingstoke: Palgrave, 1995.
84. Shireen Hunter, *Iran's Foreign Policy in the Post-Soviet Era: Resisting the New International Order*, Santa Barbara: Praeger, 2010, p. 226.
85. Published excerpts from Jalal Al-e Ahmad's diary have also appeared in Jalal Al-e Ahmad, *Safar-i Amrika* (2001).
86. Roy Mottahedeh, *The Mantle of the Prophet*, Oxford: Oneworld, 1985, p. 321.

Ahmad Karimi Hakkak, in citing conversations between Manuchehr Hezarkhani and Al-e Ahmad, notes that Al-e Ahmad's vision for the future of Iran was modeled after the Algerian revolution. See Ahmad Karimi Hakkak, *Sarguzasht-e nafarjam-e bumigerayi: roshanfikran-i Irani va gharb* (1999), p. 265.

87. Al-e Ahmad, *Safarnamah*, p. 79.
88. Ibid.
89. *Mahnamah-i Jahan-i Naw*, 1966.
90. Aimé Césaire, *Discourse on Colonialism*, trans. Joan Pinkham with new introduction by Robin D. G. Kelly, New York: Monthly Review Press, 2001, p. 7. My translation of Césaire differs slightly from that provided by Pinkham.
91. Mehrzad Boroujerdi, "Iranian Intellectuals of the West: The Tormented Triumph of Nativism," PhD diss., American University, 1996, p. 40, including n. 28.
92. Ali Shariati, Duzakhiyan-i ruyeh zamin, n.p.: n.d.; Majd, *Iran under Allied Occupation in World War II.*
93. For more on Shariati on Fanon, see Farzaneh Farahzad, "Voice and Visibility: Fanon in the Persian Context," in Kathryn Batchelor and Sue-Ann Harding (eds), *Translating Fanon across Continents and Languages*, New York: Routledge, 2017, pp. 129–50.
94. *Tawfiq*, Bahman 1348/February 1969, back cover.
95. Francis Robert Moraes, *The Importance of Being Black: An Asian Looks at Africa* (1966), p. 278. See also Charles Marion Thomas, *African National Developments* (1967), p. 175. Google Books also shows a reference to the term "Afro-Iranian" in 1967.
96. *Tawfiq*, September 1968, cover.
97. *Tawfiq*, 1969. For more on *Tawfiq* and America's involvement in the Arab–Israeli conflict, see my forthcoming book, *Between Heroes and Hostages*.
98. For more on this argument, see F. Kashani-Sabet, "Tales of Trespassing: Borderland Histories of Iran, Iraq, and the Persian Gulf," forthcoming.

## 8. CULTURAL CLEANSING AND ICONOCLASM UNDER THE ISLAMIC STATE: ATTACKS ON YEZIDIS AND CHRISTIANS AND THEIR HERITAGE

1. The authors gratefully acknowledge the funding for this research from both the Australian Department of Defence and the Australian Research Council (DE120100315). The views expressed in this chapter do not reflect those of defence or government policy.
2. Benjamin Isakhan (ed.), *The Legacy of Iraq: From the 2003 War to the "Islamic State"*, Edinburgh: Edinburgh University Press, 2015; David Kilcullen, *Blood Year: Islamic State and the Failures of the War on Terror*, London: Hurst, 2016; and Jessica Stern and J. M. Berger, *ISIS: The State of Terror*, New York: HarperCollins, 2015.

3. Nicholas Al-Jeloo, "Post-Withdrawal Prospects for Iraq's 'Ultra-Minorities,'" in Isakhan, *The Legacy of Iraq*, pp. 110–23.
4. Craig Whiteside, "A Case for Terrorism as Genocide in an Era of Weakened States," *Dynamics of Asymmetric Conflict*, 8, 3 (2015), pp. 232–50.
5. Werner Nel, "Prosecuting Islamic Extremism: Counteracting Impunity for the Islamic State through International Criminal Justice," *International Journal for Religious Freedom*, 7, 1–2 (2014), pp. 55–76.
6. Claire Smith et al., "The Islamic State's Symbolic War: Da'esh's Socially Mediated Terrorism as a Threat to Cultural Heritage," *Journal of Social Archaeology*, 16, 2 (2015); Ömür Harmanşah, "Isis, Heritage, and the Spectacles of Destruction in the Global Media," *Near Eastern Archaeology*, 78, 3 (2015).
7. Benjamin Isakhan and José Antonio González Zarandona, "Layers of Religious and Political Iconoclasm under the Islamic State: Symbolic Sectarianism and Pre-Monotheistic Iconoclasm," *International Journal of Heritage Studies*, 24, 1 (2017), pp. 1–16.
8. Chiara De Cesari, "Post-Colonial Ruins: Archaeologies of Political Violence and IS," *Anthropology Today*, 31, 6 (2015), p. 25.
9. Andrew Keller, *Documenting ISIL's Antiquities Trafficking: The Looting and Destruction of Iraqi and Syrian Cultural Heritage; What We Know and What Can Be Done*, Washington, DC: US Department of State, 2015.
10. Emma Cunliffe, "Archaeological Site Damage in the Cycle of War and Peace: A Syrian Case Study," *Journal of Eastern Mediterranean Archaeology & Heritage Studies*, 2, 3 (2014), pp. 229–47.
11. Neil Brodie, "Syria and Its Regional Neighbours: A Case of Cultural Property Protection Policy Failure?," *International Journal of Cultural Property*, 22, 2–3 (2015), pp. 317–35.
12. In documenting both the human suffering and heritage destruction inflicted on these two groups by IS, this chapter relies on several secondary sources that have meticulously recorded these events. Given the complex and asymmetric nature of the current conflict in Iraq and Syria, many of the claims made in these reports have not been verified by independent actors "on the ground" nor by the authors of this chapter. Nonetheless, reports by bodies such as the American Schools of Oriental Research, Human Rights Watch, and UNESCO employ a robust methodology and are generally balanced and conservative in their assessments.
13. Donald Bloxham, *The Great Game of Genocide: Imperialism, Nationalism, and the Destruction of the Ottoman Armenians*, Oxford: Oxford University Press, 2005.
14. Elizabeth Simpson (ed.), *The Spoils of War: World War II and Its Aftermath; The Loss, Reappearance and Recovery of Cultural Property*, New York: Harry N. Abrams, 1997.
15. Tim Winter, *Post-Conflict Heritage, Postcolonial Tourism: Culture, Politics and Development at Angkor*, London: Routledge, 2007.

16. Caroline A. Sandes, "Urban Cultural Heritage and Armed Conflict: The Case of Beirut Central District," in J. D. Kila and J. Zeidler (eds), *Cultural Heritage in the Crosshairs: Protecting Cultural Property during Conflict*, Leiden: Brill, 2013.
17. Graham Dawson, *Making Peace with the Past? Memory, Trauma and the Irish Troubles*, Manchester: Manchester University Press, 2007.
18. Benjamin Isakhan, "Creating the Iraq Cultural Property Destruction Database: Calculating a Heritage Destruction Index," *International Journal of Heritage Studies*, 21, 1 (2015), pp. 1–21; Isakhan, "Heritage Under Fire: Lessons from Iraq for Cultural Property Protection," in W. Logan, W. M. N. Craith and U. Kockel (eds), *A Companion to Heritage Studies*, London: John Wiley & Sons, 2016, pp. 268–79.
19. Robert Layton and Julian Thomas, "Introduction: The Destruction and Conservation of Cultural Property," in R. Layton, P. G. Stone, and J. Thomas (eds), *Destruction and Conservation of Cultural Property*, London: Routledge, 2001.
20. Finbarr Barry Flood, "Between Cult and Culture: Bamiyan, Islamic Iconoclasm, and the Museum," *The Art Bulletin*, 84, 4 (2002), pp. 641–59.
21. Helen Walasek, *Bosnia and the Destruction of Cultural Heritage*, London: Routledge, 2015.
22. Layton and Thomas, "Introduction," p. 12.
23. Andras J. Riedlmayer, *Destruction of Cultural Heritage in Bosnia–Herzegovina, 1992–1996: A Post-War Survey of Selected Municipalities*, The Hague: International Criminal Tribunal for the Former Yugoslavia, 2002, p. 3.
24. Like many terms in the social sciences and humanities, "heritage" is a heavily contested term, and scholars have been debating its history and theory from different methodological perspectives without providing one agreed upon definition (see William Logan, Mairead Nic Craith, and Ullrich Kockel, *A Companion to Heritage Studies*, Chichester: Wiley-Blackwell, 2016; Laurajane Smith, *Uses of Heritage*, London: Routledge, 2006; David Lowenthal, *The Past Is a Foreign Country*, Cambridge: Cambridge University Press, 1985; and Rodney Harrison, *Heritage: Critical Approaches*, London: Routledge, 2013). For the purposes of this essay, we define heritage as the tangible and intangible celebration of the past, in the present, for the future. This celebration might take the form of a monument, a statue, or a national library, but it can also be transmitted to future generations in the form of dance, songs, and stories. Needless to say, the destruction of heritage is an important part of any iconoclastic program, such as that of IS, because it targets not only the physical embodiment of this heritage but also the most abstract manifestations of a culture.
25. Eric Hobsbawm and Terence Ranger (eds), *The Invention of Tradition*, Cambridge: Cambridge University Press, 1992 [1983]; Benjamin Isakhan, "Targeting the Symbolic Dimension of Baathist Iraq: Cultural Destruction, Historical Memory and National Identity," *Middle East Journal of Culture and Communication*, 4, 3

(2011); Philip Kohl, "Nationalism and Archaeology: On the Constructions of Nations and the Reconstructions of the Remote Past," *Annual Review of Anthropology*, 27 (1998); Benedict Anderson, *Imagined Communities: Reflections on the Origin and Spread of Nationalism*, London: Verso, 1991 [1983].

26. Lynn Meskell, "Sites of Violence: Terrorism, Tourism, and Heritage in the Archaeological Present," in Lynn Meskell and Peter Pels (eds), *Embedding Ethics*, New York: Berg, 2005, p. 129.
27. Dominik Bartmański, "Iconspicuous Revolutions of 1989: Culture and Contingency in the Making of Political Icons," in Dominik Bartmański, Jeffrey Alexander, and Bernhard Giesen (eds), *Iconic Power: Materiality and Meaning in Social Life*, New York: Palgrave Macmillan, 2012; Britt Baillie and Wendy Pullan (eds), *Locating Urban Conflicts: Ethnicity, Nationalism and the Everyday*, Basingstoke: Palgrave Macmillan, 2013; Cornelius Holtorf, "Averting Loss Aversion in Cultural Heritage," *International Journal of Heritage Studies*, 21, 4 (2015); Lauren Rivera, "Managing 'Spoiled' National Identity: War, Tourism and Memory in Croatia," *American Sociological Review*, 73, 4 (2008).
28. See Max Horkheimer and Theodor Adorno, "The Culture Industry: Enlightenment as Mass Deception," in Meenakshi Durham and Douglas Kellner (eds), *Media and Cultural Studies: Keyworks*, Oxford: Blackwell, 2001 [1944]; Benjamin Isakhan, "Heritage Destruction and Spikes in Violence: The Case of Iraq," in Kila and Zeidler, *Cultural Heritage in the Crosshairs*; Sultan Barakat, "Challenges and Dilemmas Facing the Reconstruction of War-Damaged Cultural Heritage: The Case Study of Počitelj, Bosnia–Herzegovina," in Layton and Thomas, *Destruction and Conservation of Cultural Property*; Andrew Herscher, *Violence Taking Place: The Architecture of the Kosovo Conflict*, Stanford: Stanford University Press, 2010.
29. Herscher, *Violence Taking Place*; Robert Bevan, *The Destruction of Memory: Architecture at War*, London: Reaktion Books, 2006.
30. Alfredo González-Ruibal, "Time to Destroy: An Archaeology of Supermodernity," *Current Anthropology*, 49, 2 (2008), p. 150; González-Ruibal, "Embracing Destruction," in Jan Driessen (ed.), *Destruction: Archaeological, Philological and Historical Perspectives*, Louvain: Universite Catholique de Louvain, 2013; González-Ruibal and Martin Hall, "Heritage and Violence," in Lynn Meskell (ed.), *Global Heritage: A Reader*, Chichester: Wiley, 2015; Holtorf, "Averting Loss Aversion in Cultural Heritage."
31. William Logan and Keir Reeves (eds), *Places of Pain and Shame: Dealing with "Difficult Heritage"*, London: Routledge, 2009; John Lennon and Malcolm Foley, *Dark Tourism: The Attraction of Death and Disaster*, London: Continuum, 2000.
32. John Daniel Giblin, "Post-Conflict Heritage: Symbolic Healing and Cultural Renewal," *International Journal of Heritage Studies*, 20, 5 (2014); Tim Winter, *Post-Conflict Heritage, Postcolonial Tourism: Culture, Politics and Development at Angkor*, London: Routledge, 2007.

33. Bevan, *The Destruction of Memory*, p. 8.
34. W. J. T. Mitchell, *Image Science: Iconology, Visual Culture, and Media Aesthetics*, Chicago: University of Chicago Press, 2016, p. 70.
35. Irina Bokova, "Fighting Cultural Cleansing: Harnessing the Law to Preserve Cultural Heritage," *Harvard International Review*, 36, 4 (2015).
36. Like "heritage," "iconoclasm" is also a contested term with little scholarly consensus on a precise definition. A working definition of iconoclasm for this chapter is the destruction of religious images and heritage for political or religious reasons (see James Noyes, *The Politics of Iconoclasm: Religion, Violence and Culture*, London: I. B. Tauris, 2013); Stacy Boldrick, Leslie Brubaker, and Richard Clay (eds), *Striking Images: Iconoclasms Past and Present*, Farnham: Ashgate, 2013; Dario Gamboni, *The Destruction of Art: Iconoclasm and Vandalism since the French Revolution*, Chicago: University of Chicago Press, 2007; and Bruno Latour and Peter Weibel (eds), *Iconoclash: Beyond the Image Wars in Science, Religion and Art*, Cambridge: MIT Press, 2002.
37. Amed Gökçen, "Notes from the Field: Yezidism; A New Voice and an Evolving Culture in Every Setting," *British Journal of Middle Eastern Studies*, 37, 3 (2010), p. 408.
38. Garnik Asatrian and Victoria Arakelova, *The Religion of the Peacock Angel: The Yezidis and Their Spirit World*, Abingdon: Routledge, 2014, p. 1.
39. For a comprehensive view of the history and origins of Yezidis, see Estelle Amy De La Bretèque, *Paroles mélodisées: Récits épiques et lamentations chez les Yézidis D'Arménie; Littérature, histoire, politique*, Paris: 2013, p. 6; Birgül Açıkyıldız, *The Yezidis: The History of a Community, Culture and Religion*, London: I. B. Tauris, 2010; Eszter Spät, *The Yezidis*, London: Saqi Books, 2005; Christine Allison, *The Yezidi Oral Tradition in Iraqi Kurdistan*, London: Curzon Press, 2001; Axel Steinmann et al., *Yazidi: Gottes Auserwähltes Volk, Oder, Die "Teufelsanbeter" Vom Jebel Sinjar, Irak*, Vienna: Museum Für Völkerkunde Wien, 1998; Philip Kreyenbroek, *Yezidism: Its Background, Observances and Textual Tradition*, vol. 62, Text and Studies in Religion, Lewiston, NY: Edwin Mellen Press, 1995; Robin Schneider and Ernst Tugendhat, *Die Kurdischen Yezidi: Ein Volk Auf Dem Weg in Den Untergang*, Pogrom Taschenbücher 1011, Göttingen, Germany: Gesellschaft Für Bedrohte Völker, 1984.
40. Asatrian and Arakelova, *The Religion of the Peacock Angel*, pp. viii–ix.
41. Gökçen and Tee, "Notes from the Field."
42. Açıkyıldız, *The Yezidis*, p. 60; George Black, "Genocide in Iraq: The Anfal Campaign against the Kurds," in "A Middle East Watch Report," Human Rights Watch, 1993.
43. James Glanz, "Death Toll in Iraq Bombings Rises to 250," *New York Times*, 15 August 2007.
44. Associated Press and NPR reports, "General Calls Attack on Yazidis 'Ethnic

Cleansing,'" 2007; www.npr.org/templates/story/story.php?storyId=12800852. For an overview of attacks against Yezidis, see the United Nations High Commissioner for Refugees (UNHCR), "UNHCR's Eligibility Guidelines for Assessing the International Protection Needs of Iraqi Asylum-Seekers," Geneva, August 2007.

45. Açıkyıldız, *The Yezidis*, p. 202.
46. Robert Langer, "Yezidism between Scholarly Literature and Actual Practice: From 'Heterodox' Islam and 'Syncretism' to the Formation of a Transnational Yezidi 'Orthodoxy,'" *British Journal of Middle Eastern Studies*, 37, 3 (2010), p. 396. Western scholars have been echoing this epithet since the nineteenth century; see, e.g., Austen Henry Layard, *Nineveh and Its Remains: With an Account of a Visit to the Chaldean Christians of Kurdistan, and the Yezidis, or Devil-Worshippers; And an Inquiry into the Manners and Arts of the Ancient Assyrians; New Edition, without Abridgment; Two Volumes Complete in One*, New York: George P. Putnam, 1853; Alphonse Mingana, "Xv. Devil-Worshippers: Their Beliefs and Their Sacred Books," *Journal of the Royal Asiatic Society*, 48, 3 (1916).
47. Açıkyıldız, *The Yezidis*, pp. 159–60.
48. Islamic State, "The Revival of Slavery before the Hour," *Dabiq* (2014); https://media.clarionproject.org/files/islamic-state/islamic-state-isis-magazine-Issue-4-the-failed-crusade.pdf
49. Marzio Babille, "Statement on Child Deaths in Iraq," UNICEF news release, 5 August 2014; www.unicef.org/media/media_74676.html
50. UNAMI/OHCHR, "Report on the Protection of Civilians in Armed Conflict in Iraq: 6 July–10 September 2014," Baghdad: United Nations Assistance Mission for Iraq Office of the United Nations High Commissioner for Human Rights, 2014. According to this UN report, "up to 200,000 had sought refuge on Jabal Sinjar, including 75 per cent Yezidi, and 5 per cent Shia Muslims or Christians"; ibid., p. 13.
51. Independent International Commission of Inquiry, "They Came to Destroy: Isis Crimes against the Yazidis," United Nations Human Rights Office of the High Commissioner, 2016.
52. "IS Blamed for Mass Yazidi Grave Found near Sinjar, Iraq," BBC News, 28 November, 2015.
53. UNNC, "Isil May Have Committed Genocide, War Crimes in Iraq, Says Un Human Rights Report," UN News Centre, 19 March 2015.
54. Naomi Kikoler, "'Our Generation Is Gone': The Islamic State's Targeting of Iraqi Minorities in Ninewa," United States Holocaust Memorial Museum, 2015, p. 26.
55. Ibid., p. 28.
56. Inquiry, "They Came to Destroy," p. 19.
57. Ibid.
58. Michael D. Danti et al., "Weekly Report 33," ASOR Cultural Heritage Initiatives (CHI): Planning for Safeguarding Heritage Sites in Syria and Iraq, 2015.

59. HRW, "Iraq: ISIS kidnaps Shia Turkmen, Destroys Shrines," Human Rights Watch, 27 June, 2014; www.hrw.org/news/2014/06/27/iraq-isis-kidnaps-shia-turkmen-destroys-shrines
60. "At Yazidi Shrine, Armed Iraqi Faithful Recount Battling the Islamic State Group," Associated Press, 12 January, 2015.
61. Martin Chulov, "Yazidis Tormented by Fears for Women and Girls Kidnapped by ISIS Jihadis," *The Guardian*, 12 August 2014.
62. Angie Leventis Lourgos, "Yazidis in Chicagoland Fear Genocide Will Destroy Ancient Faith, Culture," *Chicago Tribune*, 24 June 2016.
63. Talha Jalal, "The Displacement of Minorities in Syria and Iraq: Implications for Human Security," in *Statelessness and Transcontinental Migration*, Barcelona: United Nations University Institute on Globalization, Culture and Mobility, 2015, p. 15.
64. Michael W. Chapman, "Yazidi Victim of ISIS: 'I Was Gang-Raped, They Call This Practice Sexual Jihad,'" *CNS News*, 6 September 2016.
65. For an overview of the factors involved in the processes of decline in population, see Betty Jane Bailey and Martin Bailey (eds), *Who Are the Christians in the Middle East?*, Grand Rapids, MI: William B. Eerdmans, 2003.
66. James Barry, "'This Is Not Our Country': Declining Diversity in the Islamic Republic of Iran," *The Muslim World*, 105, 3 (2015), p. 282.
67. For an overview of Christian communities in the Middle East, see Bailey and Bailey, *Who Are the Christians in the Middle East?*; Jean-Pierre Valognes, *Vie et mort des Chrétiens d'orient: Des origines à nous jours*, Paris: Fayard, 1994; Anthony O'Mahony and Emma Loosley (eds), *Eastern Christianity in the Modern Middle East*, Abingdon: Routledge, 2010. See also Barry in this volume for an overview of the Armenian community.
68. Joseph Sassoon, *The Iraqi Refugees: The New Crisis in the Middle East*, London: I. B. Tauris, 2010, pp. 24–7; Barry, "'This Is Not Our Country,'" p. 282.
69. Donald Bloxham, *The Great Game of Genocide: Imperialism, Nationalism, and the Destruction of the Ottoman Armenians*, Oxford: Oxford University Press, 2005; Sargon Donabed, *Forging a Forgotten History: Iraq and the Assyrians in the 20th Century*, Edinburgh: Edinburgh University Press, 2015.
70. See Barry in this volume for a discussion of the topic.
71. Todd Johnson and Gina Zurlo, "Ongoing Exodus: Tracking Emigration of Christians from the Middle East," *Harvard Journal of Middle Eastern Politics and Policy*, 3 (2014), p. 40.
72. "Iraqi Christians Flee after Isis Issue Mosul Ultimatum," BBC, 18 July 2014.
73. Eliza Griswold, "Is This the End of Christianity in the Middle East?," *New York Times*, 22 July 2015.
74. Imran Khan, "Iraq Christians Get Islamic State's Warning," Al-Jazeera, 20 July 2014.

75. Aryn Baker, "Christians and Tyrants," *Time Magazine*, 10 April 2014, p. 38. For an overview of the 2003 Iraq war and its aftermath, see Benjamin Isakhan, *Democracy in Iraq: History, Politics, Discourse*, London: Routledge, 2016 [2012].
76. Jack Moore, "ISIS to Convert Mosul Orthodox Church into Radical Mosque for Fighters," *Newsweek*, 9 June 2015.
77. Mohammad Alrubaii, Basin Francis, and Mowafaq Mohammad, "Almaseehyon baada Al-Mosul: Al-Sharq Al-Awsat lam yaed makanan salihan lil aish" [Christians after Mosul: The Middle East is no longer a viable place to live], *Al-Hayat*, 23 August 2014.
78. Alissa Rubin, "ISIS Expels Last Iraqi Christians from Mosul," *New York Times*, 19 July 2014.
79. "Isis Has Destroyed Iraq's Oldest Christian Monastery, Satellite Images Confirm," *The Guardian*, 20 January 2016.
80. "Isil Destroys Ivv-Century Church, Historical Mosque in Iraq," *Alahednews*, 26 September 2014.
81. Suadad al-Salhy, "The Full Story Behind ISIL's Takeover of Mosul Museum," Aljazeera, 9 March 2015.
82. Michael Danti et al., "Weekly Report 32," ASOR Cultural Heritage Initiatives (CHI): Planning for Safeguarding Heritage Sites in Syria and Iraq, 2015, pp. 32–8.
83. Danti et al., "Weekly Report 33," pp. 44–52.
84. Michael Danti et al., "Weekly Report 47–48," ASOR Cultural Heritage Initiatives (CHI): Planning for Safeguarding Heritage Sites in Syria and Iraq, 2015, p. 2.
85. Michael Danti et al., "Weekly Report 45," ASOR Cultural Heritage Initiatives (CHI): Planning for Safeguarding Heritage Sites in Syria and Iraq, 2015, p. 5.
86. Philip Jenkins, "Leaving Nineveh: The Last Days of Christians in Mosul," *The Christian Century*, 17 (2014), p. 11.
87. Kanish Tharoor and Maryan Maruf, "Museum of Lost Objects: Mar Elian Monastery," BBC, 7 March 2016; www.bbc.com/news/magazine-35725220
88. Dana Ballout, "Islamic State Destroys Assyrian Christian Monastery in Syria Latest Casualty in Militant Group's Campaign against Idolatry," *Wall Street Journal*, 21 August 2015
89. "Life in a Jihadist Capital: Order with a Darker Side," *New York Times*, 23 July 2014.
90. Ross Burns, "While the World Watches Palmyra, Another of Syria's Heritage Sites Risks Destruction," *Apollo*, 2016. In May 2016, it was damaged by a Russian missile that caused the destruction of the monastery (see UNESCO, "Director-General of UNESCO Deplores Severe Damage at Church of Saint Simeon, World Heritage Site in Syria," news release, 18 May 2016, https://en.unesco.org/news/director-general-unesco-deplores-severe-damage-church-saint-simeon-world-heritage-site-syria.)
91. Michael Danti and Kurt Prescott, "Weekly Report 8," ASOR Cultural Heritage Initiatives (CHI): Planning for Safeguarding Heritage Sites in Syria and Iraq, 2014.

92. Armenian National Institute, "Monument and Memorial Complex at Der Zor, Syria," Armenian National Institute; www.armenian-genocide.org/Memorial.110/current_category.72/memorials_detail.html.
93. Robert Fisk, "Jabhat Al-Nusra Blows Up Armenian Church in Deir El-Zour: A Savage Blow That Echoes through Armenian History," *The Independent*, 10 November 2014. Armenians are considered the first Christians who formed a kingdom, back in the fourth century.
94. Ibid.
95. Griswold, "Is This the End of Christianity in the Middle East?"
96. Independent International Commission of Inquiry on the Syrian Arab Republic, "Report of the Independent International Commission of Inquiry on the Syrian Arab Republic," United Nations Human Rights Office of the High Commissioner, 2016, p. 16.
97. Mindy Belz, "Militias Rout Isis from Christian Area in Syria," *World*, 29 May 2015.
98. AINA, "Isis Attacks Assyrian Villages in Syria, 4 Killed, Dozens Captured, Churches Burned," Assyrian International News Agency, 23 February, 2015.
99. Michael Danti et al., "Weekly Report 93–94," ASOR Cultural Heritage Initiatives (CHI): Planning for Safeguarding Heritage Sites in Syria and Iraq, 2016, pp. 28–9.
100. For a complete report of the damage caused to the churches along the Khabur River, see Michael Danti et al., "Weekly Report 81–82," ASOR Cultural Heritage Initiatives (CHI): Planning for Safeguarding Heritage Sites in Syria and Iraq, 2016, pp. 20–74.
101. Rebecca Collard, "Should the U.S. Prioritize Christian Refugees? No Thanks, Some Arab Christians Say," *Time*, 14 February 2017.
102. At the time of finalizing this chapter in June 2017, the battle for Mosul was apparently in its final stages and the attack on Raqqa was underway.

# INDEX

Notes: Page numbers followed by "*n*" refer to notes.